THE POLITICS OF PUBLIC SERVICE BARGAINS

The Politics of Public Service Bargains

Reward, Competency, Loyalty—and Blame

CHRISTOPHER HOOD AND MARTIN LODGE

OXFORD

UNIVERSITY PRESS

OXFORD
UNIVERSITY PRESS

Great Clarendon Street, Oxford OX2 6DP

Oxford University Press is a department of the University of Oxford.

It furthers the University's objective of excellence in research, scholarship,
and education by publishing worldwide in

Oxford New York

Auckland Cape Town Dar es Salaam Hong Kong Karachi
Kuala Lumpur Madrid Melbourne Mexico City Nairobi
New Delhi Shanghai Taipei Toronto

With offices in

Argentina Austria Brazil Chile Czech Republic France Greece
Guatemala Hungary Italy Japan Poland Portugal Singapore
South Korea Switzerland Thailand Turkey Ukraine Vietnam

Oxford is a registered trade mark of Oxford University Press
in the UK and in certain other countries

Published in the United States
by Oxford University Press Inc., New York

British Library Cataloguing in Publication Data

Data available

Library of Congress Cataloguing in Publication Data

Data available

Typeset by SPI Publisher Services, Pondicherry, India
Printed in Great Britain
on acid-free paper by
Biddles Ltd, King's Lynn, New York.

ISBN 0-19-926967-X   978-0-19-926967-9

3 5 7 9 10 8 6 4 2

Contents

List of Figures

List of Tables

Preface

This book is the product of a long-standing interest in the workings of a mostly informal institution—the understandings, or lack of them, that exist between senior public servants and other political actors over loyalty, competency, and rewards. Where are the lines drawn in the sand? What exactly is given up in exchange for what? How do those understandings grow up, mutate, and unravel? How much do they vary across different states? Such questions are not easy to answer. But they are worth asking, and increasingly so, in an age when so many bureaucratic institutions are being challenged.

Like many of those understandings themselves, it is hard to give an exact date at which our interest in this subject first developed. Both of us have some public servants in our family traditions—mostly lower-level officials, a few in more elevated positions. But what quickened our interest in such public service bargains is probably not some bureaucratic DNA in our genetic make-up. Rather it is the experience, shared with all executive government-watchers over the past twenty years or so, of observing attempts to create new models of bureaucracy that imply a different underlying 'bargain' between politicians and public servants. No one can fail to be struck by the extraordinary ideological fervour with which such issues have been debated, in what is often said to be a post-ideological age. But the hyperbolic claims and counterclaims in those debates have been linked to implicit and often very casual assertions about what the 'old' bureaucracy was like, both in its formal rules and informal conventions. It is those public service bargains, old and new, that this book aims to analyse—how such bargains vary, what holds them together, how they break down.

One key part of any public service bargain consists of reward—what those at the top levels of the state get in return for their labours and their loyalty. Twenty years or so ago, a senior Australian public servant told one of us that most of the important historical changes in the public service were reflected in arrangements for pay and reward. That observation might seem provocative for those who stress the importance of ethos and other-regarding motives in public service, but there is no doubt that in the two decades since that remark was made, issues of reward such as performance-related pay and pension rights have figured large in debates about public service.

A second key part of any public service bargain consists of the skills and competencies public servants have to offer in exchange for whatever rewards they get. This issue has also been central to historical and contemporary debates about effective executive government. Recently there has been much debate about the rise of a new politico-bureaucratic 'class' of spin-doctors shouldering aside public servants with more traditional analytic skills, and also about the growing importance said to be attached to 'delivery' skills relative to the skills involved in policy advice. Similarly, a third key element of any public service bargain consists of understandings about who is responsible for what in executive government and who is to be loyal to whom in what ways. Such agreements are often problematic, partly because of the inevitable blame-shifting games that take place between different actors when things go wrong. Issues of loyalty and responsibility lie at the heart of the much-discussed pressures to develop more managerialized and politicized senior public servants in many countries in recent years, as well as contradictory pressures for rule by autonomous econocrats and similar supposedly non-political experts.

We started to bring these ideas together into a reworking of older ideas about 'public service bargains' some years ago, while working on several intersecting projects. The experience of trying to confine our thoughts on this subject into book chapters and a journal-length paper (Hood 2000, 2001, 2002*a*) convinced us that this was a subject that needed a book-length treatment. We came steadily to the view that the changes often said to be sweeping through public bureaucracies and given the shorthand term of 'new public management' cannot be properly understood or put in context without a careful and historically grounded analysis of the public service bargains they represent.

We learnt much about bargains through interviews. But sometimes it is what is observed on the way to and from those interviews that can be just as telling in what it reveals about the life bureaucratic. We attended professional conferences and programme launches accompanied by stirring anthems and flag ceremonies. We saw British civil servants muffled up in coats and scarves, living up to stereotype by stoically typing away on their keyboards in a building whose heating system had failed. We travelled in one lift with distraught German civil servants coming back from yet another confrontational meeting with their minister, and in another that contained posters prominently warning British civil servants that '[T]here are 152 political journalists noting your every word'. We learned something about bureaucratic competency and capability on our journeys too. For instance, we witnessed one Trinidadian Permanent Secretary taking literally hands-on action to unblock the sewage drains in her building; listened to a British civil servant at the office coffee machine loudly ridiculing the idea that civil servants based in Wales should be able to speak Welsh; and observed the irony of German civil servants being sent off on courses to teach them how to write in German.

The project has taken longer than we originally planned, largely because of the many extraneous commitments that form part of the 'academic bargain' in today's world. And as these things do, the book has changed as we developed the argument in lengthy phone calls, emails, and Sunday lunchtime meetings in London. On the journey, we have accumulated many debts. We are grateful to the ESRC-funded Centre for Analysis of Risk and Regulation at LSE, of which we were both members during the gestation of this book, for providing an environment in which we could work together on this project. We are grateful to CARR and Oxford University for providing some funding for research assistance, and to Nao Kodate and Elena Bechberger for the valuable help they gave us in finding a range of material and analysing it. We are grateful to those who have read drafts of our material as we have developed it over the years, both for the insightful comments that have helped us to improve the analysis (naturally we take responsibility for errors and deficiencies that remain) and for the support and enthusiasm they offered. We would particularly like to thank Philippe Bezes, Vernon Bogdanor, Jørgen Christensen, George Frederickson, Jan Meyer-Sahling, Ed Page, Salvador Parrado, Donald Savoie, Martin Stanley and Kai Wegrich. We are very grateful to Dominic Byatt and Clare Croft of Oxford University Press for their help and support, and particularly for their understanding when our many other commitments meant that completion of the manuscript was delayed for some months. We are also indebted to Gillian Hood for preparing the index. And above all, we are grateful for the hundred-odd public servants of different kinds whom we have interviewed over a number of years, mainly in Britain and Germany, who generously gave their time to correct our misperceptions and offer often very subtle and reflective accounts of the bargains they live by and the way those understandings have been changing. We have only quoted from fifty or so of these interviews (listed in Appendix 2 at the end of this book), and by convention we do not name any of these individuals. But without them there would have been no book.

Christopher Hood
Martin Lodge

Oxford and London
Summer 2005

Part I

Surveying Public Service Bargains

1

Introducing Public Service Bargains

Jeeves, what I want from you is less of the 'well, really, sir', and more of the bucking-to spirit. Think feudally, Jeeves!

(P. G. Wodehouse, *The Code of the Woosters*, London, Penguin, 1971)

1.1. INTRODUCING PUBLIC SERVICE BARGAINS

Sir Harold Nicolson (1886–1968) was a patrician British diplomat and politician who, as a junior Foreign Office official, attended the Paris Peace Conference after the First World War. A decade or so later, comparing his diplomatic world with that of his father's generation, Nicolson concluded that a major change had occurred in the relationship between professional diplomats and elected politicians at that time. Nicolson's view was that in the 'old' diplomacy of pre-war Europe, professional diplomats—often people like him, blue-blooded or at least with aristocratic connections—had both set policy and conducted negotiations. But in the 'new' diplomacy that had emerged after the war it was a new breed of elected politicians who had taken to doing both.[1] Nicolson thought that the old understandings about what was the particular province and skill of professional diplomats had seriously broken down, producing both a state of confusion and what he considered to be a dysfunctional style of diplomacy. He thought there needed to be a new 'diplomatic bargain' based on the understanding that in a democratic age elected politicians should set policy and professional diplomats should conduct international negotiations.

A decade or so earlier, a German aristocrat–diplomat of the previous generation, Anton Graf Monts (1852–1930), diagnosed what he saw as the degeneration of the German diplomatic service between the days of Bismarck and the Weimar Republic (see Nowak and Thimme 1932: 46–53). Graf Monts

---

[1] Nicolson set out these thoughts in a biography of Lord Curzon written in the 1930s (Nicolson 1934: 387).

was bitterly critical of trends within that service consisting of what he thought to be a fatal combination of buck-passing politicians and a diplomatic service drawn from a lower class of aristocrats than in the Bismarckian era. Many of these new diplomats came from bourgeois and *nouveau riche* families and therefore Graf Monts thought they were likely to be vulgarly materialistic and to have little connection to the houses of European aristocracy. Graf Monts also criticized the new (and to him undesirable) tendency to appoint officials to the diplomatic service on the basis of their party affiliation, working under elected ministers whose political preoccupations were not well attuned to the traditional niceties of diplomacy. Like Harold Nicolson, albeit from a different political and cultural background, Graf Monts was detecting a fundamental change in traditional understandings about how German diplomats should operate and how they should relate to other actors in the political system. And Graf Monts was far from being the sole observer of German administration pointing to such changes.[2]

Three generations on from the writings of Nicolson and Graf Monts, the notion of a 'new diplomacy' is still being debated (see Davenport 2002). And it is widely claimed that equally momentous changes are in train for the conduct of executive government more generally. Over the last fifteen years or so, a huge and diffuse epistemic industry has grown up around the idea of a 'new public management' (NPM) that is claimed to be transforming older models of bureaucracy. And in the same vein as Nicolson and Graf Monts, many observers have pointed to major changes in older understandings about what public servants are expected to do—ideas encapsulated in portentous titles such as *The End of Whitehall?* (Campbell and Wilson 1995), *Breaking the Bargain?* (Savoie 2003), and *British Government in Crisis* (Foster 2005). Indeed, for those who think in Wodehousian terms, the egregious Bertie Wooster's demand for a more 'bucking-to spirit' from the faithful Jeeves (as in the epigraph) has often been echoed by politicians seeking more responsiveness and managerial get-up-and-go from their bureaucrats, and many have claimed that such demands have intensified across much of the world in the recent past. It has been commonplace for politicians and commentators alike to assert that a 'new paradigm' in public administration—emphasizing 'delivery', managerial ability, and initiative on the part of bureaucrats—is displacing more passive, autonomous, and detached bureaucratic styles associated with a past era.

---

[2] For instance, the great sociologist Otto Hintze (1964: 205) saw the German state as being in decline, moving from an ethical ideal to operating principles more like those of a business firm.

Certainly, if a linguistic makeover is all it takes to establish such a paradigm, much seems to have changed. What were once 'government officials' now in many cases go under different names and speak in a language drawn from the management schools that would be scarcely intelligible to public servants of an earlier generation. It has become commonplace for ministers, high officials, and government leaders to lecture about the need for a more Wooster-ish spirit in the public sector. And the pros and cons of the supposed new paradigm have been endlessly debated in political and academic circles, produ-cing an international 'new paradigm industry' that has depleted the forests and probably contributed substantially to global warming. From such developments we might suppose that the political Bertie Woosters of the world are indeed seeing less of the 'well, really, sir,' and more of the 'bucking-to spirit' from their bureaucrats.

But is it quite that simple? Were the practices of 'the past' as uniform and clear-cut as this onward-and-upward view of the world implies? And are present-day developments moving unambiguously towards the 'thinking feudally' attitude? If so, why is there still such variety in the relationship between politicians and bureaucrats across different political systems and different parts of the public sector? If greater political responsiveness is the leitmotif of contemporary bureaucratic reform, why is it so common for politicians to create key organizations—like central banks, safety regulators, international quangos of one kind or another—staffed by technocrats or econocrats who are apparently not subject to orders of the day from politi-cians? Why do new regulatory and ethical codes for bureaucrats, far from entrenching the sort of behaviour dogs learn in obedience classes, often seek to establish more of the 'well, really, sir' attitude? Why are reward systems for senior bureaucrats often largely insulated from political control, even in an age when some measure of *soi-disant* 'performance-related pay' has become commonplace in public bureaucracy?

Part of the answer, we think, lies in the way that 'public service bargains' (PSBs) play out, in at least two ways. First, the bargains that are struck—or come unstuck—between bureaucrats, politicians, and others, evidently develop against the backdrop of past events and practices that differ from one country or institutional setting to another. That is a point so often made by political scientists to explain the continuance of variety in the face of apparently common functional demands as to have become a cliché, but it is still important. For instance, as we shall show later, the bargain that emerged over the relationship between civil servants and politicians in western Germany after the Nazi era and the Second World War was shaped by earlier bargains, notably those that emerged during the nineteenth century, and in turn shaped the PSBs that developed after the unification of the two Germanies four decades later.

Second, the outcome of PSBs does not depend on the wants of politicians alone (any more than the relationship between Bertie Wooster and Jeeves depended only on the wants of the egregious Bertie), however forcefully those wants may be expressed. Rather, those outcomes depend on the *combined* strategic choices of all the parties to the bargain. And this is a point often made by analysts of strategy and gaming to explain outcomes that are not intended by one or more of the players in a game. That point is dramatically illustrated when armed forces overthrow their political masters in coups d'état, security services show significant political bias, or bureaucrats seek to undermine the ministers they formally serve. But there are many less-dramatic ways in which the choices made by key bureaucratic actors can shape the outcomes of PSBs. For instance, prior to the mid-1980s reshaping of the New Zealand public service, the PSB between the Treasury and the politicians of the Robert Muldoon government had broken down to the point where for some years the government paid no attention to the Chicago-school views of the Treasury and the top Treasury bureaucrats in turn chose to concentrate on issues of how to redesign the state sector for a future time when a government more sympathetic to their views should come to office (see Boston et al. 1996).

In Section 1.2 we discuss some of the dimensions of PSBs, the subject of this book. By this term we mean explicit or implicit agreements between public servants—the civil or uniformed services of the state—and those they serve. The other partners in such bargains consist of politicians, political parties, clients, and the public at large.[3] Those bargains amount to important 'informal institutions' (Helmke and Levitsky 2004) in executive government, and they can be understood as the product of some sort of equilibrium among the parties involved. This book sets out to explore such bargains and this introductory chapter aims to set the scene. What do PSBs comprise? How do they vary? And what is the significance of those bargains for understanding the politics of bureaucracy?

1.2. PUBLIC SERVICE BARGAINS AND HOW THEY VARY

To understand a PSB, like any other bargain, we need to identify what the various players gain and what they give up relative to one another and the written or unwritten understandings (or misunderstandings) that surround

---

[3] One of us has defined such bargains as 'any explicit or implicit understanding between (senior) public servants and other actors in a political system over their duties and entitlements relating to responsibility, autonomy, and political identity, and expressed in convention or formal law or a mixture of both' (Hood 2000: 8).

that relationship. In a PSB, politicians normally expect to gain some degree of political loyalty and competency from bureaucrats or public servants, and those public servants normally expect to gain some assured place in the structure of executive government, a definite sphere of responsibility and some mixture of tangible and intangible reward. Politicians often give up some of their rights to hire, fire, remunerate, or even direct public servants at will, and public servants often give up some of their rights to blame or express political opposition to the ruling regime. Political loyalty in some form is typically exchanged for discretion on the part of public servants. These standard features of a PSB are summarized in Figure 1.1 overleaf.

'So far, so bland,' as Lewis Gunn (1987: 35) once caustically put it. But things start to get less bland—and more interesting—when it comes to exactly what counts as 'loyalty', 'competency', 'rewards', and the like, because PSBs can vary widely on such matters across time and different state traditions, as well, within the respective systems across domains and position. To bring out some of that variation, Table 1.1 illustrates some of the ascertainable or measurable variations in context, reward, career, and institutional bases for the top-level public service in seven selected states.

For instance, we can contrast the sort of 'competency' (in poetic composition and general literary accomplishment) that has been required of high state officials in some mandarin state traditions, to the more workaday skills required of public servants in other contexts. And the skills and competencies required of public servants can change dramatically with the political and ideological backdrop. For instance, until the early nineteenth century, high officials of the German states were expected to be skilled state managers, schooled in the 'cameral sciences' that had developed from the sixteenth century (Maier 1966). But after the demise of autocracy, 'cameralistics' suddenly lost favour as the preferred skill base of civil servants. It was replaced by the legal training thought to be more appropriate for state administration in a *Rechtsstaat*. Similarly, in the post-imperial 'what's wrong with Britain' debates of the 1960s, many purported to find the answer in civil service competency. They argued that high state officials needed to be technically proficient in the then (briefly) fashionable Keynesian economics rather than steeped in the classics and the humanities. Thirty years later, the ability to talk in 'managementese' had become a favoured competency, at least for some.

In some cases, of course, specific skills are far less important than simple political loyalty, and political loyalty of some kind is normally central to any PSB. For instance, the loyalty part of a PSB often involves a no-strike agreement in exchange for other privileges, since strikes by some public servants can make regimes vulnerable. A case in point is that of a key section

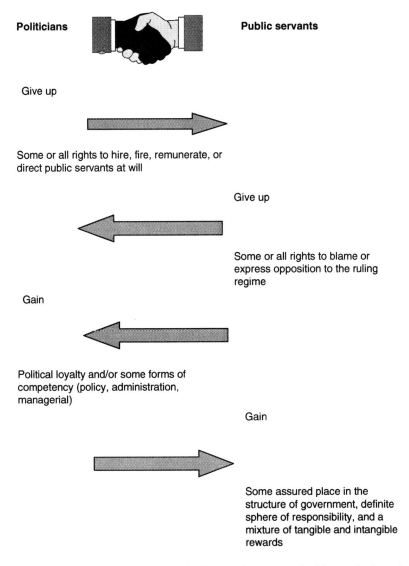

Figure 1.1   Some standard features of politician–bureaucrat 'public service bargains'

of the garbage collection workers in the tropical city-state of Singapore, who were turned into civil servants in the post-independence era (to neutralize their potential strike power in a crowded tropical city), exchanging a prohibition on striking for permanency and other civil service privileges.

Further, the party-political dimension of political loyalty in the PSB in some cases means compulsory membership of the ruling political party by public servants, as in Indonesia under the GOLKAR regime. In others it involves a ban on membership of any political party, as in the Whitehall tradition for senior civil servants. And there are various halfway stations in between, such as the practice of allocating bureaucratic posts proportionately to the electoral strengths of the different political parties in the so-called *Proporz*-democracies like Austria and to a lesser extent Germany.

The 'rewards' part of a PSB can also vary substantially. In some cases the rewards that public servants get in exchange for loyalty and competence come in the form of substantial upfront salaries, as with Singapore's top civil servants who earn million-dollar-plus salaries that would be the envy of their counterparts even in the most affluent Western democracies—but drive their own cars and buy their own apartments (see Quah 2003*a*). In other cases (like China, Indonesia, or Thailand), visible salaries even for the topmost elite have traditionally been tiny—well below what welfare recipients get in many Western states. But those tiny visible salaries reflect a more or less explicit understanding that additional earning opportunities for the elite and their families form a massive submerged iceberg of which the formal salaries comprise a tiny tip. As we shall see later, the point at which rewards arrive may also vary from one PSB to another, with substantial rewards coming during public office in some cases and after it in others.

The 'responsibility' part of a PSB sometimes means exclusive dominance of public servants over policymaking, as traditionally applied in Japan, where ministers tended to be ciphers in departmental policymaking until the Liberal Democratic Party's (LDP) long period of single-party rule ended in 1993. But sometimes the responsibility part of the bargain involves largely technical or implementing fix-it capacity, as was traditionally the case in Belgium or Hong Kong.[4] Indeed, in some PSBs, such as the US Progressive-era tradition of city-managers and (to a lesser extent) the Swedish tradition of autonomous agencies in central government, public servants have more or less exclusive control over implementation or management in exchange for direct liability for blame over such matters, and PSBs of this type have figured large in the ideas of managerial reformers elsewhere in recent decades—a point to which we return later.

PSBs vary not only in content—what exactly is exchanged for what—but also in the way they are expressed or recorded. Some PSBs (or parts of them, at least) are written in 'black letter' constitutions, as with post-1945 Germany or post-1988 Chile. Parts are often found in civil service statutes or case law.

---

[4] Though that has changed too in recent years.

Table 1.1 Some indicators of PSBs: context, reward, career, and institutional basis in selected countries

	USA	Germany	UK	Spain	France	Japan	Trinidad
Confidence in public service (World Values Survey)	High	Low	Medium	Low	Medium	Low	N/a
Approximate proportion of top public servants and political advisors to total population (in thousands)	0.024	0.018	0.076	0.233	0.092	0.057	0.54
Approximate proportion of top bureaucrats and political advisors who are 'dismissable'	0.64	0.09	0.02	0.24	0.22	0	0
Top public service pay as multiple of average earnings	4.27	3.59	5.50	2.83	4.53	3.21	5.94
Mid-level public service pay as multiple of average earnings	2.83	1.52	1.33	1.09	2.52	1.09	2.31
Automatic honours	No	No	Yes	No	No	Yes	No
Closed career pattern	No	Yes	Partly yes	Partly Yes	Yes	Yes	Yes
Constitutional entrenchment of public service	Low	High	Low	High	Low	Low	Medium
Volume and distribution of public service law	High and dispersed	Medium and concentrated	Low and dispersed	Medium and concentrated	Low and dispersed	High and concentrated	Medium and concentrated

Sources: See Appendix 1.

But many consist of unwritten conventions or understandings, even in the USA and the European Union (EU), with their highly constitutionalized style of politics. That is why the notion of PSBs can be considered as much as informal institutions as formal ones. PSBs are not only a mirror of culture, as we shall see later, but often operate through shared attitudes and beliefs rather than formal enactments alone.

Indeed, the various players may well disagree on, or have different interpretations of, what the essence of the bargain is and what counts as cheating. In his *Politics in England*, Richard Rose (1980: title page) quotes an ironic comment from Sidney Low's *The Governance of England* that 'we live under a system of tacit understandings. But the understandings are not always understood.' That certainly seems to apply to the British 'Whitehall' PSB in recent years, and is perhaps what lies behind an increasing tendency to write down the formerly 'tacit understandings' between ministers and bureaucrats, traditionally operating mainly through socialization and 'conversation' (Foster 1998) into written codes and guidelines.[5]

PSBs can vary within countries for different parts of the government or public service, as well as from one country to another, as we shall show later in this book. And they can change over time in various ways. In some cases, arrangements for the public service do not change much while overall political regimes change, as for example happened after Hong Kong's transfer in 1997 from British colonial rule to the status of a 'special administrative region' of China under its one country, two systems model. In other cases, changes in PSBs coincide with broad regime change, as happened with the Germany's shift from autocratic government to a measure of representative democracy in 1848, as mentioned earlier.

In still other cases, PSBs alter while broader political regimes remain unchanged. A notable example is that of the USA, since the US federal civil service went through numerous bargains during the country's first 200 years of existence. According to Henry Parris (1969: 29), the original bargain after independence involved permanent tenure for civil servants, but that was replaced in the 1820s by the Jacksonian party-spoils bargain that gave politicians the power after an electoral victory to put their own supporters into office in the bureaucracy for as long as they held office (Carpenter 2001: 37–46). That spoils bargain was in turn modified by moves towards a merit system of recruitment (at least for white males) during the Progressive era of

---

[5] Indeed, against a background of major disagreements about what the terms of the British bargain should be, particularly over issues of permanence, skills, and responsibility, Tony Blair's Labour government produced a draft civil service bill before the 2005 general election that was supposed to embody parts of the bargain, and was later berated by a former Cabinet Secretary, Lord Butler, for dragging its feet in reintroducing the bill after the election (*Evening Standard*, 7 February 2006, p. 2).

the late nineteenth and early twentieth century. It was modified again into a different kind of bargain after the 1960s civil rights era, with a heightened sense that the bureaucracy needed to reflect gender and race divisions in society, and in the following decade a failed attempt was made to change the bargain at the very top of the bureaucracy to create a go-anywhere corps of civil servants (Ingraham and Ban 1984). We shall look at the ways in which PSBs wax and wane later in the book.

1.3. WHY PUBLIC SERVICE BARGAINS MATTER?

PSBs matter because they can go to the heart of politics. They are part of the living constitution of any state. Scholars have long debated what are the preconditions for democracy, but any meaningful democracy can exist only if at least the police and armed forces show some sort of allegiance to the elected government. Such a bargain broke down dramatically at the end of the Fourth French Republic in 1958, when 3,000 Paris police marched on and laid siege to the *Assemblée Nationale* (Roach 1985: 112) and the army in Algeria was in open revolt. The '23 F' military coup attempt of 1981, in which members of the Spanish *Cortes* (national parliament) were taken hostage, is another case in point. And moves from authoritarian rule to representative democracy often involve tricky bargains between elected politicians and the armed services. A notorious example is that of Chile after 1988, when the constitution was rewritten to enshrine a bargain in which the military accepted a return to civilian rule in exchange for various explicit conditions. Those conditions included 'recognition of the armed forces' role as 'guardian of the nation', autonomy over internal military affairs, and a National Security Council that could call elected presidents to account (see Oppenheim 1999; Siavelis 2000). And in some democratic transitions, 'amnesty bargains' develop for public services, with the new regime explicitly or implicitly forgetting the past activities of its public servants, in exchange for loyalty to the new order. That sort of loyalty bargain was widely held to have applied to post-second World War (West) Germany and to a much lesser extent in the incorporation of East German public servants in the new Germany after unification in 1990.

Issues of how far elected politicians can control the armed forces link PSBs to the rawest kind of politics. And in any society where politics turn on race, ethnicity, nationality, or language, the question of who staffs the public service and on what terms is often the central issue in the underlying deal among different groups that holds the state together. Indeed, the idea of 'representative bureaucracy' (Krislov 1974) can sometimes be more important than electoral representation. Bargains over representation in the bureaucracy can play out in several ways, as we shall see in Chapter 2. They may take the form of job sharing for every position, division of a country into enclaves served by bureaucrats from different ethnic or linguistic groups, rotation rules where groups take it in turn to hold particular positions, or quota arrangements for distributing positions among different groups, of a kind that has been tried with varying success in many divided societies from Cyprus to Northern Ireland. Such approaches aim at securing recognition of the authority and legitimacy of the public service by the politically entrenched racial, ethnic, or language groups in society, in exchange for representation in the bureaucracy and a share of the administrative power such representation brings.

In a quite different vein from the way PSBs reflect relationships among groups in a divided society or between politicians and the security services, PSBs are also central to the managerial politics that has been so emphasized in advanced and developing countries alike in recent decades, under both New Right and Third Way ideologies. Indeed, changing the PSB often figures large in the ambitions of political reformers of various stripes. Some contemporary visions of public service reform and social improvement rest heavily on visions of the transformative effects of e-technology, but the core of the much-touted 'managerial' vision of public service change is the idea—or hope—that politicians and bureaucrats can find new ways of behaving and relating to one another. So managerial reformers often put traditional bargains between bureaucrats and politicians at the top of the list of the things they want to change.

As we will see later, some of those managerial-age reformers, like Bertie Wooster in the epigraph to this chapter, sought a more 'bucking-to-spirit' from bureaucrats in response to politicians' demands. But others, far from thinking feudally in the Wooster sense, sought more autonomy for professional managers, expert decision-makers, or regulators against the interference of politicians. And the good-governance agenda that became central to various international regimes over the past decade (including the World Bank development agenda and EU enlargement policies) also sought to change some traditional bargains between bureaucrats and politicians.

However, it is difficult to make sense of the variety of changes that are lumped together under the heading of 'NPM' without taking close account of the various PSBs that formed the starting points for current reforms in different states. Moreover, because PSBs often play a central part of constitutional (or, at least micro-constitutional) politics, the question of how they evolve and break down merits some attention. Like any convention, bargains can be subject to misunderstanding, reinterpretation, or outright cheating, as well as strategic behaviour within some accepted set of rules. Some PSBs seem to be fairly stable over time (as with the case of the French civil service), some seem to be subject to a long-drawn-out pattern of disintegration and reshaping (as with the traditional 'Whitehall' PSB), while others can break suddenly and dramatically, as seems to have happened with the Treasury and the Robert Muldoon government in New Zealand, as mentioned earlier. Such breakdowns can perhaps more often be observed as parts of the public service than for the system as a whole—for instance, when US President Ronald Reagan summarily fired all the US air traffic controllers in 1981 or UK Prime Minister Margaret Thatcher banned labour unions from her government's intelligence service in 1984.

To explain or predict the way that such conventions can develop, stick, or unravel, rational choice analysts conventionally try to identify 'Nash equilibria' in strategic interactions modelled as games (in which none of the players would be better off by altering their strategy). That kind of analysis can be illuminating, though it becomes tricky when the various 'actors' are institutions or groups rather than single individuals (see Scharpf 1997: 52–60). Other schools in political science prefer to look at the growth, change, or decline of conventions against the broad sweep of history, the activity of dominant figures, broad changes within society, or (in a more anthropological vein) against the 'thick' social context in which patterns of shared meanings develop and change. For instance, Desmond King (1995) follows this second approach in his account of how the 'race bargain' in the US federal bureaucracy changed radically over the course of a century.

Overall, PSBs offer an angle of vision on executive government that combines comparative or historical analysis of political systems with a strategic-action perspective on the making, breaking, and maintenance of the compacts between bureaucrats and other players in politics. Ernest Rutherford once declared that 'all science is either physics or stamp collecting',[6] and while political science is sometimes conceived as a kind of physics, stamp collecting is necessary too for any kind of systematic analysis. So identifying the different sorts of PSBs that are observable across states and political systems is not just a pastime for collectors of rare (or not so rare) specimens. It is a way to establish the range of patterns and possibilities, compare the starting points and (preliminary) end points of reform processes and explore the cultural, religious, and other conditions that are associated with different kinds of PSBs.

---

[6] Blackett 1962: 108. As a physicist, Rutherford naturally tended to scorn the latter.

1.4. THE ORIGINS OF THE IDEA

As noted already, for as long as anyone has written about this subject, particularly in the democratic era of the last century and a half, students of bureaucracy and politics have been preoccupied with the relationship between bureaucrats, politicians, and other actors. Such analyses include comparisons of the political-administrative nexus (Hall 1983), distinctions between 'strong' and 'weak' states (Badie and Birnbaum 1979; Heper 1992), and accounts of the difference between 'instrumental' and 'autonomous' bureaucracies (Knill 1999). Further, Eisenstadt (1958) has claimed that political-bureaucratic life has become increasingly 'bureaucratized', and Robert Putnam and his colleagues (Putnam 1973; Aberbach, Putnam, and Rockman 1981) have pointed to a change from 'classical' to more 'political' styles of bureaucracy. But the idea of that relationship as a bargain—an implicit or explicit deal among different parties, in which some x is exchanged for some y—is only recently coming to be commonly adopted.

This book aims to give the idea of PSBs a new twist and develop it further as a tool of strategic and comparative analysis. However, we do not make any claim to be the first to have framed this idea or even to have used the term. Like most ideas in political science and public administration, it has been around in some form for a long time, albeit in rather different and scattered literatures. We can identify at least three different lines of analysis from which the 'bargain' idea can be drawn, namely the idea of an 'inducements–contributions balance' in management and organizational theory, the idea of exchanges in social theory and strategic analysis, and the specific idea of a 'PSB' in Victorian Britain that was originally put forward by the late Bernard Schaffer over thirty years ago.[7]

The idea that organizational life involves a balance between inducements in exchange for contributions is a long-standing notion associated with organization theory and management. Elements of that idea long predated modern management theory. Many aspects can be traced back to Jeremy Bentham's elaborate early nineteenth-century account of rewards and punishments in institutions, for instance in his 1825 'Rules of Reward'. It is at least implicit in Adam Smith's eighteenth-century ideas, for instance, his observations of the working of British East India Company in *The Wealth of Nations*. But in

---

[7] We might possibly add a fourth kind of literature on 'pacts', namely that dealing with the historical origins of corporatism and consociational arrangements, which were based on the exchange of exclusivity in power-holding for compromise-seeking behaviour (see Lehmbruch 1998: 24–7); but the notion of a PSB is rarely explicit in this literature.

modern management theory, as it emerged from the late nineteenth century, it is the work of Chester Barnard that is conventionally seen as identifying an 'inducement–contribution balance' as central to the understanding and management of organizations. That idea figures prominently in Barnard's classic (1938) *Functions of the Executive*, and James March and Herbert Simon (1958) later developed it in their own classic text *Organizations*.

This idea is important, because problems relating to the inducements–contribution balance are seldom far to seek in public service organization. Some years ago, the *Belfast Telegraph* carried a story about a former civil servant in Northern Ireland who had forsaken the bureaucratic life to become a lap-dancer. She was reported as declaring that her new job was better-paid and more interesting than her previous work—'Oh yes, and you also feel less abused.'[8] That is (we must hope) an atypical career shift, but haemorrhage of talent from public to private sector or from poor countries to rich countries constitutes a familiar theme in debates over public sector rewards. Even the city-state of Singapore, which as we have noted has the highest-paid bureaucrats in the world (at least in dollar-equivalent salaries), was repeatedly losing entire cohorts of high-flying middle-rank civil servants in the little-tiger boom years of the 1980s and 1990s, because those middle-level bureaucrats could secure even more lucrative work in banks and company boardrooms (see Quah 2003*a*).

Looking at PSBs in terms of inducements and contributions draws attentions not only to issues of competency and proficiency—what public servants are expected to contribute—but also to what counts as an inducement for whom and when it comes in a public service career. We have already pointed out the difference between pay-as-you-go PSBs and those in which rewards come in the form of delayed gratification—pensions or earning opportunities that come after officials' retirement from office, and we shall discuss that issue further in Chapter 4. But there are also both historical and contemporary cases of bureaucrats who are never particularly wealthy at any point in their lives, as applied before the 1980s to the Scandinavian countries, Australia and New Zealand. Indeed, it used to be common to compare the bureaucratic career with an ascetic soldierly or monastic lifestyle.

If the idea of the 'inducements–contribution balance' draws attention to who gets what benefits, when and in what form, a broader literature on social exchange relationships and strategic behaviour focuses on the way that bargains can be shaped by power, the search for calculated advantage and cheating. There are at least three strands of analysis in this vein. One is a body

---

[8] *Belfast Telegraph*, 16 April 2002.

of sociological writing about exchange relationships that looks at (almost) everything from love affairs to international treaties from a social exchange perspective. The eminent sociologist Peter Blau offered one of the classic accounts of this approach in his 1964 *Exchange and Power in Social Life*. Blau showed that exchange is pervasive in social life, though not all social activity consists of exchanges, and exchanges vary both in reciprocality and in how much intrinsic value (as in friendship) they bring.[9] Partners have common interests in maintaining an exchange if both benefit from it, but conflicting interests in that each party has an interest in making the other make the greater commitment. Hence each of the partners faces the dilemma of putting pressure on the other to make that greater commitment by withholding their own commitment up to but not beyond the point where the exchange collapses (ibid. 315). Such dynamics tend to make exchanges like PSBs precarious.

Blau also argued (ibid. 22) that social exchanges are linked to power in the sense that the 'contracting parties' are often unequal in their status or the strategic resources at their command. Exchanges that are asymmetric in that sense are commonly observable, for instance in all those love affairs where one partner is more ardent than the other. Indeed, PSBs often appear to have an asymmetric quality, particularly where elected politicians claim democratic authority to unilaterally alter the terms and conditions of bureaucrats, as happened in Australia and New Zealand in the 1980s, when senior public servants were stripped of their permanent tenure. But it still takes two to tango, even if the parties to the bargain do not see themselves as of equal weight. After all, the individuals involved still have to be prepared to interact in some way—and any executive government depends for its success on people who are willing to do more than just go through the motions of bureaucratic work.

Much of the more recent writing about social exchange relationships has drawn on the theory of games and strategic behaviour, originating in its modern form in von Neumann and Morgenstern's famous analysis of 1947 and later spreading through the social sciences. The primary concern is with the analysis and identification of actor constellations and basic strategic relationships—like 'chicken', 'prisoner's dilemma', 'assurance', 'battle of the sexes'—and the array of moves open to each of the players to work out the

---

[9] Following Georg Simmel's (1950) classic analysis, Blau brought out some of the crucial differences between exchanges involving only two parties and those involving three or more (when coalitions and divide-and-rule tactics enter the picture), and in a proto-game-theory analysis brought out the common and conflicting interests possessed by partners in an exchange.

dominant strategies. Dominant strategies represent equilibria, in that they identify the points at which no player could be better off by making a different move. However, those who put the stress on 'interaction orientations' (see Scharpf 1997: 84–9) highlight the circumstances in which actors in strategic exchanges are not concerned only with maximizing their own pay-offs, but are also affected—positively and negatively—by the pay-offs other actors receive. Standard game-theory matrices that assume that players are individual maximizers and that their utilities are independent break down in those circumstances. What that would suggest is that PSBs are less likely to break down the more socially intermixed the parties are—for instance when public servants and politicians are closely linked by intermarriage and other social ties. But the Antipodean cases already mentioned suggest that such social ties by no means always counter the individual maximizing approach when it comes to PSBs.

A development of these game-theory ideas is that school of thought that sees institutions—rules, routines, conventions, public service arrangements—more generally as equilibria in social games.[10] And from a different part of the rational choice stable, institutions such as PSBs can be understood as attempts to reduce 'transaction costs'—that is, the costs associated with doing business or everyday interactions (Williamson 1986; Coase 1937)—or to increase commitment or durability of particular policies over time. The latter is the reason given by Murray Horn (1995) to explain the puzzle of why elected politicians so often seem to be prepared to give up the power of hiring and firing bureaucrats ad hoc, when it would seem to be in their short-term interests to possess such powers and use them vigorously. But 'transaction costs' are a slippery concept, and this kind of analysis can often turn into a teleological form of reasoning. Where does 'transaction cost saving' end and the preservation of the power of an exclusive social group (in gender, ethnicity, class, etc.) begin? How do we assess and weigh transaction *benefits*—for instance, of dealing with people of different ethnicity and social background to develop richer perspectives or more robust policies—as against transaction costs? These problems are not trivial. But this sort of literature at least points to some of the basic problems inherent in institutions like PSBs and the social mechanisms that can sustain them—in particular, elements of self-enforcement, third-party enforcement, and commonality of beliefs (Kreps 1990a). We shall return to these issues in Chapter 8.

---

[10] This idea is associated with the 'analytic narrative' approach (see Bates et al. 1998), but for those who see institutions as 'congealed patterns of preferences' (notably Baumgartner and Jones 1993), that congealment can be understood as representing some sort of Nash equilibrium in the strategies of a set of interacting players.

A third, narrower and much more specific vein of analysis that forms the background to this enquiry is the earlier political science and public administration literature on PSBs. The origin of such terms is often as hard to pin down as the origin of popular songs, but as far as we can discover, this phrase was first used by the late Bernard Schaffer, one of the founders of the science of development administration in the second half of the twentieth century and a leading figure in administrative science more generally up to the early 1980s (Hood 1999: 293). Schaffer used the term to denote the understanding that developed in the UK during the later nineteenth century between elected politicians and appointed bureaucrats over their respective duties and entitlements.[11] Broadly, on Schaffer's analysis, civil servants gave up some political rights (such as the right to openly criticize the policy of the government of the day) in exchange for permanence in office. And for their part, elected politicians in their role as departmental ministers gave up their right to hire and fire civil servants at will in exchange for loyalty and competence (see Schaffer 1973: 252).

The bargain Schaffer identified was never enacted into a civil service statute or equivalent constitutional form. Rather, it seems to have been what lawyers call a constructive or implicit bargain. In that sense it resembled the constructive contracts we are said to enter into whenever we buy a bus ticket or even watch TV.[12] And not every civil servant adopted it at once, or even later on, as we shall see. But, Schaffer argued, politician/bureaucrat behaviour in late-Victorian Britain could best be understood as the product of an implicit deal along these lines. Variants of the same theme developed in other Westminster-model countries, the Scandinavian parliamentary democracies, and for parts of the public service in the French and German traditions.

Schaffer's notion of the bargain that underlay the traditional Whitehall model of constitutional bureaucracy was a pioneering and characteristically insightful idea. Schaffer (ibid.) was at pains to stress the historical contingency of this 'highly complicated bargain', the long process of change that led up to it and the 'quite peculiar conditions' that were associated with it. He also—presciently perhaps—stressed the costs of the bargain and the recurring tendency of ministers to shuffle out of their part of it (ibid. 253). But his idea of a PSB can usefully be developed beyond the particular time and place for which he originally framed it, as several authors have

---

[11] At very much the same time, the late Henry Parris (1969) advanced a closely similar argument, but was slightly less explicit than Schaffer in framing the idea of a PSB.

[12] For example, the idea sometimes advanced that choosing to watch commercial TV involves an implicit contract to watch the advertisements as well as the main programmes.

begun to do (see Hood 2000, 2002*a*; Savoie 2003) and that is the task that we set ourselves in this book. In the case Schaffer analysed, public servants gave up some political rights in exchange for permanence and anonymity (and a particular pattern of rewards). But that is only one possible type of PSB out of a number of different varieties that can be observed. Indeed, the UK itself could easily have adopted the spoils bargain that began to develop in the US public service in the 1820s. In the next part of the book, we set out to explore some of the major different variants of PSB, offering both a general scheme or classification and some more detailed cases illustrating some of the key types.

1.5. OUR ANALYSIS AND THE STRUCTURE OF THIS BOOK

Having set the scene in this introductory chapter, the remainder of the book falls into three main parts. The next part sketches out some of the different varieties of PSBs that can be observed across different times and places. Such bargains, as we shall see, can vary in several dimensions—such as comprehensiveness, enactedness, individualism, as well as in the number of parties involved in the deal and the position in politics that public servants claim or accept. One of the distinctions most stressed by analysts of comparative bureaucracy is that between the idea of public servants as some sort of autonomous 'estate' in the political system, like the church or the landed gentry in early modern Europe, or as simple agents at the beck and call of politicians. Accordingly we explore 'trustee' and 'agency' bargains in the next two chapters. Building on that and adding two more binary distinctions, we identify eight different PSB types, giving examples of each type of bargain and identifying what public servants and other players exchanged for what in those cases. That is, we subdivide trustee and agency bargains into two types (representative versus tutelary trustee bargains, and directed versus delegated agency bargains), and then divide each of those four types into a further two types. Accordingly, the set of bargains that we explore, as set out in Figure 1.2, are consociational representative PSBs, selective representative PSBs, moralistic tutelary PSBs, legal/technocratic tutelary PSBs, complex delegated agency PSBs, simple delegated agency PSBs, serial loyalist-directed agency PSBs, and personal loyalist-directed agency PSBs. We supplement that analysis by some vignettes and cases bringing out changes over time in PSBs and variety among and within different state traditions.

In Part II of the book, we explore three selected—and often highly controversial—aspects of PSBs in more detail, examining issues of reward, competency

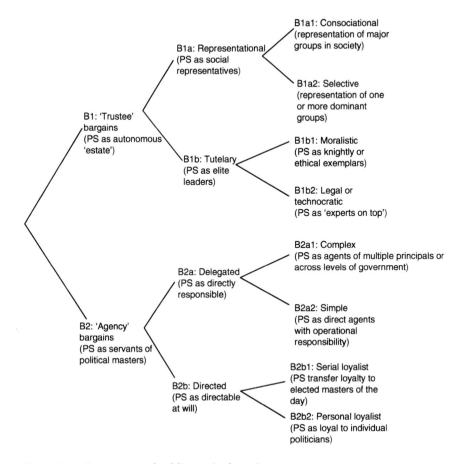

Figure 1.2 Some types of public service bargains

and responsibility, or reward. The *reward* aspect of PSBs relates, as we have already noticed, to what public servants receive in return for their labours, in what form and at what stage in their careers. Reward is also central to any PSB, from the cynical slogan, often said to originate in Soviet Russia but posted up in many offices today, that 'we pretend to work and they pretend to pay us', to the lavish rewards of nineteenth-century colonial nabobs or some individuals at the top of international organizations today. In matters of public service reward too, older conventions came under pressure in many countries during the recent past. For instance, in Australia, New Zealand, the UK, and the Netherlands, traditional pay relativities between bureaucrats and politicians disappeared, to the point where many top public servants earned more than the elected politicians they served in the guise of individualized quasi-managerial packages.

The *competency* aspect of PSBs relates to what public servants are expected to be able to know or do—something that is central to any PSB that goes beyond a simple exchange of political loyalty for patronage. New demands on competency have been made on public servants in many political systems in the recent past, with policymaking capacity becoming required of some hitherto executive public services and managerial capacity being required of hitherto policy-focused public services.

The *responsibility* aspect of PSBs relates to the matters for which public servants have autonomous decision-making power relative to politicians, as against those where they are held to be simple agents or bag-carriers. This element is also a much-debated feature of PSBs, for instance in issues over the autonomy of military commanders or the traditional Whitehall convention of anonymous civil servants who merely execute their political masters' wishes and hence cannot be named and blamed over policy or even implementation. This aspect of PSBs has also come under pressure in several developed countries, particularly of the Westminster-model type, in the recent reform era of the 1980s and 1990s. A common theme in that era was a desire to make public servants 'think feudally' in the Woosterish sense, making them directly responsible for public service delivery rather than acting as detached judicial figures disdainfully pouring cold water over politicians' half-baked policy ideas. The latter was dignified by an elaborate rhetoric of managerialism, but its political significance was often interpreted as an attempt to put public servants into the role of 'lightning rods', conducting blame for all the many faults and failings of public service delivery away from elected politicians.

In Part III of the book, we return to the issue of the making, breaking, and reshaping of PSBs. Looking at development, breakdown and change in PSBs is central for understanding the politics of contemporary public service reform, and our aim in this part is twofold. We explore what makes for 'equilibrium' in such bargains—what seems to make them endure or come apart. Such an analysis may need to take close account of the worldviews of the players—whether that be the 'Code of the Woosters', the 'law of the jungle', low-trust 'amoral familism' (Banfield 1958), or something else. However, we also aim to show that the rational choice analysis of strategic options (including cheating) available to the various players can yield important insights, especially in bringing out the equilibrium problems in managerial PSBs—a conclusion that is ironic, given the supposed rational choice origins of that type of bargain.

Finally, in a brief concluding chapter, we assess what can be learned from looking at executive government through a 'PSB' lens. What is the value—and the limits—of this approach? What light can it shed on other literatures on executive government and public service reform? And what might be the future of PSBs?

2

Trustee-Type Public Service Bargains

Similarly, the [civil servant's] relationship to his office is not one of contract, although the parties in question both give their consent and render a service. The civil servant is not employed, like an agent,[1] to perform a single contingent task, but makes this relationship the main interest of his spiritual and particular existence

> (G. W. F. Hegel (1820/1991), *Elements of the Philosophy of Right,*
> §294, p. 333)

On his way out he paused to pat Matthew on the shoulder, saying with a laugh: 'You might just as well expect stockbrokers to be ready to die for the Stock Exchange!'

> (J. G. Farrell, *The Singapore Grip*, London, Fontana 1979, p. 333)

2.1. TRUSTEESHIP AS A FORM OF PUBLIC SERVICE BARGAIN

In Chapter 1 we introduced the PSB approach to analysing executive government—an approach that focuses on what the various players gain and what they give up relative to one another, and on understandings about duties and entitlements that surround that relationship. We noted that those understandings may involve some degree of formal enactment, but are often implicit rather than a formally negotiated bargaining outcome between institutionally represented and organized groups.

As we also noted in Chapter 1, PSBs do not come in a single universal form. They vary across time, across countries, across levels of government, and across different parts of the public service. Although in contemporary economics and political science the language of principal and agent has come to be widely used to describe the relationship between bureaucrats and those

---

[1] '*Mandatarius*' in Hegel's original text.

they work for, we postpone to Chapter 3 a discussion of PSBs that centre on notions of agency. This chapter explores a rather different approach to PSBs that is at least as old as the 'agency' approach, even if less intellectually fashionable in the recent past—namely the notion of public servants as trustees (B1).

The notion of government as a trust and those who govern as trustees is a long-standing idea in writing about politics in the English-speaking world. It is an idea that is most famously associated with John Locke's *Two Treatises of Government*, originally published in 1690. The notion of trust comes from equity in the English legal tradition, and a trust is an instrument (intentional or 'constructive') that vests the legal ownership of property in hands other than those of the beneficiaries. Trustees and agents are subject to some common legal obligations, but the relationship between trustee and beneficiary differs from that of principal and agent (which we discuss in Chapter 3) in several ways. For example, the relationship of trustee and beneficiary is not created by a contractual agreement between those parties; trustees do not legally 'represent' their beneficiaries in the same way that agents represent their principals, and trustees do not bring their beneficiaries into contractual relationships with third parties in the way that agents do. Most important for our purposes, trustees are not subject to control by their beneficiaries, though those beneficiaries can take legal action to compel trustees to fulfil the terms of the trust (see Pettit 2001: 28).

Trusts are ubiquitous in the English legal tradition, though the instrument does not appear in the same way in the Roman-law tradition (Burn 1996: 49). A well-known and controversial example of the application of the trust instrument in the UK is for occupational pension schemes. Here the trust form has been used legally to segregate the assets of a pension fund from those of the employing firm or institution and to give employees the legal right to take action against the fund managers for failing in their duties. Neither the segregation nor the legal right would be legally feasible if pension entitlements were merely a matter of the contract between employer and employee, as has sometimes been proposed (ibid. 8).

We can think of a 'trustee bargain' in government as an analogous agreement—enacted or 'constructive'—between public servants and other key actors in the political system. In a trustee bargain, public servants are expected to act as independent judges of the public good (i.e. the interests of their beneficiaries) to some significant extent, and not merely to take their orders from some political master. The notion of a trustee relationship implies that public servants possess a domain of autonomy in which they exercise discretion in a way that is not subject to commands or control from elected politicians. Rather, they are subject to a fiduciary duty not to allow their personal interests to conflict with their public responsibilities and can be disciplined or removed from office for failing in this duty. Accordingly, under a PSB of the trustee type, the tenure and rewards of public servants are not under the direct control of those for whom they act, the skills and competencies they are expected to show are not determined by the instrumental interests of elected politicians, and loyalty lies to an entity that is broader than the elected government of the day.

That might seem like an idealist, other-worldly, or pre-democratic view of public service—'stockbrokers ... ready to die for the Stock Exchange', in the words of our second epigraph. But in fact, conceptions of public service relationships that approximate to a bargain of this type are not far to seek. For instance, in the EU, both the politically appointed Commissioners and the civil servants beneath them are formally bound to an exclusive 'duty of loyalty to the [European] Communities' (*European Commission Staff Regulations Handbook*, Art. 11), and in that sense are not expected to act as the 'agents' either of their own national governments or of the EU Parliament and the Council of Ministers. Something broadly similar goes, formally at least, for German civil servants who (at least since the 1919 Weimar constitution (Art. 130), normally considered to be embraced by Art. 33(5) of the 1949 Basic Law of the West, which was in turn extended to unified Germany after 1990) are expected to be loyal to the constitution and its values, not simply to the government of the day.[2] *The Bundesbeamtengesetz* (§52 (1) and (2)) specifies that civil servants serve the whole people, not just one party, and must consider in their actions the welfare of the general public and show commitment to the constitution and its preservation. That document also specifically provides for circumstances in which civil servants are only subject to the law and are not obliged to implement directions from superiors (§55).

Those are both examples of bargains roughly approximating to the trustee form that are system-wide and enacted in constitutional documents or similar formal provisions. But trustee bargains may be implicit or unwritten and they may be partial—applying only to some of the public service. For instance, in democratizing states with a strong tradition of military involvement in politics (such as Brazil or Turkey) the military often lay claim to a 'trustee bargain' in at least two related ways. One, as brought out in Samuel Finer's (1962: 33–9) classic analysis of *The Man on Horseback*, is the common military claim to the right to act as the 'trustee' of the constitution or national interest at large, the guardian of the nation which intervenes in politics when it considers that national interest to be threatened by a civilian government

---

[2] Indeed, the 1972 *Extremistenbeschluss* (much debated at the time) extended the principle of constitutional loyalty by prohibiting association with organizations deemed as threatening the constitutional principles of the (then West) German Basic Law.

(as in the classic Brazilian tradition of the military's claim to exercise *poder moderator* (Stepan 1971: 4).

The other is the right to a substantial degree of autonomy in the running and deployment of the military machine itself, in some cases in exchange for non-involvement in civilian politics. The classic example of this type of bargain is perhaps the concept of the military as a *Staat im Staat* that developed in Prussia and Germany in the early era of democratization, with the military placed outside the normal constitutional and political processes and accountable only to the monarch. Even the Weimar Republic did not establish formal subordination of the military but instead relied on a 'partnership relationship' of equals (Hornung 1975: 35–42 Finer 1962: 47–51). Many political scientists have argued that successful democratization in many cases depends on the ability to conclude a bargain with the military that strikes a balance between 'agency' and 'trusteeship' and thus avoids long periods of military rule (Feaver 2003: 4–10).

Nor is the military the only significant part of the state apparatus that frequently lays claim to a strong element of 'trusteeship' in its relation to other parts of the political system. In contemporary times, much attention has been directed to non-majoritarian organizations in the economic sphere, particularly independent regulatory authorities and central banks such as the US Federal Reserve and the famous (West) German Bundesbank, which was often held up as a model for others to copy during and after the glory days of the post-Second World War German economic miracle (Schmidt 1989). As with the military case, the 'trustee' element involves being cast as a guardian of national interests rather than as an agent at the beck and call of the elected politicians of the day.[3] Earlier enthusiasts for this kind of PSB include the famous economist John Maynard Keynes (1952), who explicitly advocated 'public sector trusts' independent of direct control from elected politicians (see also Hood and Jackson 1991: 89–90). The argument goes that such a guardian in its policy decisions will set aside political pressures designed to advance the short-term interests of powerful interests in favour of longer-term and wider interests of the society and economy as a whole. Some of the elements of that sort of bargain can be found in legislation and in the formal terms on which the office-holders are appointed (e.g. in the statutes governing UK network regulators that limit ministerial influence to 'guidance' in specified areas, rather than 'direction' and the appointment of the president of the German cartel authority as a lifelong appointee rather than a political civil servant). Similarly, and arguably most explicitly, the European Treaty requires

---

[3] Even though the term 'agency' is often—confusingly—used to describe independent regulatory organizations.

the European Central Bank to seek 'price stability' as its primary goal (Art. 105 (1)) and prohibits the taking of any instructions from any other organization (Art. 108).

In other cases again, we can find bargains that are partly of an agency kind, but with an element of trusteeship about them, at least in the understanding of some of the parties. As we shall see later, in Chapter 6, aspects of 'trusteeship' apply even to civil servants in the Westminster/Whitehall family,[4] even though the bargain those civil servants operate under is often described both by officials and scholars as if it were a purely agency role of taking or anticipating orders from elected ministers.

In all of these cases, what we find is either a formal provision that the public servants involved have, an element of autonomy in the way they exercise their responsibility, or a strong unwritten understanding to the same effect. In both of those types of 'trustee bargain', the observance of the bargain is potentially problematic. What is to prevent one or more of the parties from cheating or reneging on the deal? In the case of the unwritten understandings, what happens when the understandings are no longer understood by one or more of the parties? How does actual practice relate to what is set down on paper? At this stage we set aside the issue of cheating and observance of such bargains, postponing our exploration of that issue to Chapters 7 and 8.

In using the term 'trustee' to designate this class of bargain, we do not mean to imply more than a loose analogy with the English law of trusts, any more than John Locke seems to have implied a strict parallel in his famous description of the relationship between governors and governed as a trust.[5] Indeed, to draw a Locke-type analogy between public service and trusteeship in law is tricky in several ways. First, according to many contemporary commentators critical of what they call the 'Anglo-American' approach to public management, something approximating to a trusteeship approach to PSBs is more commonly found in Continental-European Roman-law jurisdictions, even though, as noted earlier, the concept of trust *à la* Locke comes from the common law. Second, within England itself, the concept of trust in law has historically been applied to private law relationships rather than to

---

[4] Those trusteeship elements are generally less explicitly recognized than in the case of the German *Bundesbeamtengesetz* cited earlier, though in derived Westminster/Whitehall systems such as Trinidad and Tobago, it was common for the responsibility of permanent secretaries for all aspects of administration (under the general direction and control of the minister) to be written into independence constitutions (e.g., Art. 85 of the Trinidad and Tobago constitution) (TT1).

[5] For instance, Laslett argues that Locke's famous 'right of revolt', allowing for the trustees to be overthrown by the beneficiaries if they fail in their trust, contradicts a key prescriptive principle of trust law, indicating that 'Locke did not intend to go further in his references to trust than to make suggestive use of legal language' (see Locke 1960: 113).

those between public servants and the Crown (see Burn 1996: 49). Third, the notion of trusteeship stretches the concept of a 'bargain', in that trust relationships in law do not result from agreements between trustees and beneficiaries. But they do depend on bargains of another type, between those individuals who create a trust and those who agree to exercise it. And in a broader sense, there has to be an underlying social understanding about the acceptability of trusts as an institution for such a relationship to continue in existence.

In Section 2.3, expanding on what was said in Chapter 1, we sketch out some varieties of PSBs that approximate to some notion of trusteeship. But in the next section we briefly consider what sort of conditions seem to be conducive to 'trustee-type' PSBs.

2.2. WHY TRUSTEE BARGAINS?

It is not difficult to see why 'trusteeship' might have figured prominently in PSBs in pre-democratic and colonial settings. They echo visions of 'enlightened absolutist' monarchy and aristocracy as 'servants of the people' in the vein of the Prussian king Frederick II (Frederick the Great, who reigned from 1740 to 1786), who saw his role as that of 'first servant of the state' (see Johnson 1975). But on the face of it there is something of a puzzle as to why anything approximating to a 'trustee' PSB should survive into an era of egalitarianism and democracy. In a democratic age, why has the trustee bargain not been consigned to Lenin's famous (and indeed overflowing) 'dustbin of history'?

One possible answer—perhaps the most obvious one—might be historical lag. By that we mean the commonly observed tendency of long-established institutions to take time to respond to changes in their environment. It would hardly be surprising if state bureaucracies only came into line with the move to electoral democracy after significant delays, because of general institutional 'stickiness' and inertia. Indeed, such delays are central to Michael Moran's explanation (2003) for the persistence of what he calls 'club government' in Britain (see also Marquand 1988). Moran sees club government as the persistence of attitudes and institutional practices redolent of the era of aristocratic government for a century or more into the age of electoral democracy. And similar processes have been observed in many other countries. For instance, the post-Second World War creation of the *Ecole Nationale d'Administration* (ENA) in France, designed to establish a legal-economic counterpart to the eighteenth-century specialist elite schools for mining and road engineering (*Ecole Nationale des Mines* and *Ecole Nationale des Ponts et Chaussées*) is said to have had the effect (intended or otherwise) of perpetuating the rule of a privileged caste of Paris-based senior civil service families (see Hayward 1983: 123–8).

The historical lag explanation, of 'trusteeship' ideas as a hangover from an earlier aristocratic or colonial political regime, probably has some force. But it seems unlikely to be the whole story, for at least three reasons. First, as we noted earlier, new forms of trustee-type bargains keep emerging during the democratic age, particularly with the enthusiasm for taking key tasks of economic management out of the hands of elected politicians and giving them to independent experts of one kind or another. Second, there is no obvious reason why a notion of 'trusteeship' should have been the prevailing bargain for the public service in an age of monarchical or aristocratic government rather than an agency-type bargain. The reverse seems equally plausible—after all, state officials might just as well be regarded by those monarchs or aristocrats as domestic servants to be ordered about at will.[6] One senior British civil servant in an interview recalled to us that he was indeed treated very much like the family butler or estate steward by aristocratic Conservative ministers of thirty years before (UK19). Third, and relatedly, the notion of 'trusteeship' does not seem to be closely linked to the particular features of 'club government' identified by Moran. Rather, the established PSB in the UK, at central government level at least, is conventionally seen in comparative perspective as an 'agency' form, whereas some of the leading examples of the 'trustee' form can be found in 'legalistic' state traditions like that of Germany that do not possess what Moran sees as the defining features of 'club government'.

So while tradition and historical inertia may well play a part in explaining why we see 'trustee' bargains in a democratic age, such forces do not seem to fully explain either the cross-national differences that can be observed or developments over time. So what else might account for what we observe? From standard themes in institutional analysis, we might identify three 'usual suspect' reasons for why something other than an agency form of PSB might develop in an age of electoral democracy—namely checks and balances, blame avoidance, and commitment politics of various kinds.

The 'checks and balances' argument is normally put in normative or doctrinal terms. It goes that in a liberal democracy (as opposed to 'Jacobin' forms of unchecked majoritarianism), the power of elected politicians needs

---

[6] Moreover, the emergence of trustee-type bargains in Europe is normally dated at about the turn of the nineteenth century, even though some other trustee-type institutions, such as the Chinese Imperial censorate, have far earlier origins.

to be balanced by independent sources of administrative power, at least for some functions where there might be particular risks of corruption, conflict of interest, or naked use of the legal powers of the state as a weapon against political opponents. Such arguments have often been used to justify a measure of autonomy in the hands of public servants such as tax assessors, census officials, public prosecutors, even intelligence officers and political police. And giving autonomous power to enlightened technocrats fired by zeal for the public interest is often seen as a recipe for successful economic policy, as we have already noted.

However, for this idea to explain (as opposed to justifying) the development of trustee-type PSBs, one or all of the three mechanisms would have to be at work. First, the idea itself might generate general approval. Second, those who have a clear interest in an autonomous public service might have the power to bring that about. Third, perhaps a variant of the second, politicians themselves might have an interest in promoting checks and balances that limit their own power.

General approval of the checks-and-balances ideas might be expected to be strongest in those democracies in which unchecked exercise of power by elected politicians has produced deeply illiberal policies in the past, as in the case of Germany. The force of interests in pressing for public service autonomy might be expected to be strongest in political systems where major economic interests are fearful of pressures on elected politicians to pursue policies unfriendly to firms or investors. Autonomous public servants controlling key aspects of economic policy may in some circumstances serve to reassure business interests, seeking ways of entrenching property rights and currency stability against 'political risk'. And politicians themselves might support public service autonomy in various circumstances. For instance, Bernard Silberman (1993: chs. 2–3) suggests that conditions of high uncertainty about political elite succession, paired with a 'social network' leadership structure, will tend to make politicians behave in that way.

Such ways of securing political commitment have been much discussed. In a well-known analysis, Brian Levy and Pablo Spiller (1996) have set out an array of political commitment mechanisms that can protect investors and business firms against raids by 'expropriating' governments, though they do not explicitly include trustee-type PSBs in that catalogue. But Murray Horn (1995) makes much of the 'commitment' argument to explain why politicians often seem to follow a self-denying course in giving up powers to appoint, dismiss, and promote public servants at will. Horn's argument goes that governing groups who face a risk of being supplanted by others with different policy preferences at a future election will prefer to trade 'fingertip control' over their civil servants in the present in exchange for denying such control to their successors, provided that legal or institutional arrangements can be devised to do so. That is perhaps a special case of the ironic observation that the strongest supporters of any given policy are often the strongest opponents of giving the government of the day substantial discretion in operating such policies (see Bendor and Moe 1985; Scholtz 1991: 122).

Such commitment arguments might account for the emergence of 'trustee-type' PSBs sometimes. But in Horn's own transaction-cost argument, 'commitment costs' are only used to explain why or when elected politicians prefer one form of agency bargain to another. His analysis seeks to explain when politicians choose a personal-loyalist form of agency bargain (in which incoming elected office-holders appoint their own agents) as against a serial-loyalist form in which a permanent civil service serves successive elected office-holders. Something more basic would seem to be needed to make such an explanation work for trustee-type bargains, such as those 1980s/1990s ideas about 'pacted transitions to democracy' that many political scientists identified as key to the emergence of electoral democracy in numerous cases in the so-called third wave of democratization in the 1970s and 1980s, particularly in Latin America.[7] The idea of a pacted transition, which we touched upon in Chapter 1, is that a successful shift to democracy in such cases involves elites from a pre-existing regime driving the sort of bargain with pro-democratic elites in which each side achieves a 'minimax' position (i.e. a strategy that minimizes the chances of maximum loss).

If checks-and-balances politics can play out in such ways, blame-avoidance motivations might also account for trustee-type PSBs, even and perhaps especially in a post-aristocratic age. In most of the literature about blame avoidance and blame management in political science, the issue for elected politicians as institutional designers is not so much the prospect of having policies, or even the entire constitutional order, undone by successors of a different political stripe, as of the risks of being blamed for failures in policy and administration. The 'blame-avoidance' argument goes that elected politicians in deciding institutional arrangements will in some way weigh up the relative advantages of 'credit claiming' (which comes from being directly in control when things go well) with 'blame shifting' (which comes from being able to disown responsibility when things go badly), and give autonomy to other institutions when the expected advantages of blame-shifting exceed those of credit-claiming (see Fiorina 1982, 1986).

---

[7] See Huntington (1991), Whitehead (2002: 36), O'Donnell, Schmitter, and Whitehead (1986), Colomer (1991, 1995, 2000), and contrast McFaul (2002). For a brief discussion of 'transitional justice' as it applies to public servants after regime changes, see Elster (2004: 92).

So from this perspective, we might expect trustee-type PSBs to be favoured if politicians prefer to avoid blame for bureaucratic activities than to claim credit for them, and specifically if: (*a*) politicians believe a trustee-type PSB will in fact help deflect blame away from themselves; (*b*) politicians believe the workings of executive government are more likely to be unpopular than popular with voters at large; and (*c*) politicians' risk preferences are such that they prefer to avoid losses than to have a chance of gaining credit. So in that light we might interpret trustee-type bargains as what are most likely to be preferred by elected politicians with a strong negativity bias—in the sense that they prefer blame avoidance to credit claiming. Such motivations are often also invoked to explain developments such as apparent self-denial on the part of elected politicians giving up control over specific economic policies to autonomous public servants (see Weaver 1986, 1988), though less commonly to trustee-type bargains of a more general type.

We often find multiple possible explanations of the same institutional forms, and indeed such forms may be produced by multiple causes. It seems hard to deny that trustee-type PSBs often involve some historical lag. But if that was all there was to it, we might expect such PSBs to steadily disappear over time without any significant development of new trustee-type PSBs. Yet, on the contrary, shifts to electoral democracy may produce a shift *towards* trustee-type bargains of a type that did not exist in the earlier era as part of a 'pacted transition' process. And the development of capitalist democracy in the current era of 'globalization' may also create new pressures for trustee-type bargains as a means of reducing the risk to business from exposure to decisions by vote-seeking politicians. The logic of political blame-avoidance considerations in such an era may point in a similar direction, at least for some types of trustee bargain. So what sort of variations are possible on this theme?

2.3. SOME VARIETIES OF TRUSTEE BARGAINS

Treatises on trust law distinguish different categories of trust, for instance in distinguishing trusts that are expressly created by the settlor from those that are implicit or constructive, private and public trusts, overt and secret trusts, trusts for predetermined beneficiaries and trusts with a more open remit (see, e.g. Oakley 1998: 35–43). In the same way we can identify more than one form of trustee-type PSBs. One of the fundamental issues in any trust arrangement is the relationship between trustees and beneficiaries, and the same applies even more to government. For instance, in a pension trust, should the trustees be representative of the pensioners (or future pensioners) whose funds are held in trust? Or should those trustees be drawn from individuals who are exceptional and exemplary in some way to exercise their duties without fear or favour? In the same way, public servants in some kinds of trustee-type PSBs are conceived as representatives of the society they serve, while in others they are anything but. Accordingly, following the analysis we foreshadowed in Figure 1.2, we can distinguish between 'representational' and 'tutelary' sub-types of the trustee bargain, which differ in the nature of the office-holders and the principles on which they are selected.

2.3.1. Representational Forms of Trustee-Type Bargains (B1a)

At the heart of what we call a 'representational' form of trustee bargain is an understanding that the public service should be representative of the society it serves in some way, for instance in terms of geography, gender, race, language, or class. And such understandings are not far to seek in many societies. As we noted in Chapter 1, issues of who is represented and how do not apply only to elected legislatures. The representativeness of the non-elected public service is often just as politically salient as that of the legislature, if not more so (Subramaniam 1967; Krislov 1974; Esman 1997).

Understandings about representativeness in bureaucracy can operate at various levels. They may apply to the top levels of the public service, the supposedly 'commanding heights' of power in the state, as in the case of the legal requirement that the German federal civil service should reflect the federal nature of the state. And they can also apply to the 'street-level bureaucrats', like police and teachers who operate in the front line as the visible presence of state activity and public service delivery (Lipsky 1980). In a representational bargain, the implicit or explicit exchange is between support for the state or the regime by the groups that are represented and a significant share in the administrative power of the state. And representation through the bureaucracy comes to take on aspects of 'trusteeship' when that representation is expected to imply some degree of independent action by those bureaucrats as part of some broader political settlement, and not just the role of a robot programmed or directed by others.

Representative bargains involving an element of trusteeship can vary in several ways, and we can distinguish here between 'consociational' (B1a1) and 'tutelage' (B1a2) varieties, as mentioned briefly in Chapter 1. Under the consociational form (B1a1), all parts of society obtain some 'fair share' of public service positions in exchange for support of the regime. Such an arrangement has come into prominence in political science during the last thirty years or so as a result of the work of Arend Lijphart (1968, 1984) who in successive works has propounded consociationalism as a key device for the stable liberal-democratic government of divided societies.[8] By divided (or plural) societies, Lijphart means societies that are divided on racial, linguistic, ethnic, or religious lines (rather than social class divisions) without any cross-cutting cleavages, and by consociationalism he means a system of governance that combines four main features, namely a grand coalition of the elites across the segmented groups in the society, a veto on the part of each group in the society, autonomy in the hands of each group in running key public or community services such as education,[9] and a large element of proportion-ality in electoral systems and government bureaucracy. The latter means recruitment and promotion rules designed to ensure that all the main groups contending for a share of power in the society are represented at all levels in the public service.

'Consociationalism' turned into a major and influential research pro-gramme in political science, even though Lijphart's claims for consociation-alism as a system of governance have been much criticized (e.g. by Barry 1975; Bogaards 2000), on grounds that include methodology, alleged anti-democratic tendencies, and underlying logic. It is not our purpose to weigh such claims here, only to note that the consociational school highlights the way that representation within bureaucracy is often a key part of implicit or explicit conventions about the governance of divided societies. However, most of the literature on consociationalism focuses on arrangements for electoral representation, consultation arrangements, and equal funding of public services for the various groups in divided societies (Rauderaad and Wolffram 2001). Consociational representation within the public service has received much less attention, even in the countries originally identified by Lipjhart as exemplars of consociational arrangements, namely the Nether-lands, Belgium, Austria, and Switzerland (Klöti 2001).

Such consociational arrangements for the public service can take various forms. The first, as highlighted by Lijphart, consists of maximum delegation of public services to units in the population that are small enough to be socially homogeneous, coupled with rules of equal funding. An example is equal funding for state and private denominational schools in societies with a strong religious divide, as introduced in 1917 in the Netherlands. The second consists of doing work through teams rather than single officials, for instance

---

[8] And in that sense an alternative to the government of such societies by politics of homogenization, such as integration, assimilation, or outright elimination (see McGarry and O'Leary 1993).

[9] As in the application of the 'subsidiarity' doctrine in numerous European states (see Hood and Schuppert 1988: 19).

when police patrol in pairs representing the key groups in a bipolar society. In some cases military units can be operated on the same principle, as Horowitz (1985: 464) claims to have applied to the Lebanese army prior to the civil war of 1975–6, when the army split up along ethnic and religious lines. A third consists of rotation rules, such that members of the different social groups successively hold key offices in the bureaucracy as an alternative to dividing up the positions on a job-share or dual-key basis.

A fourth, perhaps a variant of the second, consists of ethnic quotas or broad proportionality rules for the bureaucracy, even if the casework is not done in pairs or in teams. Examples include the nationalities quotas within the European Commission bureaucracy (see Page 1997: 41–68; Hooghe 2001: 177–9) and other proportionality rules such as those applying to the public services in pre-1975 Lebanon (parity between Muslims and Christians for administrative posts)[10] or in the divided state of Cyprus before its partition in 1974, when the constitutionally prescribed ratio of Greeks to Turks was 70:30 in the civil service (Art. 123 of the constitution) and 60:40 in the armed forces. This PSB proved precarious, in that conflict over the implementation of those quotas, especially those for the civilian bureaucracy, was one of the key steps in the chain of events that led to the island's partition. Some consociational agreements for bureaucracies, such as those embodied in the changes to the former Royal Ulster Constabulary (Northern Ireland's police force) as part of the 1998 Belfast Agreement brokered by the UK and Irish governments (McGarry and O'Leary 1999), can involve elements of all of those four devices.

In contrast to the share-out-the-power consociational form of representative PSB are those forms of representation in the public service that give disproportionate administrative power to one particular group in the society as part of some broader social settlement or system of rule (B1a2). A traditional example is the idea that aristocrats or landed gentry should disproportionately staff the higher reaches of the civil or military service. Rulers from Frederick the Great of Prussia to Britain's Queen Victoria and the Saudi royal family have favoured this idea, partly no doubt from some general prejudice in favour of blue-blood, but also to reduce the possibility that demands for radical social and political change would resonate with those holding key offices in the military and bureaucracy.

However, the notion that the public service should have some sort of trustee role disproportionately representing some favoured group in society is by no means confined to some aristocratic past. Ideas about selective

---

[10] Unlike political posts where the ratio between Christians and Muslim was fixed at 6:5 (and further distinctions within each 'commune'), reflecting the population distribution in 1943.

representation can be found in the contemporary era as well. In many countries, the public service has been conceived as an organ of the state that should disproportionately represent a particular group as an established estate of the realm—such as the *bumiputra* Malays in post-colonial Malaysia or Afro-Trinidadians in post-colonial Trinidad and Tobago. At independence in the 1960s, Eric Williams' PNM regime reflected the notion that the more educated, nationalistic, and urban Afro-Trinidadian group of the population (largely descended from African slaves who had been freed in the early nineteenth century) represented the backbone of the nation. In all of these cases, implicit understandings about the representational bargain were overlaid on what was ostensibly an agency-type civil service,[11] and in the latter case the one-sided selective representational bargain established in the 1950s and 1960s came to be challenged a generation later as Indo-Trinidadians[12] demanded a greater degree of representation in the higher ranks of the bureaucracy hitherto dominated by Afro-Trinidadians.

As in this case, selective representation PSBs often reflect ideas and assumptions about 'ethnocracy', the rule of one ethnic group over another (Horowitz 1985: 446–52). Such ideas and assumptions are pervasive, often as a legacy of non-democratic forms of rule. Examples include parts of the former Soviet Union and in those ex-colonial societies where armies and bureaucracies were recruited along ethnic lines. Under British colonial rule in Africa and Asia, the 'officer class' in the military was frequently drawn from regions and ethnic groups quite different from those from which the mass of soldiers came, often from the peripheral regions least affected by colonial administration. That governing strategy inevitably set the scene for post-colonial politics and indeed coups d'état (ibid. 527), particularly where such officer class groups differed sharply from civilian governments based on different ethnic constituencies as to what the PSB for military and civil administration was to be.

2.3.2. Tutelary Forms of Trustee-Type Bargains (B1b)

Selective representation of the kind just discussed comes on the borderland between representational and tutelary forms of PSBs. In contrast to the

---

[11] That limited element of trusteeship was written into the constitution and apparently underpinned by a Public Service Commission, a standard device used in Westminster-model systems outside Westminster for civil service appointments and promotions. But one senior Trinidadian civil servant (TT3) told us that under Eric Williams, the assumption was that public servants were 'one of us'—that is, Afro-Trinidadian and PNM supporters.

[12] Largely descended from indentured labourers brought over from East India to work in the plantations after the freeing of the slaves in the early nineteenth century.

ideal representational form, tutelary trustee bargains reflect an understanding that public servants should be far from representative of the wider society, or even of some favoured group within it. Instead, the understanding behind the bargain is that public servants comprise exceptional and unusual individuals who exercise a trusteeship role on behalf of society at large.

Such a bargain involves the exchange of status and discretionary power for special moral or technocratic competence. It is a trustee bargain in the sense that it involves a degree of autonomous administrative power that goes well beyond the role of a 'servant'. And it is tutelary in the sense that it involves a strong form of 'merit' selection that is not alloyed by considerations of political or social representativeness. It is the sort of model that Plato put forward for his ideal republic, with an ascetic elite of philosophers trained for lifetime service in government. That vision has been influential in the Western tradition, and the analogous Confucian ideal of entrusting the powers of government to an elite of morally upright and cultured individuals remains influential in East Asia.

At first sight, we might suppose such ideas to belong to a pre-democratic age of snobbery and elitism. But tutelary kinds of bargain are still important. Variants of them—usually for parts of the public service rather than all of it—can still be found in the contemporary age. And there are two important variants that we will briefly discuss here. In one variant, the tutelary trustees are selected on the basis of their exceptional moral and cultural qualities, and in the other, they are selected on the basis of their exceptional technocratic skills and expertise.

We call the first variant 'moralistic tutelary' form of trustee PSB (B1b1). Examples of it, already mentioned, include the Confucian scholar-official tradition of Imperial China and the still powerful vision of Japanese bureaucrats as *Samurai* or ascetic knightly warriors in the service of the state (inherited from the pre-Meiji Tokugawa era). In this kind of PSB, what public servants offer are moral and cultural qualities that make them fit to govern, and not primarily or necessarily technical or subject-specific expertise. The ideal is of high-minded public-spiritedness on the part of those who govern the state at the upper levels, not the technical skills associated with 'policy wonks'. As we shall see later, this form of trustee PSB has been attacked on several fronts in Japan. The 'trustee' part of the bargain was formally weakened with the removal of the bureaucracy's independent powers of regulation in the post-Second World War constitution, and accompanying reductions in its former pay and privileges (see Kasza 1988). More recently, especially since the end of the Liberal Democratic Party's (LDP) long period of single-party rule in 1993, politicians began to move to a more 'agency' conception of the civil service.[13] But the 'moralistic tutelary' tradition at least remains important as the backdrop for such debates.

The other variant discussed here is a notion of technocratic trustees more associated with the German bureaucratic tradition (B1b2). That variant reflects Georg Hegel's ideal (noted in the first epigraph) of public servants as impartial experts or technocrats making decisions on behalf of society as a whole rather than according to the interest of any single lobby group (see Shaw 1992: 386). Indeed, in this tradition, it is precisely the superior subject-expertise, analytic and technocratic skills of the public service that allows it to withstand the pressure of particularistic interests in exercising its 'trustee' role. Such bargains are commonly found both in long-established state traditions and in contemporary institutional developments.

The German public service is perhaps the leading example of a state system that has traditionally stressed the ideal of 'technocratic trusteeship' underlying the PSB. That idea seems to have developed as part of the official legitimization of the place of bureaucrats in the state as the managerial state associated with eighteenth-century absolutism took a different form from the early nineteenth century (Gillis 1971: 215). The notion of bureaucrats as legal experts in the *arcanae* of legislative drafting and steeped in the details of the policy domains they dealt with developed as part of the post-1810 world, but it remained an animating vision of the PSB for well over a century after that. Indeed, as we have already noted, after the Nazi regime subverted the independence of the legalistic German bureaucracy, the tutelary trustee role after 1945 was entrenched, for the then West Germany, in constitutional and legal standards that were also safeguarded by judgements from the Federal Constitutional Court. A very different bargain developed in the former East Germany, as we shall see.

Moreover, as we have already noted, the notion of public servants as technocratic trustees has been much favoured in particular economic domains, particularly regulation, competition policy, and central banking as a means of insulating such domains from pressures by elected politicians deemed to be too responsive to particularistic (so-called rent-seeking) interests.[14] Again, as already noted, the German case contains some of the classic

---

[13] The extent to which the reality of public service behaviour and attitudes falls short of the ideal of knightly asceticism has been the subject of much debate too, particularly with criticism of the once-taken-for-granted practice of civil servants taking well-paid jobs after leaving the bureaucracy (see Nakamura and Dairokuno 2003), which we discuss in Chapter 4.

[14] These developments are often seen as special to the last few decades, but they have earlier antecedents. For instance, semi-autonomous public corporations were widely favoured as an instrument of public policy in the middle years of the twentieth century, for very similar reasons of insulating economic management from raw political direction.

examples of this vision of the tutelary-technocratic PSB, notably in the case of (West) Germany's Bundesbank in the age before the advent of the euro in 2000. Despite relatively weak formal institutional safeguards protecting its autonomy in rate setting, the Bundesbank became known throughout the world as a 'technocratic trustee' in managing the economy by stressing the need for such trusteeship as the only way of avoiding the sort of economic destabilization that was widely held to account for the collapse of the Weimar Republic. Another very important (West) German example is the development of 'technocratic tutelage' in the competition policy domain from the late 1950s. The famous 1957 law against restrictive practices in the former West Germany entrenched the institutionally autonomous position of the competition experts in the Federal Cartel Office. But equally important in promoting the autonomy of the Cartel Office, and that of the once-legendary Federal Economics Ministry, was the notion that the pursuit of broad 'ordo-liberal principles' by relatively autonomous expert trustees were essential both for economic recovery after the Second World War and for the West German version of liberal democracy.

Similar, often watered-down versions of those technocratic trustees have been widely advocated and adopted in different societies over the last two decades. Independent central banks have often been claimed to be the best way of achieving the stable monetary policy needed for economic development, and independent regulators, particularly for competition, have become widely advocated and, to a large extent, instituted as a central element in economic management in an era of strong international competition.[15] Georg Hegel seldom gets the credit for such institutional architecture, but the underlying PSBs are in essence the sort of expert trusteeship that he advocated nearly 200 years ago.

2.4. CONCLUSION

Even in what is often portrayed as an age of successively advancing 'waves' of democracy (Huntington 1991), the notion that public servants should not merely be at the beck and call of elected politicians, but also have some independent sphere of action in the public interest, has by no means faded away. Indeed, that notion has been applied in numerous cases to police, and to regulate those elected politicians themselves, in forms such as special prosecutors, parliamentary commissioners for standards and especially electoral

---

[15] For central banks, see Barro and Gordon (1983), Franzese (1999), McNamara (2002).

officers, in classic Hegelian form. And that idea has also been widely used to wall off certain fields of economic policy from the discretionary power of elected politicians through various kinds of 'non-majoritarian' institutions for regulation and economic management. So what we have called the trustee-type bargain is not just a relic for antiquarians. In fact, it seems very unlikely to disappear altogether, even if some of the forms discussed in this chapter are less common than others.

We sketched out earlier some of the possible ways that we could account for the development of trustee-type bargains. We suggested that not all trustee-type bargains could be explained as a kind of historical lag in which government bureaucracy adapts to the advent of electoral democracy only with significant delays. That 'lag' explanation seems to apply mainly to the selective form of representational trustee PSB and to the 'moralistic' type of tutelary trustee PSB, because there is no obvious blame-avoidance explanation for either of these forms. The political commitment explanation might account for several kinds of trustee PSBs, but it may be harder for the moralistic trustee variety to provide policy 'lock-in'. The blame-avoidance explanation is another plausible explanation for various 'technocratic' forms of tutelary trustee PSB, but it seems to fit less obviously for the representational varieties discussed here. The judgement of experts in particular may be easier to distance from the general political process than applies to the representational types of PSB. Accordingly, there seems to be no single all-purpose way of accounting for every form of trustee-type PSB, at least out of the three 'usual suspect' explanations we discussed earlier, and it seems likely that multiple causes are at work.

We started this analysis by characterizing a trustee-type PSB as one in which the tenure and rewards of public servants are not under the direct control of those for whom they act, the skills and competencies they are expected to show are not simply determined by the instrumental interest of elected politicians and indeed, their loyalty is not simply to the elected government of the day. In the next part of the book, we will be delving further into the reward, loyalty, and competency dimensions of PSBs such as those discussed here. But before turning to that issue, we discuss the 'agency-type' group of PSBs in terms similar to those used here.

3

Agency-Type Public Service Bargains

It was Miss Crawley's habit to accept as much service as she could get
from her inferiors; and good-naturedly to take leave of them when she no
longer found them useful...

(W. M. Thackeray (1848), *Vanity Fair*, London, Nelson, p. 175)

3.1. THE PERVASIVE ANALYTIC LANGUAGE OF PRINCIPAL AND AGENT—AND THE QUESTIONS IT BEGS

Rational choice theorists transformed the language—if not necessarily the substance—of bureaucracy theory in the 1970s and 1980s by introducing the terminology of 'principal' and 'agent'. For that strain of theory, control over bureaucracy was like the relationship between principals and agents who are supposed to act on their behalf.[1] The notion was popularized by the 1980s British sitcom *Yes, Minister*, in which devious civil servants sought to outwit and outmanoeuvre their often inept ministers. The principal–agent language suggests that bureaucrats are to be understood as potentially wayward agents who are liable to act in ways that are not good for their political masters—for instance by shirking, or even sabotage.[2] Since it is assumed that agents will tend to put their own interests ahead of the interests of the people they work for, it follows that control by those 'principals' will be problematic, meaning that much analytic attention needs to be paid to the costs and difficulties of monitoring and direction.[3]

---

[1] The landmark contribution is William Niskanen's (1971) much-cited analysis, and since then a massive literature on the subject of 'agency costs' has developed. For a critical review see Jones 2003: 403–6.

[2] Sabotage is distinguishable from shirking in that it is itself a form of work (see Brehm and Gates 1997: 28–34).

[3] Economists have tended to highlight the potential of control loss through information asymmetry between principal and agent and consequently high costs incurred by principals in monitoring agents (see also Wilson 1989: 154–75). Two standard and linked ways for principals

Following this conception, a conventional way of thinking about principal–agent relationships in representative democracy is to cast elected politicians as agents of the electors, top public servants as agents of the elected politicians, and front line public servants as agents of the top public servants. When executive government is looked at in that way, principal–agent relationships are everywhere, and so are the strategic problems of control where the interests of principal and agent diverge.

Though present-day institutional economists and rational choice political scientists as a rule use the terminology of principal and agent very loosely, their language of principal and agent is a half-buried metaphor. The metaphor comes from the law of agency, which is a key part of the law of contract—though 'principal–agent' theorists tend to pay scant attention to the niceties of the law of agency in practice or to the way it deals with the information-asymmetry problems that economists focus on in analysing relationships among different actors.[4]

In English law, agents are people who establish contractual relations between two parties—those that they act for (their principals) and third parties (Hanbury 1960: 1–2). Standard examples include estate agents in real estate transactions, auctioneers who sell property on behalf of their owners, literary and theatrical agents who broker contracts between writers and publishers or artists and movie or theatre companies. The law of principal and agent deals with all the complex issues of liability and obligation that arise in relations between principals and third parties with whom their agents have put them in contact. It also deals with the relationship between principals and agents, for example, in what kinds of information the agent is obliged to render to the principal and what competencies can reasonably be expected of the agent (ibid. 50; see also Beatson 2002).

Even this sketchy account of the law shows how the 'agency' metaphor differs from that of 'trusteeship', the alternative standard legal metaphor for government that we discussed in Chapter 2. It is true that trustees and agents in English law are under some common obligations, including limitations on the ability to delegate their own powers and the obligation not to put themselves into a position where duty conflicts with interest (e.g. in

---

to respond to that problem are to concentrate on so-called fire-alarm, rather than police-patrol, approaches to oversight (which cut down on the time required for oversight by principals) and to use third parties—auditors, inspectors, consultants, special appointees—as overseers of the competency and diligence of the agent.

[4] The information-asymmetry problem is normally dealt with in contract law by imposing fiduciary duties of good faith and full disclosure on both parties: the relationship between principal and agent in English law is normally taken to be a contract *uberrimae fidei* (see Hanbury 1960: 67).

themselves buying property they are responsible for selling). But there are also some fundamental differences. Whereas trustees are expected to act in the interests of beneficiaries, and are subject to legal sanctions if they flout those interests, they are not expected to do the bidding of those beneficiaries. But under the law of agency, an agent is expected to follow the lawful orders of the principal, and the principal is in turn held to be responsible for the actions of the agent.[5]

Of course—as is the way with any complex body of law—there are important limits and exceptions to both of these rules. But our general point is that some PSBs more closely resemble the relationship between a principal and an agent than the 'trustee-type' arrangements that we discussed in Chapter 2. And the purest and most simple form of such a bargain is one in which the principal in some way directly controls the reward and tenure of the agent, the skills and competencies required of the agent are those needed to do the principal's bidding, and the agent's only loyalty is to the wishes of a single principal, who in turn takes responsibility for the acts of the agent. To be more specific, in a PSB that resembles agency relationships in law, public servants:

(1) enter into arrangements with third parties for which their political masters, considered as principals, are liable;
(2) are expected to do what their political principals ask, within the limits of constitutionality and legality that would apply to any agency relationship;[6] and
(3) are under some fiduciary duty to make the fullest disclosure about their activities in their communications with their principals.

In such an arrangement, public servants accept those responsibilities in return for some quid pro quo that is known to both parties and fixed by some sort of agreement between them.

As Chapter 2 showed, numerous PSBs do not map very closely onto the concept of agency in law. And indeed it is odd that economists, who normally take a pride in parsimony and precise use of language, chose to take their terminology from a rather special part of contract law, rather than using simpler legal terminology, such as that of employer and employee. But the concept of an agency PSB is still important for several reasons.

---

[5] Following the doctrine that *quis facit per alium facit per se*, that is, the notion that the agent's actions are construed in law as those of the principal (Beatson 2002: 681).

[6] Those limits include, at least since the post-1945 Nuremburg trials and the 1961 Eichmann trial, norms of international law that go against an 'only following orders' defence on the part of those who portray themselves as mere agents of an all-powerful principal (see Arendt 1964). Even in ordinary contract law, in the USA at least, contractual bargains are potentially subject to being struck down by the courts as 'unconscionable', for instance on grounds of duress (see Posner 1986: 104).

Such a bargain in its pure form may be the exception rather than the rule, but in many important cases, elected politicians and public servants have indeed related to one another in something approximating to an agency bargain as described earlier. Indeed, the relationship between elected politicians and direct political appointees often resembles that sort of bargain, as in the case of the *Persönliche Referent* in the German bureaucracy. Probably the best-known example is that of Günter Guillaume, who was appointed personal adviser to the (West) German Chancellor Willy Brandt in 1972 and triggered Brandt's resignation in 1974 after being exposed as a spy for the East German regime—a classic case of a principal being held responsible for the acts of an agent.

Moreover, something approximating to an agency relationship is often seen as a necessary condition for bureaucracy in democratic government. After all, if public servants are not 'agents', how can representative democracy be possible? Such reasoning leads many champions of democratization to aim for a more 'principal–agent-like' relationship between elected politicians and bureaucrats. As we have shown in Chapters 1 and 2, while the German PSB was recreated in 'trustee' style in the post-Second World War West German constitution, the post-war Japanese constitution moved the Japanese PSB into what was at least ostensibly a more agency form, in a reaction against the former watchword 'exalt the officials, despise the people' (Nishio 2004: 145). Post-colonial governments have also often sought to develop more of an agency style of PSB in their efforts to bring formerly autonomous colonial bureaucracies under the heel of their new political masters. A case in point is Lee Kuan Yew's People's Action Party (PAP) government of Singapore in the early 1960s, which sharply cut back on the allowances of the senior ranks in the bureaucracy for a few years in the aftermath of independence, dramatically bringing home to the senior bureaucrats the desirability of being responsive to the wishes of the new government (see Quah 2003*a* and contrast Lee 1998: 318).

Even in the established democracies today, many schemes for reform in executive government are intended to make the relationship between politicians and public servants more 'agency-like' in several ways—the 'bucking-to' spirit that we discussed in chapter one. In fact, for scholars such as Moshe Maor (1999), that theme of increasing the principal's control over the agent—more than the achievement of 'efficiency' in terms of value for money—was the basic driving force behind the much-discussed 'NPM' movement of the 1980s and 1990s across a number of parliamentary democracies. Some of the themes in that movement included:

- increasing politicians' control over tenure and reward arrangements, for instance, by removing indefinite tenure from departmental heads or making political adviser positions a staging post to regular civil service appointments;

- increasing the emphasis on 'delivery' skills relative to those of judgement, policy advice or adjudication, particularly linked with; and
- more elaborate control systems in the form of politically set targets and performance indicators to ensure that the agent follows the principal's wishes.

If the agency bargain and its variations merit attention for such reasons, at least three issues deserve to be explored. First, the corollary of the question we asked in Chapter 2, is the puzzle of why the pure form of agency bargain should *ever* be diluted. Politicians in a democracy are under strong pressure to apply quick fixes to intractable problems, to run a tight political ship in the face of inertia, plotting and sabotage, and to outmanoeuvre or roll over their many opponents. We might expect them to want bureaucrats and public servants to be as closely as possible under their thumb in those circumstances. So why is it that we so often find agency bargains diluted in ways that put significant decisions and key issues of staffing (such as appointment, tenure, and reward) out of the direct control of political 'principals'? Why would elected politicians in a democracy settle for less than a total 'agency' bargain with their public servants, and when would they prefer such a bargain?

Second, how do agency bargains survive in the face of all the political stresses and strains to which executive government is subject? You hardly need to be a fully paid-up rational choice theorist to see that both sides may have both motive and opportunity for cheating on any such bargain. Quite apart from all the general reasons why employers and employees might want to cheat on the bargains they have struck with one another,[7] there are particular cheating motives and opportunities that apply to the politician–public servant relationship. For instance, politician principals might want to try to escape political heat by shuffling off responsibility for the actions they have ordered or civil service agents might seek to carry out their orders in a way that follows their own inclinations and interests rather than what their political principals intended. These are far from imaginary dangers, and the historical record is full of examples of such deviations. Indeed, Max Weber (1968: 990–4) pointed out some of the problems a century ago, before principal–agent terminology had become the dominant language for discussing such issues in economics and political science.

---

[7] This situation has been formalized in the so-called 'Trust/Honor Game' (see Kreps 1990b), as elaborated by Gary Miller (1992) in a landmark analysis of employer–employee games over piece-rate rewards.

Third, what are some of the different forms that agency bargains take? How and why do they vary in matters of reward, competency, and loyalty or responsibility? Most of this chapter is devoted to exploring different forms of agency bargain in historical and comparative perspective, since we postpone to Chapter 8 a fuller analysis of the factors that underpin or undermine PSBs. Accordingly, in the rest of this chapter, we first consider the factors that prompt political systems to adopt agency-type bargains, and then look at some of the main variants of agency PSBs.

3.2. WHEN DO POLITICAL SYSTEMS ADOPT AGENCY BARGAINS?

In Chapter 2, we identified three 'usual suspect' reasons for why elected politicians should settle for less than a total agency bargain with appointed public servants: checks and balances, commitment, and blame avoidance. To the extent that there is something in these standard and well-established lines of argument, their corollary is that the agency bargain will be particularly attractive in at least three kinds of circumstances, which may well be related. First is where checks-and-balances arguments do not carry much weight either with the electorate at large or with the main players in the political system. A slightly different, albeit somewhat tautological, way of putting the same point is to suggest that 'agency bargains' may tend to develop most strongly where there is only a single 'veto player' in the political system, using the well-known language of George Tsebelis (2002). A second condition favourable for the development of agency bargains would be circumstances where commitment issues do not figure large in politics. A third condition favourable for agency PSBs would seem to be circumstances where blame avoidance by the use of some degree of autonomy on the part of public servants is either politically unnecessary or politically impossible.

So what exactly are *those* circumstances? Such questioning can potentially take us into an infinite regress, but a possible argument might be that those 'agency-friendly' conditions can be found at two ends of a democratic spectrum. One is in the type of democracy where there is so little party turnover (or expectation of such turnover) in government that checks and balances, commitment, or blame avoidance are scarcely an issue. An example of that type of political system is the tightly run city-state of Singapore, which at the time of writing had been governed by a single political party since 1959 and had had only three prime ministers in nearly fifty years. In that regime, where opposition parties were weak to the point of invisibility, and any intrusive media questioning of the actions and running of executive government hardly existed (except perhaps in internet sites run by individuals out of favour with the governing regime from outside the country), none of the three 'usual suspect' explanations (checks and balances, commitment, and blame avoidance) for diluting agency bargains has much force.

In such types of regime, the notion that the public service should form any kind of judge-type semi-autonomous power checking the power of other elements of the governing group cannot be expected to carry much weight. If the established governing coalition expects to win elections and remain in power more or less indefinitely, Horn-type 'commitment' arguments for relaxing a pure agency approach will not weigh very heavily either. And in political systems where opposition groups and even media have little opportunities to offer sustained and well-informed criticisms of the conduct of executive government, there is likely to be only occasional need for scapegoats or lightning-rods to deflect blame away from the rulers. In political soil of that type, the agency type of PSB seems likely to develop in a fairly pure form.

However, favourable conditions for agency-type PSBs also seem to be found in democracies with precisely the opposite political characteristics. By that we mean conditions in which the political future of any governing coalition is highly uncertain and so is the behaviour of possible successors who might emerge after future elections. The governing group is exposed to constant, intense, sustained, and sophisticated public questioning about its executive actions by all too well-informed and credible critics. Elected politicians are so little respected that that they are routinely and heavily vilified whatever they do, and the media and public at large are programmed to regard them as guilty until proved innocent.

In such conditions, the governing group is likely to feel that with so many entrenched and well-armed opponents, turning the public service into yet another branch of the opposition is the last thing they need. If the behaviour of possible successors following an election defeat is unpredictable, any governing group cannot tell whether a strategy of 'autonomizing' the public service will be respected by their successors. After all, such a group might immediately abandon such autonomy and go for spoils appointees on a tight rein. In such conditions, diluting an agency bargain in the hope of preserving policy stances into the future is likely merely to cramp the style of the current governing group without necessarily doing so for its successors. The same applies if the cultural and social climate is such that incumbent politicians will always be the first to incur blame from the media, opposition parties, or government at large, irrespective of detailed institutional arrangements.

If politicians are going to get the blame for everything that goes wrong in executive government whatever they do, they might as well go for a purer form of agency bargain and the extra ability to micro-manage the bureaucracy that goes with it.

Such conditions were perhaps approximated in those countries of Central Europe that witnessed a transfer of power to the opposition after their first democratic elections. For instance, Jan Meyer-Sahling (2004) argues that in the case of Hungary, the regular electoral turnover in office between the former socialist governing party and other parties in the 1990s and early 2000s meant a continuous 'clean out' of public servants who were seen as too close to the previous regime, thereby disabling any move towards the kind of 'depoliticized' civil service (with a trustee-type PSB) that was being advocated by the great and the good in international organizations. In fact, high levels of discretionary control by politicians over their public service agents seem to have been a feature of post-communist transitions of this type (ibid. 97).

On this argument, it would seem most likely to be the political systems somewhere between those two extremes that provide the most favourable conditions for departure from some kind of agency bargain. Those 'in between' political systems are those in which the use of the public service as one of a set of checks and balances is neither 'unthinkable' nor redundant. They are political systems for which electoral upset is a real possibility, but the behaviour of probable successors towards the bureaucracy is reasonably predictable, and where governing politicians are neither routinely vilified nor so well-armed that they have little to fear from critics.

This analysis in principle applies to both the directed and delegated forms of agency bargain, because it will be recalled that the latter differ from trustee bargains in that delegation is readily alterable or revocable altogether. The analysis may also help answer the second question posed earlier—namely why agency bargains do not continually collapse under pressures to renege by both sides. After all, just like trustee bargains, agency bargains are potentially subject to cheating on both sides. Agents cheat, through shirking or sabotage when they do not carry out their principals' orders or behave according to their expectations—for example, when they leak information that is supposed to be confidential to pursue their own political agendas, when they lie to or mislead their principals, when they delay or drag their feet, or when they pick and choose the parts of the principal's orders they obey rather than ignore. Principals cheat when they deceive or double-cross their agents, for instance, by issuing deliberately ambiguous instructions, keeping their agents in the dark about their true wishes or other important information, or when they blame their agents for carrying out their own wishes. As we shall see later, both kinds of cheating are common enough.[8]

3.3. HOW DO AGENCY BARGAINS VARY?

3.3.1. Delegation and Direction

Turning to the question of how agency forms of PSB can vary, politicians dealing with public servants on an agency basis face at least two basic choices. Do they delegate their powers to their agents in some way, working on an arm's-length basis, or do they keep their agents on a short leash, giving them precise orders on a daily basis? In the latter case, agents work on the principal's instructions, like stockbrokers who buy or sell specific stocks when instructed to do so by a client, or soldiers who follow their orders of the day. In the former case, agents work within a general framework agreed with the principal, with discretion to operate within that framework, like a stockbroker who has discretion to buy or sell stocks on behalf of a principal within some set of agreed parameters or objectives. The military equivalent arises in those sorts of cases where units operate (e.g. behind enemy lines) with general orders but a high degree of discretion in matters such as what targets to attack, when or how. Now in both cases, the agent acts for the principal, and the job of the agent is to carry out the principal's wishes in some sense, not to act as a guardian of some constitutional framework or in any fiduciary or trusteeship capacity. But the operating conditions are very different. In one case, principals have their agents at their beck and call to follow the whims of the moment, while in the other the principal has the agents operating on a long leash.

Both approaches have their costs and benefits. For instance, the former approach may ensure responsiveness in real time but exposes politicians to a heavy burden of day-to-day direction, while in the latter case, the principal is less burdened with micro-management, but runs the risk that any particular actions may run against what the principal might have wanted at that moment. Anyone who has ever had a management job will recognize that dilemma. So principals might well want to mix and match or switch sequentially between the two strategies—for instance, putting agents on to autopilot

---

[8] But agency bargains do not always seem to degenerate into 'double-double-cross' situations noted earlier, and political systems with traditions of agency-type bargains rarely seem to switch wholesale to trustee-type bargains. Rather, they seem to develop islands of trusteeship in a sea of agency and/or switch among different forms of agency bargain.

when the principal goes away but going on to an orders-of the-day basis when the principal returns.

In the principal–agent version of the theory of the firm in economics, in which the principal controls the reward of the agent, successful delegation is ordinarily expected to depend on the extent to which reward arrangements can align the agent's interests with those of the principal. One standard way to do that in private business is to make the agent agree to rewards that depend on the stock price of the corporation. And there has been a vogue for new forms of performance-related pay in public bureaucracies in recent decades or so (see Ingraham 1993), but as we shall show in Chapter 4, arriving at anything resembling the stock-price basis of reward in government and politics is difficult. The strong form of agency bargain, in which public servants agree to elected politicians directly controlling their rewards, bonuses, promotion, or preferment during and after public service, is much rarer than bargains in which politicians agree to civil servants controlling most or all of these elements for themselves, or delegate them to other organizations not fully under their control.

However, we often find a mixture of short-leash and long-leash types of agency PSBs. In parliamentary systems, ministers often surround themselves with an immediate entourage of beck-and-call-type agents—the *Persönlichen Referenten* and *Leitungsstäbe* of the German bureaucracy, the political advisers and personal staff in the Whitehall bureaucracy, the French *cabinets*, or the Washington spin doctors of more recent vintage—while other agents work on a more delegated basis, to be summoned or instructed only occasionally, or controlled through formal delegation frameworks. Politicians who fear cheating by agents working on a delegated basis may be attracted by the prospects of balancing them with agents working on a short leash. And such a strategy may also help them do a little cheating themselves.

3.3.2. Multi-Principal and Single-Principal Bargains

A second way in which agency bargains vary concerns the extent to which the agency bargain involves a single principal or multiple principals. Whereas 'trustees' do not have principals, once we move to the world of principals and agents, at least four variants are possible: a single agent may serve a single principal; multiple agents may serve a single principal; a single agent may serve multiple principals; and multiple agents may serve multiple principals.

Principal–agent theory in economics generally starts from the single-agent, single-principal situation, but bureaucratic facts often mean that who exactly counts as the 'principal' for whom bureaucrats are agents is far from clear. One of the long-standing themes of the literature of public administration over a century or so is the multiple accountabilities to which public servants are often exposed, making them agents of more than one principal. So what are such 'agents' to do when their various principals place contradictory demands on them—for instance, in a parliamentary system when their departmental minister and the prime minister are at loggerheads, when different signals and messages come from their first-line managers and from those at the top of the hierarchy, or when they get different messages from line-of-command superiors and regulators or overseers of various kinds? Many debates about the proper conduct of public servants (e.g. over leaking of information) turn precisely on who is to be counted as their most important 'principal' or 'stakeholder', as we shall see later.

Similar problems occur where the political principal delegates tasks or responsibilities to a group of agents rather than to a single person. In this case, it is the potential for conflict (and shirking or sabotage) among the various agents that may make the single principal–multiple agent bargain problematic in several ways. Multiple agents may shirk by free riding on each others' efforts (Miller 2000); they may sabotage each other's work to make their own contribution more visible (Horn 1995); and the aggregation of the various delegated activities 'up the chain of hierarchy' may prove problematic (see Bendor, Glazer, and Hammond 2001: 246). Where multiple agents confront multiple principals, the two sets of potential sources of conflict and tension become compounded.

Both the single and multiple-principal agency bargains can vary in space or time. A bureaucratic agent may serve a single principal in space in the sense that he or she answers to a single superordinate authority at any one time, such as a single minister or department. And such a bureaucratic agent may serve a single principal in time in the sense that he or she serves only while one specific individual remains in office. As we noted in the first chapter when we commented on the variable dismissability of public servants (see Table 1.1), the epitomy of the second type of bargain is normally taken to be the USA, where thousands of top civil service positions in the first three or four rungs of each department change hands with every new president. The justification for such a system is that principal-specific tenure limits the influence of a permanent bureaucratic elite and augments the power—and funding—of political parties (see Carpenter 2001).

Agency bargains may also involve multiple principals in space or time. A bureaucratic agent may serve multiple principals in space when he or she answers to two or more separate superordinates, such as different ministries, levels of government, or even different jurisdictions. A bureaucratic agent may serve multiple principals in time if he or she works for succeeding generations of superordinates. The parallel in the latter case is with those family retainers in aristocratic houses who might serve several generations of heads of the family. The agent is on permanent or indefinite tenure in the service of the 'house' and passes from one particular principal to another. That is the traditional basis of the British and Japanese PSBs.

The latter type of agency bargain might seem to go against the grain of politics, because it surrounds politicians with those who have served or may serve their political enemies, in contrast with the spoils-type bargain, in which the agent serves only during the tenure of a particular principal. It is often said that spoils-type agents have a personal interest in prolonging the tenure of their principals (or helping them go onwards and upwards) in a way that a 'serial-principal' agent does not. As one former UK political adviser pithily put it to us, 'It is...a relationship clearly identified by one objective, you want [your political master] to succeed' (UK10).

3.4. FOUR TYPES OF AGENCY BARGAIN

3.4.1. Directed forms of Agency Bargain (B2b)—'Personal Loyalists' and 'Serial Loyalists'

Putting the two sets of distinctions discussed in Section 3.3 together, we can identify at least four types of agency-type bargains, following the branching-tree approach that was laid out in Figure 1.1. Broadly, we can distinguish delegated (B2a) and directed agency (B2b) bargains, and between simple and complex agency bargains. Directed bargains are those where public servants have no independent responsibility or liability of their own. They approximate the English legal notion of agents as people who bring a principal and a third party into a contractual relationship, but are themselves invisible in the sense that they 'drop out' of that relationship as contracting parties. The implication is that public servants act at the bidding of the politicians for whom they work, and that even if they do not, politicians accept responsibility for their acts as if they had given specific directions. Under directed forms of agency bargain, public servants exchange day-to-day loyalty to the politicians for whom they work for access to the confidential counsels of those politicians and a measure of anonymity when it comes to public praise or blame.

Within the directed form of agency bargain, we can distinguish two further subtypes, in terms of the kind of loyalty that public servants offer and perhaps the degree and kind of anonymity they get in exchange (which in turn has implications for the reward and competency dimensions of the bargain). Personal advisers to ministers or spoils appointees, already discussed, are common examples of such 'personal loyalist' form of agency bargain (B2b2), in that the agent's loyalty is to a particular individual rather than to an office. Personal loyalists of this kind rise and fall with their particular 'principal', and, as we have already noted, that linkage arguably means that their minds are concentrated on the advancement of that individual, to the exclusion of other or wider interests.

In practice, even for public servants appointed on that sort of tenure, the lines of loyalty often seem to be more complicated than that simple picture suggests. For example, temporary political advisers appointed by ministers in Germany and Britain often have loyalties to the political party in government as well as to their immediate political boss,[9] and indeed advancement may depend on the former as well as on the latter. So such individuals may live in a state of uncertainty as to whether they have a 'personal loyalist' or a 'serial loyalist' bargain, given that reappointment depends on the preferences of an incoming minister.

The other type of directed agency bargain is what we call the serial loyalist type (B2b1). 'Serial loyalists' as the label implies, undertake to be loyal to the individual in office at any one time, and transfer loyalty from one office-holder to another. As we have already noted, the best-known example of the serial-loyalist type is the Westminster-system Schafferian bargain, in which public servants are expected loyally to serve any government of the day in exchange for being granted anonymity and tenure. The 'serialism' and the 'loyalism' is starkly embodied in the famous 1985 'Armstrong memorandum' issued by the Head of the UK (home) civil service, Robert Armstrong, at the height of the Thatcher era. The memorandum declared:

Civil servants are servants of the Crown. For all practical purposes the Crown in this context means and is represented by the Government of the day.... The Civil Service serves the Government of the day as a whole, that is to say Her Majesty's Ministers collectively.... The duty of the individual civil servant is first and foremost to the Minister of the Crown who is in charge of the department in which he or she is serving.... It is of the first importance that civil servants should conduct themselves in such a way as to deserve and retain the confidence of Ministers, and as to be able to establish the same relationship with those whom they may be required to serve in

---

[9] A point made to us by a former Labour political adviser in the UK (UK2) and by a former Conservative political adviser who defined himself as a 'Tory slave' (UK6).

some future Administration.... In the determination of policy the civil servant has no constitutional responsibility or role, distinct from that of...ministers (Armstrong 1989, orig. 1985: 140–1).

As we shall see in Chapters 6 and 7, there are some important exceptions to the 'agency' view of the UK's PSB, and in any case numerous senior civil servants did not see their relationship with politicians in quite such starkly 'agency' terms as is conveyed by the Armstrong memorandum.

There are, of course, cases that can cut across these types or constitute hybrids of them. Consider three kinds of possible complications. First is the French *cabinet* system, in which members of a minister's *cabinet* are personal loyalists in the sense that their tenure as members of the *cabinet* ends when the minister steps down, but most *cabinet* members are permanent civil servants who are likely to serve in some senior capacity under governments of different types. The same applies to the *cabinets* of commissioners in the EU Commission, which are within the gift of each individual commissioner, but consist only partly of the commissioner's personal following brought in for the purpose. The *cabinets* also comprise regular commission officials and national government civil servants 'parachuted' in to the commission by their member states, and in both cases the individuals can expect a more or less permanent career, either in the commission or in their national government.[10]

Second, in the UK, some appointments to the 'regular' civil service during the Thatcher and Blair governments were widely claimed to have overtones of 'personal loyalism' about them, in so far as the public servants concerned have been seen as the protégé of the minister who pressed for their appointment. But this variant can also be quite nuanced: one such Whitehall appointee told us it was a distinct advantage to him when the minister who had pressed for his appointment to a senior position left office shortly afterwards, so that he was not seen as a stooge of that particular politician (UK20). Third, particular individuals may cross from one category of 'directed' bargain to another, as in the case of former regular civil servants in the UK system who reappear at a later date as personal-loyalist political advisers or vice versa. Traffic from positions that involve a personal-loyalist variant of agency bargain to positions involving a form of trustee bargain is also common in German bureaucratic careers. Something similar can happen with appointments to the higher spheres of the Commission directorates in the EU.[11]

[10] Hooghe (2001:186–7) argues that a period spent in a Commissioner's cabinet was seen as a primary route for high-flyers within the Commission's own staff to reach top positions in the institution.

[11] See Hooghe (ibid. 60).

3.4.2. Delegated Agency Bargains (B2a)—Simple and Complex Types

Contrasting with the 'directed' form of agency bargains, where public servants have no formal sphere of delegated responsibility (though they may well have substantial delegation in practice), are those forms of agency bargain where public servants have some formal 'space' for independent activity (B2a). The delegated form of agency bargain approaches the 'trustee' form, but differs from it in so far as public servants of this kind are not independent judges of the public interest. Rather, they take their orders from their elected principals, and those principals can change or remove any discretionary powers they have granted without change of a constitutional type.[12] They are like those forms of agency in the law of contract in which the agent has substantial discretion—like stockbrokers working on a discretionary basis for their clients—but still serves the principal under discretionary terms that can be changed at will. Under the delegated agency bargain, the political principal and the public servant agree on a framework, set by the principal, within which a zone of discretion is obtained by the public servant, in exchange for direct responsibility for outcomes within that zone of discretion.

The delegated form of agency bargain has been much advocated in recent years, particularly within the Westminster-model tradition where the traditional constitutional form of ministerial responsibility has been interpreted to mean that ministers take the blame for acts of their 'agents' even (in extreme versions) if those ministers were unaware of what their agents were doing and had given no explicit instructions about the actions that come into question. Constitutional historians argue about whether there was really any time in which ministers routinely fell on their swords for actions of their 'agents' that they had neither explicitly sanctioned nor been aware of. But it has been common, at least since the 1960s (for example, with the collapse of the Vehicle and General Insurance Company in 1969: see Gunn 1972), for ministers to name and blame civil servants directly for actions of which they were not informed or aware (see also Polidano 1999: 214). Indeed, it is now a stock blame-avoidance gambit of ministers under pressure to deny knowledge of the actions in debate and put the blame on civil servants. What ministers seem to be seeking here is a modern form of Machiavelli's famous principle of delegation, in which things that go wrong or prove unpopular involve delegated responsibilities, but credit is claimed for whatever proves to be successful or popular.[13] Whether this sort

---

[12] Of course the delegated agency bargain also comprises some mutual understanding about whether and how such changes will occur, giving rich scope for conflict and cheating.

[13] 'Princes give rewards and favours with their own hands but death and punishment at the hands of others' (Machiavelli 1961: 106).

of modification of the traditional Whitehall bargain proves to be viable in the longer run is something we will discuss later in the book, particularly in our discussion of the loyalty aspect of PSBs in Chapter 6.

In a more 'mentionable' development, delegated agency bargains have been popular in managerial reforms, particularly in the 1990s vogue for breaking up formerly monolithic bureaucracies into separate agencies headed by senior public servants operating within a framework agreed by ministers, but with some discretionary space as to how to achieve the objectives they have been set. Such bargains have been much advocated as a means of putting more emphasis on managerial or delivery skills by agency chief executives, and of being able to link reward with observed performance against targets. The agreed framework serves as the formal basis for the bargain under which responsibility is delegated, and in most forms, the notion is that the principal is responsible for the policy settings or targets (and the outcomes, good or bad, which achievement of the specified targets may lead to), while the agent is responsible for whether or how far those targets are achieved. In practice, such bargains often break down under political pressure, and indeed many have argued (following Gregory 1995) that such frameworks are inherently limited in the extent to which they can clarify lines of responsibility in all possible contingencies (contrast Polidano 1999).

As with the directed form of agency bargain, we can distinguish at least two forms of delegated responsibility that falls short of trusteeship or judge-type autonomy. One is what we call the simple delegated agency bargain (B2a2), in which there is a single 'principal' and a single 'agent', as with the case of an agency CEO who agrees a framework for delegated responsibility with the single minister who has sole, or at least major, authority over the policy area in question. That dyadic approach is the sort of vision of the delegated agency bargain that has been propounded by the various managerial prophets of delegated responsibility within civil service systems, and was a particular feature of the contractualization of the employment relationship between ministers and their chief executives (formerly permanent secretaries) in New Zealand after 1988.[14] Such an approach lends itself to the various forms of strategic behaviour that dyadic relationships can involve, including the problem of *ménage à trois*, as one or both of the parties introduce another player. We discuss that problem further in Chapter 9.

---

[14] Even the famous New Zealand contractual reforms were not a pure case of an agency bargain, insofar as chief executives were appointed by a 'trustee-type' third party, the State Services Commission rather than directly by ministers (who, however, had veto power over appointments under the 1988 State Sector Act).

By contrast, under a complex delegated agency bargain (B2a1), we do not find a single principal dealing with third parties through a single agent. Instead, in the complex type, there are multiple principals or multiple agents (or both) in the formal relationship from the outset. A commercial analogy is the case mentioned earlier of the auctioneer in English contract law who acts, at least at one point in the transaction, as the agent of both the buyer and the seller. Such cases are also not far to seek. For instance, to the extent that delegation of responsibility occurs within the US federal civil service (and such delegation has hitherto been very limited, in contrast to the rash of agencies in the UK), the agency bargain involved is bound to be complex, in so far it must be agreed by the two main 'principals' involved, the Congress and the Executive branch.[15]

Even within the UK, we can find numerous cases of delegated arrangements. For instance, the Driver and Vehicle Licensing Agency had the Department for Transport as its main principal, but also several other ministerial principals when it came to meeting targets concerned with crime, environment, and 'modernization'. And delegated agency bargains in divided government systems will tend to be complex rather than simple, making such bargains vulnerable to deadlock and hold-outs. The more 'complex' the agency bargain in this sense, the more likely it is that the agent will either have virtually unchecked discretionary power as a result of being able to play off the various principals against one another's problems, or, on the contrary, that will have no effective delegation at all as a result of the different and probably contradictory preferences of the multiple principals involved (the classic multiple-masters problem).

3.5. CONCLUSION

In this chapter, we have pursued the pervasive notion of politicians and bureaucrats as principals and agents, and explored the kinds of bargain that can be reconciled with that view. There are numerous PSBs that fit the notion of politicians as principals and bureaucrats as agents, though the contract-law metaphor needs to be stretched a bit to describe bureaucratic relationships. And we have seen that such agency bargains come in a variety of forms rather than a single one, and they can change over time from one form to another.

---

[15] And it is of course a drastic simplification to treat 'Congress' as a unitary principal, given the distinct committee systems of House of Representatives and the Senate (see Hammond and Knott 1996; Bendor, Glazer, and Hammond 2001: 244–6).

Reversing our analysis in Chapter 2, we earlier explored conditions in which agency-type bargains might emerge—in which considerations of checks and balances, commitment, and blame avoidance carried little weight. The conditions may vary from one variant of agency bargain to another, but we suggested that those conditions were broadly likely to be found at extremes of a democratic spectrum, in which there is either no effective party turnover (one-party states) or continuous party regime change (such as those of Central Europe).

We also suggested that forms of agency bargain can change over time. As we noted in Chapter 1, the civil service of the post-independence USA seems to have had a form of 'serial loyalist' bargain, later shifting towards a more 'personal loyalist' bargain in the 1820s in the Jacksonian era. And several of the changes that have taken place in Westminster-model-type countries under the label of 'NPM' have been in the direction of a form of delegated agency bargain for at least some key civil servants. The aim has been to put those agent-type civil servants into a more formal arm's-length relationship with their politician principals. But when politicians try to finesse such bargains to try to achieve the political nirvana of a system of executive government in which blame flows downwards in the bureaucracy while credit flows upwards to ministers, the metaphor of 'agency' begins to wear thin, and as we shall show in Part III, the underlying bargains needed to realize any such outcome are precarious and vulnerable to cheating on all sides.

Part II

Three Dimensions of Public Service Bargains

4

Reward in Public Service Bargains: Pyramids, *Noblesse Oblige*, Turkey Races, and Lotteries of Life

"When you retired, you see, from your last ambassadorial post, you got a duty-free allowance, known as your cellar, a certain amount of wine you were allowed to bring back to England as a privilege. The exact number of bottles was never fixed: it was left to your discretion, and everyone was happy. Until one fine day Sir This-and-that turns up with ten, twenty times what was reasonable. And that was it. As from the next day, no more allowance. No more cellar."

"Ruined it for everyone. What appalling selfishness."

"Indeed, I hope I needn't ram home the moral. In other areas the custom has grown up over the years of people in certain positions being deemed to be entitled to certain privileges. Of—and this is the point—a modest and limited order. And everyone is happy, until..."

"Until someone goes beyond what is reasonable."

(Kingsley Amis, *The Old Devils*, London, Hutchinson, 1986, pp. 90–1)[1]

You need a decent level of reward, otherwise we would read the job adverts for half of the day.

(German civil servant, D7)

4.1. THE CENTRALITY OF REWARD IN PUBLIC SERVICE BARGAINS

Reward forms a central component of PSBs. Table 1.1 showed how upper-level public servants in seven countries compared in terms of their risk of dismissal, the extent to which they had to compete for promotion with 'lateral entrants', their expectations of gaining state honours 'with the rations' as they

---

[1] This anecdote is said to refer to Sir Gladwyn Jebb (later Lord Gladwyn, 1900–96), a British diplomat and later Liberal-Democrat peer, who was British ambassador to Paris from 1954 to

moved up the ladder, and their earnings as a proportion of average earnings. That table showed substantial variety in all of those elements, but such comparisons are necessarily rough-and-ready. That is because, in contrast to other areas of statistics, readily comparable figures about the earnings of top public office-holders are remarkably hard to come by even in what is supposed to be an age of transparency (see Hood and Peters 1994). So in this chapter we aim to probe behind those numbers to get at some of the more qualitative aspects of reward in PSBs.

We pointed out in Chapter 1 that at least since Chester Barnard's *Functions of the Executive* (1938), it has been conventional to think of all organization as based on some exchange of contributions for rewards. The implicit or explicit agreements that develop over pay, perks, and other kinds of rewards can sometimes be subtle and precarious, as the first example in the epigraph shows. But who or what controls the rewards of public servants (be it the market, their peers, parliamentarians or other political masters, or some mix of those three) is always central to the politics of PSBs.

So it is not surprising that those who wish to reform bureaucracies and change bureaucratic behaviour—whether it be to reduce corruption or shirking, make bureaucrats more responsive, more entrepreneurial, more independent, or whatever other purpose it is that the reformers seek—often see the reward component of the PSB as the most important thing they have to change to achieve their goals. For example, a decade or so ago, the World Bank (1993) in a review of the 'Asian miracle', praised Singapore's controversial policy of paying its ministers and high civil servants salaries on a par with top jobs in the private sector. The Bank argued that such an approach should be generally applied across Asia in exchange for commitment to high performance and clean government. Making some heroic assumptions, it claimed that high pay for top public servants caused better economic performance for two reasons. High pay attracted more competent individuals to public service, and high pay produced less corruption, which in turn lowered 'transaction costs' for business and pushed up economic growth. Moreover, perhaps stretching credulity for most of its readers, the Bank argued that the pay bargain espoused by Singapore involved principles that were 'readily applicable to any society' (World Bank 1993: 174; Hood and Peters with Lee 2003: 5–7).[2]

1960. The official rationale for the 'cellar' allowance was that diplomats needed to have a cellar to be able to entertain as part of their official duties and that they deserved to be protected from tax loss if they were recalled at short notice. Sir Patrick Reilly, British ambassador to Paris from 1965 to 1968, claimed to have been 'almost the last, if not the last' ambassador to have enjoyed this privilege (Correspondence and Papers Concerning the British Embassy, Paris, 1965–82, Bodleian Library, Oxford, MS. Eng. c.6879, fol 142).

  [2] One of our interviewees in Trinidad shared this view enthusiastically (TT5).

At the opposite end of the argument are those socialists, egalitarians, or populists who argue that the rewards of high public servants should be representative of the incomes of those they rule, if they are to stay in touch with the everyday concerns of the governed (see Hood and Jackson 1991: 54–5).

But debates over the reward component of PSBs do not turn only on how much public servants should be paid. How they should be paid is also a subject of long-standing debate. For example, from Adam Smith and Jeremy Bentham up to modern 'efficient wage' theorists, one recurring variant of 'economic rationalism' has consisted of the doctrine that variations of pay-for-performance should be adopted as the central part of a public service pay bargain in which (as Adam Smith (1937: 678) famously put it)

Public services are never better performed than when their [public officials'] reward comes only in consequence of their being performed, and is proportionate to the diligence employed in performing them.

Others have reasoned about the 'how' of the reward bargain in rather different terms. For instance, from Georg Hegel through Max Weber and onwards, many accounts of public bureaucracy have seen the reward side of PSBs as including elements of permanence, career progression, relatively generous pensions after service, and an income that is steady, if often modest by the standards of top business earnings. It is often assumed that such a reward bargain will be especially attractive to risk-averse individuals who would rather have secure but averagely paid employment and a guarantee of relative comfort in their old age, rather than gamble on the chance of winning the jackpot in the lottery of business life. Reflecting that sort of view, one British interviewee who entered the civil service in the 1970s told us he had seen the civil service reward package at that time as akin to buying at the sort of department store that offered good value for money though not necessarily the trendiest items or the very lowest prices for customers prepared to take high risks or willing to shop around (UK4).

From this perspective, the standard bureaucratic reward bargain consists of an acceptance of a comfortable lifetime income in exchange for relative security, and perhaps intangible 'psychic income' in other forms, such as respected social status or intrinsic satisfaction of working for government. Some of our interviewees made much of the satisfaction they gained from shaping policy or services for the public good. Some saw the pleasures of the job as coming from being close to exciting decisions (UK10, UK22) and powerful ministers, even 'having fun' (UK10), while one German interviewee, perhaps living up to stereotype, saw it as coming from officially recognized status: 'The nameplate on the door costs nothing, but everyone can see where

I am ranked' (D3). Comfortable pay, linked with a satisfying job, was Georg Hegel's recipe (the so-called alimentation principle) for a professional public service that would not be captured by sectional interests (see Hegel 1991: §294).[3] That alimentation principle became entrenched in German civil service law,[4] and it was echoed by many of the bureaucrats we interviewed (as in the second epigraph to this chapter), even though it is unlikely that any more than a handful of them had any direct knowledge of Hegel's views on the matter.

What we have sketched out earlier are only some of the possible ways of reasoning about the reward bargain.[5] But it shows some of the variety both in theory and practice. What public servants get for their pains and when they get it can vary substantially, and who counts what as a reward can vary too. Even for those PSBs where the 'deal' on rewards has traditionally approximated to the conventional Weberian-Hegelian view sketched out earlier, the outer reaches of the reward bargain around this core can vary widely. For instance, in the British and German diplomatic services with which we began this book, one essential part of the bargain up to the early twentieth century was the demonstration of a private income by the aspiring (usually aristocratic) diplomats, requiring the less wealthy aristocrats[6] to marry into wealth (Röhl 1994: 151–2).

Moreover, even the 'core bargain' over bureaucratic reward is not invariably a Hegelian acceptance of relatively modest lifetime rewards in return for relative security and 'psychic income' in the form of status and putative job satisfaction. In some cases, the life bureaucratic by no means involves a monkish renunciation of riches, but is rather a route—sometimes *the* route—to opulent rewards. We noted in Chapter 1 that colonial government in the eighteenth and nineteenth centuries provided an opportunity for some colonial officials to make staggering sums. The notion that an overtly opulent lifestyle was appropriate for colonial officials often seemed to be interlinked with more or less explicitly racist ideas, as with the case of the Public Services Salaries Commission in colonial Malaya of 1919, which pronounced that: 'unless a European can earn a wage on which he is able to live decently as a

---

[3] See Hood and Peters (1994: 2), Avineri (1972: 159–60).

[4] BBG §79: 'Der Dienstherr hat im Rahmen des Dienst—und Treueverhältnisses für das Wohl des Beamten und seiner Familie, auch für die Zeit nach Beendigung des Beamtenverhältnisses, zu sorgen. [. . .]'. ['As part of his work—and loyalty relationship, the employer has to provide for the well-being of the civil servant and his family, also for the time following the end of the civil service relationship.']

[5] See also Hood and Jackson (1991: 55–61), Hood and Peters (1994), Hood and Peters (2003).

[6] Of which Anton Graf Monts was one.

European should, he merely brings discredit and contempt upon the European community' (quoted by Quah 2003*a*: 146–7).

Such colonial and racist arguments are rightly discredited today. But there are contemporary counterparts to those lavishly paid colonial nabobs, in the world of privatized or quasi-privatized public service providers, international bureaucracies and even in a few national bureaucracies, notably that of Singapore, which has already been mentioned. But state service can be a principal road to riches even where official salaries and perquisites are low, as in the many developing countries where a post in the state bureaucracy (particularly in one of the so-called 'wet' parts of government that have access to a rich flow of funds from international development agencies), can constitute a major earnings opportunity for officeholders and their families (see Hood and Peters with Lee 2003: 10).

Further, even for those cases where the traditional reward bargain has been some version of the Hegelian 'alimentation bargain'—of steady and comfortable rewards being exchanged for a lifetime of impartial public service—some important changes can be observed. For example, in many countries, the salaries for senior civil servants were traditionally related to those of elected politicians, with a pecking order that put the latter at the top, with department heads and everyone else taking their allotted place down the line. That is still the pattern in Germany and the USA, where at the time of writing it was still considered unthinkable for any bureaucrat to be paid more than the top elected politicians.[7] Yet over the past few decades that understanding has changed in several countries, with the link between politicians' pay and bureaucrats' pay broken by the adoption of pay schemes notionally based on performance, with senior central and local government civil servants now in what was once the unthinkable position of earning more than the elected ministers who head their departments, as has happened in Denmark, the UK, Australia, and Sweden (see Christensen 2003: 64–65).

Once-hallowed relativities have been overturned in some other cases as well, for instance, in the UK's executive agencies in central government, several of which have been headed by managers pocketing substantially more than the heads of the policy departments or even the head of the civil service. That development in the 1990s caused major upsets for some departmental civil servants (see Hood 1998*a*). Indeed, in a valedictory lecture in 2005, the outgoing British Cabinet Secretary, Sir Andrew Turnbull (2005), put this problem high on the list of civil service issues he had failed to solve. In a

---

[7] The German Federal Law for Ministers specified that ministers were to earn 1 1/3, the Federal Chancellor 1 2/3 of the basic salary that would apply to increment B11—the salary class applicable to state secretaries (BMinG §11).

slightly different vein, one senior UK departmental civil servant that we interviewed dismissed the problem in a light-hearted tone, implying that the high relative salary levels for the agency chief executives were a kind of 'joke', acceptable as long as the agency CEOs were 'not misled by the relative salary levels' into thinking they were not subordinate to the topmost civil servants who were really in charge (UK18).

4.2. REWARD BARGAINS: FOUR PATTERNS

Building on such observations, this chapter picks out and discusses four types of reward bargains that emerged from the reflections of public servants we interviewed. We label those four strains or dimensions '*noblesse oblige*', 'pyramids and escalators', 'turkey races', and 'lotteries of life'. These four types are neither mutually exclusive nor jointly exhaustive, and there is considerable variety to be observed within each one of them, but they have been chosen because they represent some of the major differences in reward bargains over time and among countries that we have observed. To some extent they fit onto the various worldviews identified by grid-group cultural theory[8]: pyramids and escalators can be considered to echo some of the features of the hierarchist worldview, while turkey races link to individualism, *noblesse oblige* patterns can have at least ostensible echoes of egalitarianism, and lotteries of life are the fatalist version of reward bargain. We summarize these four types in Table 4.1 and they form a convenient starting point for a discussion of variety in public service reward bargains.

4.2.1. Pyramids and Escalators

What we call the 'pyramids and escalators' form of reward bargain involves two elements that are logically separable but in practice often seem to go together. One is a structured hierarchy of rewards and the other is a 'stairway to heaven' pattern, in which advancement is relatively predictable. Such a pattern can be seen as part of a bargain in which rewards follow rank in a predictable way in exchange for integrity, loyal service, following rules and making judgements.[9]

The pyramid element means that rewards reflect a stable and well-understood order of precedence. In such a world, those at the top of the

---

[8] See Douglas (1981), Thompson, Ellis, and Wildavsky (1990), Hood (1998*b*).
[9] See Horn (1995: 111–131) for a transaction cost based analysis of the escalator approach to public service rewards

Table **4.1** '*Noblesse oblige*', escalators, lotteries and turkey races: four elements of reward PSBs

'Lottery of life' bargains	'Pyramid and escalator' bargains
Non-automatic or predictable rewards	*Structured pattern of reward*
Agreement to live with the upsides and downsides of a reward 'casino'	Expectations of orderly and predictable progression
'Turkey race' bargains	'*Noblesse oblige*' bargains
Variable rewards	*Relative self-restraint at the top*
Agreement to rewards based on individual competition	Agreement to a double imbalance structure with relatively less generous pay at the top

food chain get the most of whatever is going—be it salaries, honours, travel conditions, other perks such as lavish offices—and the rest get proportionately less according to their place on the ladder of status. You know where you are in a pyramid—especially if you are at the bottom of the heap. Differentiation according to grade and rank may be reflected not only in pay and allowances, but also appear in all the other badges of status—for example, single or shared offices, size of office, furniture, and floor coverings (and what is on the door plate, as emphasized by the German interviewee we quoted earlier). In some times and places, it has even extended to family and marriage arrangements, as in the old maxim in the British army that subalterns might not marry without permission, captains and majors were free to marry, and colonels had to marry.

The other element of the pyramids and escalators form of reward bargain consists of a 'stairway to heaven', in which rewards and career progression in the bureaucracy follow a predictable path, as far as anything can be guaranteed in this life. Those entering some public service systems have fairly definite expectations of how they will be rewarded a decade or more hence if they follow the rules and meet ordinary expectations of ability and hard work. Seniority-based pay is central to the traditional Japanese reward system, in private firms as well as in government bureaucracy,[10] and we found strong elements of 'predictability expectations' over rewards in both the German and British cases too. A representative German interviewee put it like this: 'the *Dienstherr* says, "For the demands I am making on you—which are "torture"—I will give you a predictable future' (D4). A younger British interviewee also expressed expectations of some degree of predictability:

---

[10] Though at the time of writing, the Japanese government was floating the idea of moving away from this sort of pay system, as many private firms had done, towards a UK-type pay structure with larger elements of performance pay (see *Japan Times* 10 July 2004 'Civil Servants Now Face Performance-Related Pay'). Similar moves had been agreed in Germany to make civil service pay—for new entrants—more flexible.

Coming in as a fast streamer, you are told that you are there because you are expected to make it to Principal within 4–6 years ... I would imagine that most fast streamers expect to be promoted to principal within four years, but hope to get to Assistant Secretary within 6–8. . . . (UK7)

In the German case, predictability included an incremental pay system (once common in Britain too, albeit in a different form) in which pay depended on years of service as well as on grade, rather in the same way that most contribution-based pension payments do. That age-related incremental scale system meant that two people of different ages at the same grade could earn very different amounts. For instance, two people on grade A13 doing the same job could have a pay difference of nearly two-fifths, simply because one had celebrated thirty or so more birthdays in the bureaucracy than the other. It even meant that in some cases, superordinates could earn less than their subordinates. Perhaps not surprisingly, this escalator system was being challenged at the time of writing. As one of our German interviewees put it:

The 30-year-old *Regierungsrat* earns less than the 60-year-old *Regierungsrat* because the former has progressed through [fewer] increments. The justification was, this [difference] is because of loyalty or experience, it was impossible to promote everyone and this was a way of compensating [for lack of promotion]. For young people, this appears strange ... (D4)

Another German interviewee, reflecting a trustee-bargain view of the civil service role, justified this traditional age-related pay escalator as a means of safeguarding independence through security, and thought that it contributed to a healthy system of checks and balances in the state machine: 'Being troublesome is very important for politics' (D2).

Pyramids and escalators are logically separable forms of bargain. But they are arguably linked, in that one (perhaps the only) reason for the lower ranks to accept a structured hierarchy is the expectation that the sweets of higher reward will come to them with the passage of time. And contrariwise, if one of those two elements is removed or weakened, the other is likely to come under pressure. So, if the escalator stops—for instance, if lateral entry disturbs previous expectations of steady advancement through the ranks, or if economic crisis means that all bets are off—the reasons for those in the middle and bottom of the heap to accept a differentiated reward pyramid become weaker. Indeed, exactly that happened in Trinidad and Tobago in the 1980s, and 1990s, when 'structural adjustment' policies agreed with the World Bank involved pay cuts for the bureaucracy that in effect meant the pay escalator was going in reverse (TT4).

4.2.2. '*Noblesse Oblige*' or Rent Non-seeking

In the recent past, one common pattern of reward in public services was one in which those in the lower ranks of the bureaucracy were fairly generously rewarded relative to their counterparts in the private sector, while those at the upper levels earned less than their counterparts in the higher ranks of business and the more highly paid professions. This pattern, sometimes (if perhaps tendentiously) referred to as 'double imbalance' (Sjölund 1989), meant that there was a pay discount at the top of the public service and a pay premium at the bottom. In fact, as we showed in Table 1.1 for seven countries, there was substantial variety in the difference between the proportions of average earnings commanded by top public servants as against mid-level officials. But we call the pattern of relatively low top earnings *noblesse oblige*, because it seems to imply a degree of knightly self-restraint on the part of senior civil servants that, at first sight, seems to be wholly at variance with those forms of public choice theory that depict top bureaucrats as rapaciously self-serving rent-seekers. To the extent that *noblesse oblige* bargains can be observed in some times and places, it suggests either that there is something that is not captured by that rent-seeking perspective, or at least that top bureaucrats can sometimes be singularly unsuccessful in their rent-seeking aspirations.

More generally, such a bargain seems to involve the exchange of legitimacy—recognition of the right to rule—for some self-restraint, at least over the more obvious aspects of reward. What top public servants get in exchange for an element of self-denial is the sort of respect and acceptance that, in an egalitarian culture, goes to ascetic rulers who choose to ride bicycles and walk on linoleum floors.[11] Indeed, Tocqueville (1946: 143–4) in his famous *Democracy in America* argued that such a bargain was in effect the price of rulership in a democracy of the type he observed in the early nineteenth-century USA. Tocqueville thought that pressure from voters, the majority of whom were not wealthy, would limit the modest salaries that would be allowed to high office-holders.[12] But, if the figures we presented in Table 1.1 are anything to go by, those pressures do not seem to apply with equal force in all contemporary democracies.

---

[11] Of course, in other kinds of culture—as in Jon Quah's case of colonial Malaya, already mentioned—anything other than a lavish and opulent lifestyle on the part of rulers will be seen as mean and contemptible.

[12] Such a bargain has potentially paradoxical consequences for democracy, in that it may produce incentives for corruption in government and may even lead to *de facto* aristocracy, in that the middle class may not be attracted to public office by that sort of PSB (see Hood and Peters 1994: 11).

Why should top civil servants accept restraint or relatively modest rewards in a *noblesse oblige* pattern? What could be the quid pro quo—the other side of such a bargain? Is it just the empirical fact, sometimes ignored by the cruder forms of self-interest theory, that some human beings get pleasure from self-denial? That pleasure may come from religious conviction that abstinence now will be rewarded in the next world, or in its secular version with the gratification of feelings of socialistic solidarity with the mass of humanity. There is no doubt that such attitudes and beliefs are widespread in some societies, and indeed, as we noted in Chapter 1, it has been common for public servants in some times and places to see their calling as involving monk-like acceptance of (relative) poverty. In the early twentieth century, leading British public servants such as Beveridge and Haldane liked to compare the conditions of state service with the vows of poverty and self-sacrifice taken by soldiers or monastic orders (see Thomas 1978: 42, 158; Barker 1997: 39), and in the nineteenth century Sir Arthur Helps declared that 'there should be men in office who love the state as priests love the church' (Schaffer 1973: 39).[13]

That monkish metaphor points to a bargain embodying at least a pledge of poverty and obedience—perhaps not necessarily chastity, though celibacy has certainly been required of state officials in some historical cases, including the mamelukes of the Turkish sultan in the eleventh century (see Coser 1974: 159). And working for the state, like a religious calling, is valued for its own sake in some way—low rewards are exchanged simply for inner satisfaction, for those individuals who get their kicks from the bureaucratic life. If, as one senior British civil service interviewee wistfully told us, 'By and large in the civil service, nothing you do is ever recognized' (UK8), what are the compensating benefits? One German civil servant saw them in the 'narcotic' effects of involvement in policy-shaping:

When you do [policy in the domain the interviewee worked in] for such a long time, it corrupts you. I don't want to do a routine job, I want to be stretched politically. It is like a drug. (D20)

If that is what the *noblesse oblige* bargain involves, it would seem to be as much with the deity or top civil servants' inner selves as with other human actors. But a PSB involving low material rewards may involve a quid pro quo that amounts to more than a warm inner glow. It may be reflected in social respect

---

[13] Rather later, Lord Bridges (1950: 32) in *Portrait of a Profession* drew parallels with academic life, but bemoaned the fact that the British civil service lacked 'the expressions of corporate life found in a college. We have neither hall nor chapel, neither combination room nor common room'.

that comes from being in a high status if lowly rewarded profession, perhaps linked with the acquisition of medals, titles, or honours that are seen in some circumstances as partial substitutes for high material rewards. In the British case, we were told by some that honours and related perquisites were very important because, '... in these jobs where you are under great stress and fairly lonely, people watch for every signal minutely' (UK19). Another interviewee (UK25) told us that honours almost came with the rations for the economic regulators that emerged in the 1980s: 'It is part of the package [though] it is not written down. Even [name] who really fell out with the [name of department] when he was [name of regulatory office], he was given a CBE. [Name], who is regarded by many people as quite mad ... went away with a CBE.' Indeed, it used to be said in Britain that honours and titles were a compensation for the higher salaries that public servants would otherwise demand, and at least one interviewee put this argument to us. But as we showed in Table 1.1, there is no obvious inverse relationship between top-level public service earnings and the automaticity of honours in the seven cases we summarized there. For instance, top German civil servants were paid over 25 per cent less than their be-medalled UK counterparts[14] at the time of writing.[15] Indeed at the very top of the tree, the most highly paid British Permanent Secretaries—those most likely to have knighthoods or other orders of chivalry bestowed on them—earned more than two and a half times the salaries of their ungarlanded German counterparts. What one person or group sees as *noblesse oblige* may not be seen in that way by others.

However, there are at least two variants (perhaps weaker forms) of the *noblesse oblige* bargain in which self-restraint on the part of top civil servants is balanced by something more substantial than medals and official titles. One is the pattern which applied in the late (and by some lamented) Soviet Union and its satellite states and is common in much of the developing world today, in which top state officials are paid salaries that look tiny but are only the exposed tip of a much larger reward iceberg. And that hidden iceberg itself can come in several forms. It may consist of in-kind perks that enable those officials to live in luxury, but are more or less hidden from public view—the

---

[14] As indicated in Table 1.1, at the time of writing, the German honours system did not provide bureaucrats with any automatic honours. That system had moved decisively towards rewarding public service 'on the ground' (individual acts of self-sacrifice and bravery, and the like) in the late 1980s and early 1990s, while an attempt to move in the same direction by the then British Prime Minister John Major in the early 1990s did not greatly reduce the total number of awards granted to top UK bureaucrats (see Philips 2004).

[15] In 2004, German state secretaries' 'B11' pay level provided them with approximately £94,200 per year, while in 2003 British permanent secretaries earned between £118,750 and £251,500 per year (Bundesbesoldungsordnung, *Civil Service Yearbook* 2004).

special shops for the *nomenklatura,* official housing, health care, cars,[16] western products, vacation, retail, and leisure facilities that are all provided by the state for its favoured officials.

The other comes in the form of a range of earnings opportunities for state officials and their families on the basis of their official position. Max Weber (1968: 963–5) thought that a defining condition of modern bureaucracy was the separation of official and private life, but across much of the world there is a tacit and sometimes explicit understanding that state officials will make up for their modest official salaries by other kinds of earnings on the side—from police officers 'moonlighting' as security guards to more dramatic forms of corruption and extortion. Accordingly, while relatively low material rewards for high public service are commonly observable across much of the world, the quid pro quo in the underlying bargain often involves more than intrinsic satisfaction. And that is why purchase of public office, even for jobs with tiny salaries, is historically common. For instance, Voslensky (1984: 189) argued that earnings-opportunity offices such as public prosecutors were purchased for quite large sums in parts of the Soviet Union during the Brezhnev era, even though the official salaries that went with these jobs were very low.

If one weaker variant of the *noblesse oblige* bargain involves modest official salaries balanced by substantial hidden rewards or earnings opportunities, the other involves exchanging restraint at one point of a career by more substantial rewards at another point. 'Good things come to those who wait', says one proverb and 'live now, pay later', says another contradictory one. The first pattern seems to be more common than the second, although PSBs certainly vary in terms of how 'end-career-loaded' reward patterns are. 'Live now, pay later' was the line taken by the famous 1854 Northcote-Trevelyan report on the British civil service, which sought to lock the 'best and brightest' from the universities into a public service career by pay levels that would look attractive to raw recruits but not to those who had made a success of careers in other walks of life. Such pay levels would therefore allow the state to obtain the services of talented people later in their careers on relatively modest terms: 'A young man who has not made trial of any other profession will be induced to enter the civil service on much more moderate remuneration than would suffice to attract him a few years later' (C 1713, 1854: 8).

The contrary proverb, 'Good things come to those who wait' is reflected in many public service reward packages that include relatively generous retirement pensions, traditionally often comprising a substantial proportion of

---

[16] For instance, in the former German Democratic Republic (GDR), most citizens had to wait for years to obtain a humble Trabant car, but bureaucrats were given superior cars (with the model dependent on their status), and their ministers rode in dark blue chauffeur-driven Volvos and Peugeots (see Wagner 1998: 117).

final salary and involving no employee contribution. But the delayed-gratification variant of the *noblesse oblige* bargain is perhaps epitomized by the Japanese tradition, mentioned earlier, which reserves the pinnacle of reward for later in the career. This variant of the *noblesse oblige* bargain works through the *Amakudari* or 'descent from heaven' system, in which early retirees from the civil service in their mid-fifties go on to better-paid jobs in the public and private sector in a highly institutionalized way after thirty years or so of less well-paid work (Colignon and Usui 2003). Here, the implicit bargain is that public servants accept modestly paid work for decades (thus living up to their favoured public image as an ascetic knightly group of *Samurai*, rather than materialistic money-grubbers) on the understanding that opportunities for much higher earnings will follow later. Those former civil servants become wealthy as a result of working for a succession of public corporations or private firms in the final decade or so of their working lives or move into leading political positions in LDP governments.

On a variant of 'efficient wage' theory[17] it can be argued that a delayed-gratification bargain of this type encourages civil servants to establish a reputation for effective work, rather than aiming for apparent successes which will soon be revealed to their fellow-insiders as illusory. Indeed, Ramseyer and Rosenbluth (1993: 116) argued that the *Amakudari* system gave Japanese civil servants (especially those from the finance and industry ministries) strong incentives to be responsive to politicians, because politicians controlled the substantial element of post-retirement earnings in the lifetime-income stream. As they put it, 'LDP leaders mitigate . . . agency slack by requiring bureaucrats to post their post-ministerial salaries as bonds that they forfeit if they fail to implement LDP preferences. During their time at the ministry, the bureaucrats work for less than their spot-market wage . . . . If they implement those [LDP] preferences faithfully, they receive the shortfall as high salaries in the jobs they get after their mandatory retirement from government service.'[18]

But how 'efficient' such a bargain is depends on what efficiency is taken to mean. If the big rewards come only after a long period, it may encourage a time-serving approach to staying out of trouble rather than risk-taking that may bring large policy pay-offs. Moreover, any delayed-gratification reward

---

[17] The idea rediscovered by economists in the 1960s that it may make sense for employers to overpay workers relative to the spot price of their labour at some periods of their careers (see Phelps 1968; Stiglitz 1974).

[18] Horn (1995: 62) has argued from a slightly different perspective that bureaucrats who want to keep open the prospect of remunerative employment outside the bureaucracy in a future life have an incentive to maximize their long-term labour market rate by showing themselves to be competent, particularly in dealings with business.

bargain is risky and precarious, because it relies on a high degree of trust by civil servants that politicians and the private sector will in fact deliver on such an end-career-loaded deal, and in principle either or both of those parties could abandon the bargain (see Miller 1992, 2000). So this kind of bargain is definitely not for a low-trust society. It seems likely to develop in a highly institutionalized form only when public servants have good reasons to trust the other parties to the bargain with a large part of their lifetime earnings. After all, opportunistic politicians might rat on the deal. They might choose to benefit from all those decades of hard and modestly paid toil from their officials, but then decline to deliver when it comes to what was supposed to be payback time (thus, in effect pocketing what Ramsayer and Rosenbluth describe as the 'bond' of post-retirement earnings). And even if the politicians did not behave like that, such a deal could collapse if the private corporate employers decided to pull out of their part of the arrangements, for instance, if they came to see the import of an annual quota of superannuated fifty-something public servants as bringing more costs than benefits to their businesses.

Nor is that just an abstract possibility. In the early 1990s, rising public criticism of the descent from heaven system as 'sleaze' by Japanese voters (especially a new generation of female voters) and a reluctance on the part of some large corporations to continue participating in a system that was arguably less useful in a world where major Japanese companies wished to compete in global markets meant that the future of the traditional end-loaded reward system came to be seen as increasingly problematic by potential top civil servants (see Nakamura and Dairokuno 2003: 115). *Amakudari* to the private sector dropped substantially over the fifteen years to 2003,[19] and more civil servants left in mid-career. It is commonly said that the changes in *Amakudari* reduced applications for the civil service examination from the topmost graduates from the law faculty of Tokyo University (the elite school that was the traditional route into the top civil service) between the early 1990s and the early 2000s (see also Suleiman 2003: 196–7).

4.2.3. Turkey Races

In the run-up to the Christmas holiday of 2002, it was reported in the British tabloid press that an extra element of competition was being introduced into the festive proceedings by a cheap publicity stunt to make Christmas turkeys

---

[19] See Annual Report on the authorization of former civil servants' employment by for-profit companies, 1982, 1986, and 1989; *Nikkei Newspaper*, 4 April 2004). These numbers do not cover the commonly utilized and perhaps increasingly preferred exit route to public corporations (*Tokushu Hojin*, the so-called 'amakudari à la carte').

race for their freedom (*Evening Standard*, 10 December 2002, p. 5). The idea provoked outrage from animal rights campaigners, who understandably thought a race to determine which animals would go free and which would end up in the festive cooking pot was carrying competition to the point of indignity. However that may be, for some civil servants, the reward bargain somewhat resembles the deal offered to those unfortunate Christmas turkeys, in that what they get depends on pitting their individual effort and skill against that of everyone else, or at least on their ability to perform at an acceptable level in the bureaucratic race.

Max Weber (1968: 963–5) thought fixed money salaries (as opposed to fees or other forms of reward) were a defining condition of modern bureaucracy, in business as well as in government. But modern institutional theory takes a more differentiated view. Indeed, as has already been noted, reward bargains involving payments according to performance had been advocated by 'economic rationalists' long before Weber's day. Variable rewards were at the heart of the scientific management movement that developed from the late nineteenth century, and variable rewards came back into fashion from the 1970s in a different guise that had more impact for senior civil servants. As we noted in Chapter 3, along with the development of 'principal–agent' approaches to analysing firms and organizations from the 1960s came the idea of pay bargains that made the rewards of agents depend on how well they serve the interests of their principals. One of the ways of solving the principal–agent problem in big firms was therefore seen as making managers' rewards depend on the stock price of the corporation, which principals (stockholders) were assumed to want to maximize.

There are real problems, which we will not go into here, about applying this solution even to that particular form of the principal–agent problem. But briefly consider the possibility of applying a variant of that kind of reward bargain to deal with principal–agent problems between politician principals and bureaucratic agents. Suppose that we start with the conventional assumption that politicians want to win elections, and further assume that their chances of winning elections are measured by their opinion poll ratings, which function as the equivalent of stock prices. The implication would be a reward bargain in which senior bureaucrats' rewards would depend on the standing of their (politician) principals in the opinion polls. The interesting question for this analysis is why 'efficient reward' bargains of this type have not emerged in public bureaucracies, in contrast to their stock-price equivalents in business corporations.

Part of the answer probably lies in the sheer technical difficulty of establishing such a reward bargain in a formal way. A bargain of that type might be easier to establish for the personal staff of a president or prime minister than to civil servants working for a departmental minister in a conventional parliamentary system. But even in the former case, it could not apply in those numerous cases where presidents face term limits over re-election, as with the traditional one-term rule in Mexico. And for departmental civil servants in parliamentary-government systems, anything approximating to such a bargain would raise serious problems of incentive alignment. For instance, should their rewards depend on the poll standing of the government as a whole? That would be like rewarding the managers of one corporation by the performance of a general stock-market index, like the Dow or the Nikkei—yet movements in such an index might be weakly or even negatively related to the stock price of any one corporation as affected by its managers' efforts. Those civil servants whose well-managed departments were islands of perfection in a sea of government incompetence would not be selectively rewarded, and those whose individual fiascos were outweighed by the efforts of other departments would not be punished.

However, if to avoid that difficulty departmental civil servants' rewards were made to depend on the poll standing of the individual ministers they serve, the result might well be a heightened form of the interdepartmental battles that are apt to be endemic in government. Reward-seeking civil servants would have even more reason to support their ministers' jockeying for popularity against rival ministers, by doing as much as they could to block or sabotage the efforts of other departments. And if all, or even many, senior civil servants behaved like that, the conduct of executive government would be anything but harmonious and cooperative. That in turn might well *reduce* the poll standing of the government as a whole—exactly the opposite of what the 'principal' is assumed to want.

One potential way out of this difficulty might be a reward bargain for politicians in which individual ministers' rewards depended on the poll standing of the prime minister or the government as a whole (though that would not necessarily be problem-free). But the problems of developing a PSB that would relate bureaucrats' rewards to politicians' electoral chances do not end there. The stock of corporations is traded regularly, though stocks can be suspended from trading, and market signals may be of varying reliability, notably when trading volume is low. But elections are events that take place at discrete intervals. What politicians want is a result on a particular day. Opinion poll ratings are valued to the extent that they are valid proxies of election outcomes, but a survey reading at t_0 does not necessarily predict electoral outcomes at t_n.

Indeed, the conventional theory of 'political business cycles' assumes that politicians may have to court unpopularity with the voters at some points during their term to compensate for the largesse distributed to voters at other points. For instance, they may need to take the unpopular step of raising taxes and charges after an election to build up a 'war chest' to finance popular vote-winning giveaways before the next election.[20] To the extent that politicians follow that sort of 'rhythm method' in their electoral strategy, a pay bargain that linked civil servants' rewards to the poll standing of their political masters at all points of the electoral cycle would be far from 'optimal' for aligning the interests of principal and agent. A more sophisticated predictor of likely electoral outcome would be needed, weighting the principal's opinion poll standing at any one time for the point in the electoral cycle and linking it to other elements of a political forecasting model. But any such weighting would inevitably strain at the limits of available technology and knowledge.

Finally—and raising an even more fundamental difficulty—there are snags arising from the likelihood that the opinion poll rating (or expected electoral result) of the principal depends to a substantial extent on the principal's own behaviour, and not just on the behaviour of the agents. For example, politicians may damage their poll ratings or electoral prospects by their personal financial misconduct or sexual exploits, such as extramarital affairs or unsuitable liaisons with their staff, and such activities can hardly be put down to the behaviour of their agents. Indeed, paradoxically, for the political variant of the optimal reward bargain to function in the face of such difficulties, it would be necessary for the agent to be able to control the principal, following the maxim 'stop me before I kill again'. Yet that is precisely the reverse of what optimal rewards and the direction of control in principal–agent theory was supposed to be all about (see also Miller 2000).

Such difficulties are not trivial, and probably explain why optimal reward bargains are hard to devise for public servants in a way that even approaches the idea of linking managers' pay to the stock price of the corporation they work for (deeply problematic though that is in practice too). Accordingly, the 'turkey race' form of reward bargain for public servants tends to come in one or both of two forms. One consists of competition for increased reward in a race for promotion. That kind of competition can be fierce, even in a closed-career structure, if the numbers coming in to the high-flier entry grades are high relative to the positions available at the top and their exit options are limited, for instance, in economic recessions when jobs in private business dry up. For all the talk of 'competition' as the watchword of the contemporary world of public services, the equivalents of today's public servants in their grandparents' generation in the slump of the 1930s often faced much tougher de facto competition (to enter the public service in a world of fewer private

---

[20] See Kalecki (1943), Nordhaus (1975), Alt and Chrystal (1983: 125), Alesina, Roubini, and Cohen (1997).

sector career options, to gain promotion in generally smaller bureaucracies, and to secure a comfortable income without the exit options in the private sector that are available today).

Some of our older Whitehall interviewees saw pyramids and escalators giving way to a turkey race to reward. Many of them said that older conventions of a system that 'looked after' its career staff and had some aspirations to plan their careers had moved substantially towards a 'turkey race' for promotion or even staying in the service. One such interviewee said, 'The new deal is that you will look after yourself in an environment where the risks and rewards are sharper' (UK5), and another, reflecting on thirty years in Whitehall, argued:

Nowadays ... it [promotion] is a free for all. Whereas there was a strong element in the past of 'Norman has done jolly well as an Assistant Secretary for ten years, he has only six years to go, so let's put him in as Under-Secretary of ...,' that would not happen any more. We are much more ruthless. If Norman is plodding on as an Assistant Secretary for ten years, then it is more likely that we are going to talk with him about an early exit. ... (UK1)

Indeed, some saw such a move in the direction of a 'turkey race' as something that was weakening Whitehall's traditions of civility. One interviewee suggested that it meant those who wanted to look after their careers needed to deploy an increasing amount of overt 'muscle':

It is increasingly a confrontational thing. If you are a fast-stream 7 and you want to stay in, then you are pressing to be in ... [such-and-such a] job and then two years later you are pressing to be out of it ... you may 'evaporate' if they don't [move you to another high profile position]. (UK9)

A variant of 'turkey race' competition for promoted posts consists of competitions that are open to lateral entrants as well as existing public servants. That has traditionally been used in Norway, albeit within a small labour market, and has been introduced into other civil service systems (notably that of the UK) in more recent times. But the other main form of 'turkey race' takes the form of competition for variable bonuses or 'performance pay', which has been much advocated and in many places applied as a recipe for controlling bureaucracies over the last few decades. For determining the intensity of the 'turkey race' that such systems comprise, the key factors are the difference between the 'safety net' (the guaranteed minimum wage) and the 'jackpot' and the probable extent to which any one individual can expect to exceed the safety net—something that is relatively predictable in those performance pay regimes, such as that of the UK at the time of writing, in which there were fixed quotas for the proportions of staff in the competition to be given performance-pay awards.

The bonuses or performance awards can be linked to performance against quantitative performance indicators or targets (as in the case of the chief executives of the UK's executive agencies) or other measures that are more or less objectively identifiable. A traditional case in point is that of naval commanders who were rewarded according to the value of the ships they captured in many countries, including the USA until after the Civil War. An example current at the time of writing, albeit perhaps less direct than the naval commanders' prize money, is the pay regime for senior civil servants in Singapore, in which a component of salaries was related to the overall performance of the Singaporean economy, with bonuses when gross domestic product (GDP) grew strongly and pay cuts when GDP fell (see Quah 2003*a*: 153–5). Such a pay bargain was presumably intended to focus bureaucratic minds on the importance of securing business prosperity and economic growth.

More commonly, though, variable reward to top civil servants comes in the form of bonuses resulting from qualitative ratings of their performance made by superiors. It could be argued that such performance ratings are the closest that 'turkey race' reward structures can normally get to incentive alignment with politicians' goals, though politicians rarely decide such bonuses on their own. Even then, there is more than one possible type, and such bonuses can be linked to group or individual performance, or change from one emphasis to the other, as has happened in the UK over the past ten years, where an initial heavy emphasis on rating individual performance came to be transformed into a heavy emphasis on team bonuses below the topmost ranks, though bonuses remained individual at the top.

4.2.4. Lotteries of Life

In orthodox accounts of modern bureaucratic functioning, following Max Weber, advancement and reward in state service depends on a combination of seniority and merit. And as already noted, the reward bargain in the cases we investigated included some element of relatively guaranteed progress in exchange for a measure of ordinary diligence or aptitude. But in those cases there was also an irreducible 'lottery' element. By that we mean an element of reward that depended on unpredictable matters relatively independent of individual skill, desert, or sagacity. One of our very senior British interviewees, perhaps with excessive modesty, saw his advancement essentially in lottery-type terms:

So I got, by luck and chance . . . jobs of a degree of interest and responsibility that were well in advance of what most people entering at my level . . . were getting . . . I was dead lucky. (UK4)

Others pointed to the unpredictable downside events—the snakes rather than the ladders of chance—that could finish a career. One of our British interviewees thought that such downside chance factors tended to affect public servants in local authorities closer to the front line of service delivery rather than their regulators and overseers in Whitehall:

People in local authorities carry quite a lot of responsibility for real delivery which if it goes wrong can be very tragic. A death of a child in care may cost you your job and that of the head of social services.... (UK14)

Religious believers may think themselves certain of their reward in heaven, but such factors mean that earthly rewards for public service are always chancy to a greater or lesser degree. For instance, the intrinsic satisfaction to be gained from working at the higher levels of government (something that many of our interviewees stressed, as has already been noted) may decline or disappear if conditions of work are changed in unexpected ways. Politicians may take less interest in policy advice from their civil servants (see Campbell and Wilson 1995). Public respect for the public service as a profession may decline. And the reputation of particular departments can change as well, as emphasized in a comment by one German civil servant on the plummeting prestige of a once-renowned department

There are numerous civil servants who suffer from this loss [of prestige], especially the older ones who have witnessed other times. It is tough to sink so deep, [to find] that your own significance has gone down so much. (D21)

Similarly, as we have already noted, expectations about future prospects may be disappointed. The prospects of obtaining lucrative employment later in a career to compensate for the lean years working for government may be dashed. What might once have been widely accepted supplementary earnings opportunities from the job—for instance from writing or public speaking—may come to be proscribed or deemed as 'corruption'. Benefits in kind may disappear too. Indeed, all these types of changes can readily result from reform programmes or regime change that could not easily have been predicted by those who entered the bureaucratic career twenty or so years ago. And at the time of writing, proposed changes in public service retirement pension arrangements that lengthen the working lifetime needed to achieve the maximum pension payment had provoked protests and even strikes from civil servants in France and Britain, who saw such changes as undermining the reward bargain they thought they were signing up to.

In one sense, such changes might be seen as no more than particular instances of the way that life in general can be a lottery. But the lottery element we are concerned with here relates to more or less explicit understandings that reward in the public service will depend on matters that are independent of seniority or of merit as ordinarily understood.

Much of that unpredictability turns on the hard-to-call twists and turns of political fate, including imponderables such as what the hot topics will turn out to be at some indefinite future time, or what balance of factions or political forces will hold sway in the future. But it also comes from other features of human relationships (D6). Where will friends and enemies be distributed in a complex organization at any point in time? Who else, with what attributes, will happen to be available for preferment at key junctures in any individual's future career? What other chance factors will go up to put an individual in the right or wrong place at a critical time? In Joseph Heller's great novel *Catch-22* (1961), some of the characters in the ramified Second World War military machine obtain largely unmerited rewards and advancement as a result of random twists of fate, while more deserving characters fail to do so for the same reason. Every complex bureaucratic system has something of a lottery element about it for the players, and the reward bargain in such an organizational setting involves an agreement to play in that casino in exchange for whatever the outcome of the gamble turns out to be.

Apart from the imponderable x-factors and the political or social changes that even the greatest experts often fail to predict, there are two common 'lottery' elements that come into reward bargains. One is when political party or party-regional affiliation shapes preferment, as has increasingly been claimed to apply to Germany over the past thirty years (see Derlien 2004) and applies to the 'posts of confidence' in the political-adviser part of the civil service in the UK, as well as to a larger number of quango appointments. The other common lottery element arises when individuals do not know whether they will be exposed to outside competition in ascending to any particular higher job in the state service, or whether they will be competing only with the known quantities of colleagues already in the public service.

4.3. MIXES AND COMBINATIONS, TRENDS AND TENDENCIES

The four patterns of reward bargains represent variety in emphasis and they obviously overlap. We can think of them as circles on a Venn diagram, albeit with four overlapping circles rather than the conventional three of such a diagram (leading to geometrical difficulties with 'overlapping overlaps'). For example, *'noblesse oblige'* is often linked to escalators and pyramids. 'Turkey races' are often linked with lotteries of life, for instance, when it is not clear according to what performance criteria one is being evaluated against, or how large the potential reward is likely to be. 'Escalators' and 'pyramids' also often involve a considerable lottery element, especially given the uncertainty about the level to which the 'system' will 'look after' individual civil servants—the big uncertainty highlighted by several of the interviewees we quoted earlier.

Triple hybrids are also commonly observable. *Noblesse oblige* can be mixed with both escalators and lotteries, and similarly escalators can be mixed with lotteries and turkey races. But though hybrids seem to be common, each public service system has its own distinct emphasis among these types of bargains. And the mix of bargains can differ from one level of government to another: the PSB mix in the EU Commission is different from that applying in the national governments of many of the member states, and in many cases, the local or regional government PSBs are different again.

The mixes can change over time as well. Many of our interviewees saw a shift from a mix of *noblesse oblige* and pyramids and escalators towards turkey races and lotteries. What has traditionally been taken, as least from the Weberian perspective as the essence of modern bureaucracy—a reward bargain of the 'pyramids and escalators' type—seems to have been in retreat in a number of countries. As we have already noted, older relativities were upset with the rise of a new class of executive managers at the top of the civil service in the UK. Several countries witnessed a breakout movement by some high public servants trying to get away from the link with politicians' pay. Those 'escapees' sought a new pay bargain in which senior public servants got higher salaries than the politicians they serve, often under the guise of performance-pay regimes (Christensen 1994). Several of our British interviewees argued that such changes were producing a *sauve qui peut* environment for public servants, who had to adopt increasingly attention-seeking strategies of career advancement. One argued

The organization was increasingly unable to look after people, because it became increasingly evident that the ministerial input into career advancement was becoming bigger. And therefore people . . . felt that they had to be seen, they had to be recognized individually. (UK4)

What we have called '*noblesse oblige*' reward bargains seemed to be in some retreat too. There had been some move away from the older 'double imbalance' pattern in some former Swedish-model states, with sharply increasing pay for those at the top and relatively static pay (and job outsourcing) for those at the bottom. However, there still seemed to be a current pay discount relative to top company salaries in the upper reaches of most public services,[21]

---

[21] Singapore is the most obvious exception, and even there, the aspiration to parity was proving hard to maintain at the time of writing.

although generous and in most cases non-contributory pension entitlements have to be taken into account in drawing the comparison. The Japanese deferred-gratification variant of the *noblesse oblige* bargain seemed to be under pressure too, possibly because it depended on the ability of one side in the bargain to trust the other to deliver later. Lower-trust relationships arguably lend themselves more to reward bargains of the 'pay as you go' type, which economize on trust.

While these two strains of reward bargain seem to have weakened a little, 'lottery of life' and 'turkey race' bargains were perhaps becoming correspondingly stronger. The 'lottery' element of reward bargains can be expected to increase with shifts towards more open party-politicization of civil services, as happened in the German civil service since the 1950s, and according to observers like Maor (1999), in many other parliamentary systems since the 1980s in one form or another, including more 'posts of confidence'.

The 'turkey race' element seems to have changed too in some ways. While the long (largely) peacetime boom of the developed countries in the late twentieth century arguably weakened the competition from the best and the brightest to get into public service, other forms of competition were stepped up, perhaps as a compensatory move. More performance-related pay elements were introduced in many countries, and more lateral entry in a few. To the extent that lateral entry to the public service from outside supplements or replaces a closed-career pattern (or can be expected to do so in the future), the 'lottery' element will increase. Lateral entry may increase within the public service too, if formerly separated corps form a common pool for promotion. Certainty may decline if incremental pay scales dependent on length of service are abandoned or truncated, or their future status is doubtful. And certainty may also decline if a larger element of pay becomes variable, thus increasing the 'lottery' component relative to the certainty component. As any turkey could tell you, what are intended to be turkey races can easily turn into lotteries of life.

5

Competency in Public Service Bargains: Wonks, Sages, Deliverers, and Go-Betweens

> Mere prattle without practice is all his soldiership...
>
> (Iago (speaking of Cassio) in Shakespeare's *Othello*, Act I, sc. i)

> It is one thing to know what you want to achieve, but the skill of government is doing it in a way that brings it about without side effects that you don't want.
>
> (British civil servant interviewee (UK8))

5.1. BUREAUCRATIC COMPETENCY DEBATES—OLD AND NEW

Some wags might dismiss the phrase 'competent authority' as an oxymoron, in the same way that some people see 'military intelligence' or 'sense of the meeting' as contradictions in terms.[1] But, as we noted at the outset (and as Bernard Schaffer (1973: 252) pointed out long ago) competency, in the sense of ability, skills, or experience, forms a central part of any PSB that goes beyond simple exchange of patronage for political loyalty. Rulers, political leaders, and even warlords always need some modicum of ability in their executive apparatus if they want to survive or achieve their goals. For instance, the Al-Qaeda attack on the USA on 11 September 2001 did not just require a handful of fanatics willing to die for the cause. Those individuals needed to acquire the training and technical knowledge to be able to fly large commercial airliners, disengage themselves from complex ground control systems, for instance, by turning off transponders, overcome cabin and cockpit staff

---

[1] Or perhaps even a paranym, a term sometimes used for words that means the opposite of what they say. For instance, the British magazine *Oldie* (20 March 1992, p. 3) in a tongue-in-cheek 'Dictionary for Our Time' defined 'highly capable' as 'official description of any minister not up to the job'.

without firearms, and control a large group of desperate passengers (see National Commission 2004, ch. 1). Equally, after the Al-Qaeda attack, pointed and insistent questions were raised about the competency of the US intelligence and security bureaucracy, given that massive organizations of experts with budgets running into billions of dollars failed to gather, put together, and act upon intelligence about preparations for that devastating attack (ibid. chs. 11, 13). In rather, sharper vein a generation before, Norman Dixon's classic (1976) *On the Psychology of Military Incompetence* had claimed that the British military tradition tended to produce a lethal mixture of out-of-date skills with a dysfunctional organizational style.

Nor are concerns about public servants' competency only about life-and-death issues of that kind. For instance, politicians often complain about the communication skills of their public servants, and indeed one of our German interviewees recalled how a particular minister furiously tore up the prepared speeches written for him by the departmental speech-writer, in front of invited audiences (D12). And bureaucrats themselves often complain about the abilities of their colleagues or subordinates. For instance, one senior German civil servant commented to us about the variable quality of the documents coming up the line to him from his subordinates:

Three out of ten [memoranda] are unnecessary and the writers have not thought about whether the information [they provided] was important for me ... I read them and think, this person has not reflected enough. At least three of the other seven are too long, that is, three pages are used to provide information that could have been conveyed on one to two pages. Among the other four, which do give me important information, two are poor in terms of presentation, poor German or poor formulation, and two are good, with clear and precise information. (D19)

Of course, competency in the sense of ability is not all that is typically wanted from public servants in exchange for competency in the sense of legal power. Honesty and loyalty are often of the essence too, to say nothing of social qualities such as the ethnic, confessional, or social class qualities that have so often been bound up with the PSBs. In many times and places, such qualities of political or group 'belonging' have had to be traded off against skills and competency, and such trade-offs have come in many different varieties. One type of trade-off is found where rulers or those in high positions within an institution choose to surround themselves with loyal mediocrities, sacrificing high ability in their subordinates for the peace of mind that comes with the expectation that a court full of nonentities will not produce any credible challengers for the crown. The legendary J. Edgar Hoover, director of the US Federal Bureau of Investigation (FBI) from 1924 to 1972, is said to have chosen that kind of trade-off, since it was said of him that 'Hoover lives in the past surrounded by aged or incompetent men who have spent their careers looking backward and telling [him] what he wants to hear.'[2]

The opposite kind of trade-off between loyalty and competency, familiar in studies of revolution, consists of the case where new regimes have to make use of military or civil officials whose skills and expertise are needed but whose hearts-and-minds commitment to the new order is uncertain because of their association with the previous regime. The Communist regimes of the twentieth century often had to balance 'redness' and expertise in their state apparatus after they came to power (Moore 1959: 159–88), just as dynastic monarchs before them frequently had to balance a desire to have their military and civil government led by their own aristocratic relatives with a need for ability in the higher ranks of the state apparatus. Such a balance can be hard to achieve. After all, Frederick the Great of Prussia had to abandon his instinctive aversion to government by a college-trained middle class after the evident failures of blue-blooded bureaucracy (Johnson 1975: 55); and after the debacles of the Crimean War, the British Queen Victoria and those who thought like her had to reconcile their aristocratic desire for executive government by 'gentlemen' with the need for a modicum of competency in the public offices.[3]

We will discuss honesty, loyalty, and responsibility as elements of the PSBs in Chapter 6, but this one is concerned with the competency elements of such bargains—that is, what skills, knowledge, or ability are called for in exchange for the right to exercise administrative power. Identifying this element can be tricky. Official competency frameworks and formal documents describing the knowledge and skills required of public servants can of course give us some clue to the nature of public service 'competency bargains' and how such bargains change over time. For instance, the fashion for new competency frameworks for the upper levels of the public service that spread across several European countries in the 1990s typically made much of leadership and managerial abilities, in contrast to the stress traditionally laid on subject-matter expertise in many of those countries.[4] But such statements were often quite vague, with some of the central desiderata, such as the ability to wield effective political power, left implicit. So one way of pinning down the most valued competencies in the public service is to work back from

---

    [2] A statement from an anonymous letter written in 1968 and quoted by Gentry (1991: 600); see also Theoharis and Cox (1988: 108).

    [3] 'The queen...let it be known that she had misgivings lest competitive exams "fill the public offices with low people without the breeding or feelings of gentlemen"' (Mueller 1984: 212).

    [4] This stress on identifying public service competencies in that era reflected a fad that by that time was just past its peak in US private corporations, where it had enjoyed a boom in the 1980s under the influence of management gurus like Richard Boyatzis (1982). But in fact that private-

frequently recurring lines of criticism of failures and shortcomings in skills or ability, to identify the missing qualities that such criticisms are directed to. At least four such lines of criticism seem to be commonly found.

One consists of charges of lack of leadership, direction, orderly management, and effective discipline, resulting in the failure to achieve desired 'results'. Public servants are often accused of poor ability to manage public organizations effectively, inability to run a tight ship in which major lapses do not routinely occur, inability to lead, or work cooperatively within, teams in an organization, and other failures in management or corporate functioning. From this viewpoint (often expressed by both politicians and bureaucrats), much of what goes wrong in government stems from weak organizational leadership, poor project management, and commonly occurring behavioural or managerial lapses such as failures in joint working, lack of well-defined and commonly understood procedures and rules and poor communication within public organizations.

A second common line of criticism consists of charges of lack of appropriate individual skills and knowledge relevant to the art of governing. It is common for public servants to be criticized for lack of expertise, or knowledge that is out of date, as in the stereotype case of the army that fails because its soldiers have been prepared to fight the last war but not the present one (see Wilson 1989: 14–18).[5] Over the last twenty years or so it has been common for public servants to be criticized for poor understanding of information technology, paralleling the average teenager's views of the older generation's ability to operate modern electronic gadgetry. Such criticism is embodied in all the numberless clichés on the theme of 'industrial-age bureaucracy in the information age'[6] that have been uttered over the last decade or two by those with millenarian visions of bureaucratic salvation through information technology.

But public servants are often accused of lacking other necessary skills as well, such as language ability (a problem identified as a source of the weakness of US intelligence about the groups responsible for the 11 September 2001

sector competency boom had itself been preceded by a competency framework, 'Revised Core Qualifications', introduced for the then new Senior Executive Service in the US federal government in 1979 (Flanders and Utterback 1985; United States Office of Personnel Management 2001: 8). Although the novelty of these competency ideas was probably exaggerated by those engaged in selling them, the new behavioural stress did represent an attempt to change the emphasis at that time away from policy knowledge and the ability to offer sage counsels to something more managerial.

  [5] Indeed, as a teenager in the early 1960s, one of us received military training in how to fight the previous war (Second World War), with equipment from the war before that (First World War) and an instructor who was a veteran of the war before *that* (the Boer War).

  [6] The phrase used in the Clinton-Gore 'National Performance Review' of 1993 in the USA (Gore 1993: 3).

attack on US cities), knowledge of management ideas or professional training in economics. The latter was the central plank of a famous attack on the British mandarinate in the late 1950s by Thomas Balogh (1959), and indeed, when things go wrong in government, critics often find that the fault lies with 'a bunch of amateurs'[7] in charge. The implication (satirized in the famous Major-General's song in Gilbert and Sullivan's *Pirates of Penzance*, listing that officer's command of a set of arbitrarily prescribed facts and theories)[8] is that the most important competency quality of public servants is to have their heads full of the most up-to-date professional knowledge in fields of expertise related to government.

A third common line of criticism is directed at failures on the part of public servants to be able to 'think outside the box', in management jargon—to be too institutionalized in thinking, too dull and predictable and not capable of coming up with left-field ideas or dramatic new perspectives. Here the notion is that public servants lack the ability to think outside a set of bureaucratic tramlines or to act in other than institutionalized or stereotyped ways. This sort of criticism of bureaucratic failings is of long standing, going back at least to Charles Dickens's biting satire (1857/1998: ch. 10) on the 'Circumlocution Office' (aka the British Home Office) in the nineteenth century, and Robert Merton's account (1940) of bureaucratic dysfunctions in the mid-twentieth century, but it is still commonly encountered. For instance, one UK interviewee described to us a thrusting New Labour minister's frustration with the apparent inability of his departmental civil servants to come up with any interesting strategic or policy ideas in meetings:

He was then expecting the officials to have a fantastic chance to pour out ideas, but they would come to the meetings and say, 'What do you want, Secretary of State?' And he would say, 'I have some ideas, but aren't you guys doing any thinking?' (UK2)

A final common line of criticism goes that public servants are too blinkered by narrow departmentalism and lack the mentalities and capabilities necessary to work effectively across the 'silos' into which the world is institutionally and culturally divided—within government, between governments, between sectors and social groups within society[9]—even though the central problems of

---

[7] The title of a trenchant book on Australian government and administration by James Cumes (1988).

[8] The song is said to satirize the ideas of Sir Garnet Wolseley, later Viscount Wolseley (1833–1913), author of *The Soldier's Pocket Book for Field Service* (1869). It may also satirize the views of Sir Edward Hamley (1824–93), commandant of the staff college Sandhurst 1870–7 and author of *The Operations of War* (1866)) who thought knowledge of military history was more useful than 'military science' in achieving success in battle (see Bradley 2004).

[9] See Mayntz and Scharpf (1975) for a classic analysis of 'negative coordination'.

governing typically require the ability to work in that way. The argument goes that when public servants cannot straddle such boundaries, good ideas, effective communication, and common-sense improvements tend to come to grief at the cultural and bureaucratic fault-lines between groups, organizations, and jurisdictions, and that any problem, however important, that cuts across such boundary lines tends to be automatically placed in the 'too hard' basket (see Wilson 1989: 181–5; Bardach 1998: 164–84).

From the perspective of such critics, many bureaucratic failings can be put down to ethnocentrism, ethnic or racial exclusivity, and other forms of cultural or institutional blindness that prevent the sort of information gathering needed to develop effective policy, handicap joint working across boundary lines, and stop effective communication.[10] That was the message of Pat Moynihan's *Maximum Feasible Misunderstanding* (1969), which put the dramatic failures of the 1960s US community-action programme down to the cultural segmentation of a system in which technocratic lawyers and economists in Washington failed to anticipate how the programme would unintendedly develop as a potent political weapon by those who were disaffected with the political establishment at that time. Similarly, business people often criticize the bureaucrats who regulate or oversee them for a cast of mind and background that makes it impossible for them to work effectively across the boundary line between the business firms and the bureaucracy, and such views are often reflected in various 'changing places' initiatives designed to broaden the social understanding of public servants, whether it is to sleep out with the homeless or work in penthouse suites for banks or oil companies.

As is often the way with criticisms of government and public servants, such lines of criticism tend to conflict with one another in the (usually implicit) assumptions they reflect about what the most important competency qualities of those individuals should be. And if put together, they imply more or less impossible demands on any mere mortal, even of the Platonic philosopher-king school. Moreover, examples such as the generic management competencies fad of the late 1990s show that the skills and abilities that a regime calls for from its public servants are not a set of eternal verities, even though there are many recurring features. Moods and demands can change over time.

Nor are those competencies the same in every contemporary state, because they reflect the purposes, values, and preoccupations of the regime. If government documents are to be rendered in poetry (as Thomas Hood (1911, orig. 1836) supposed to apply in the Ottoman state of his day), then poets will

---

[10] Indeed, quite apart from the ordinary cultural and linguistic limitations that handicap most mortals, it is historically common for particular bureaucracies to be dominated by socially exclusive associations that further narrow their cultural span.

be needed in government service. If legal process is the cultural be-all and end-all of the political system, as it was in the *Rechtsstaat* regime that replaced absolutism in Germany in the mid-nineteenth century, judges and lawyers will be the most important public servants. If science and engineering is the basis of the regime—as some have argued to apply to the former Soviet Union, and to a lesser extent to France—then engineers and science professors will be wanted to run the state. Of course, the relationship between supply and demand can often be two-way in politics, and a government service full of poets may well find reasons for 'poeticizing' every tax demand or legal summons, just as a bureaucracy full of lawyers may see a pressing need to tackle any problem with heavy-duty legalese.

So competency bargains also come in more than one form. Here, reflecting the four types of criticisms that were briefly discussed earlier, and again drawing on the views of those we interviewed, we focus on four selected types, which are summarized in Table 5.1. As in chapter 4, these types map to some extent on the various worldviews identified by the grid-group cultural theory. The first type, reflected in the US city-manager tradition, puts the ability to run organizations and deliver results through the government machine in its various forms, as the central competency required of public servants. A second puts the emphasis on 'boundary spanning', the ability to move among different 'worlds' and bring them together without being able to use a trump card of hierarchical authority—a skill traditionally associated with diplomacy but often also argued to be a central ability of public service more generally, particularly in contexts where there is no central point of authority. A third is concerned with the substantive skills and knowledge of public servants in the sense of technical or quasi-technical knowledge—the tradition of *Fachkompetenzen* (substantive knowledge of the technicalities of policy) in the German state system. And a final type is concerned not so much with technical or subject-specific expertise as with the sort of intuitive skills in political counsel that cannot be 'schooled', and that often involve the ability to look at the world in unpredictable and unconventional ways.

To some extent, the kind of competency bargain that focuses primarily on the technical skills or knowledge that each public servant is expected to possess has something of a hierarchist character in cultural-theory terms, since it is high in both group and grid (professional rules and institutional knowledge). By contrast, the sort of competency bargain that puts the stress on boundary spanning is high in group but not in grid, since it precludes any chain-of-command approach. The sort of competency bargain that puts the stress on a single person's ability to deliver 'results', rather than just obeying rules, has an individualist character, since it is low in both group and grid. And the kind of competency bargain that centres on intuitive and unpredictable

Table 5.1 Wonks, sages, deliverers, and go-betweens: four elements of competency
PSBs

'Sage' bargains	'Wonk' bargains
Statespeople in disguise skills	*Technical or Fachkompetenz skills*
Provision of intellectual or moral insight	Provision of technical knowledge and judgement
'Deliverer' bargains	'Go-between' bargains
Skills of (creative) execution	*Boundary-spanning skills*
Provision of the ability to get things done	Provision of the ability to work across different worlds

skills in counselling over rulership has something of a fatalist character, in the sense that such skills are not readily programmable or replicable, and do not easily fit into a notion of progression by well-understood principles. But this ordering is meant to be heuristic rather than definitive, and we do not want to suggest anything more than a loose association with the grid-group categories.

5.2. 'WONKS' WITH SPECIFIC SKILLS AND KNOWLEDGE: FACHKOMPETENZ-TYPE COMPETENCY BARGAINS

In some versions of competency bargain, public servants are expected to be 'wonks'. They obtain the right to rule over particular fields in exchange for the specific skills or knowledge that they possess. For Hans Mueller (1984: 280), the 'dream' of the eighteenth-century cameralists such as Justi was that 'the ideal state could be governed by experts who knew the technical and material resources of the society and consciously guided that society into the paths of economic development'. Justi was neither the first nor the last to have had such a dream, and it has recurred in numerous different forms since then, for example, in the faith in impartial professionals in the Progressive era in the USA and in the post-Second World War development movement.

As already noted, the German word *Fachkompetenz* sums up much of the essence of this kind of competency, and that term came into official use as part of an understanding that state competencies in the legal sense—official authority or jurisdiction—should be matched by possession of appropriate technical and subject knowledge to an advanced degree on the part of the state's officials. Technical competency has been central to accounts of the development of modern bureaucracies at least since Max Weber (1921/1980: 551), who in discussing *behördliche Kompetenzen* emphasized the importance of recognized qualifications to underpin bureaucratic authority as well as appropriate division of labour. And indeed, it is conventionally expected that the *Fachkompetenzen* of state officials will be reflected in general respect for their technical expertise and subject knowledge among those they deal with. In the German tradition, the notion is that the skills and knowledge of such officials can be respected even by those experts and citizens who disagree with the state's policies or seek to evade its laws. One German interviewee declared that 'I have to be the best in terms of expertise, otherwise I cannot convince anyone' (D19). Another told us, 'Academic knowledge is the basis, the matrix with which we work...' (D16), and a third (D4) said that 'even for a head of unit, [technical] expertise is...important'.

Of course, as all of those interviewees were at pains to add, a stress on *Fachkompetenzen* does not necessarily imply that public servants live in some politics-free world in which technical expertise is never problematic or challenged, or that presentational skills are unimportant in the policy process—quite the reverse. But in a world dominated by *Fachkompetenz* views of public service competency, subject experts run the state and their skills and knowledge are not transferable across public policy domains. It would be as inappropriate to have a monetary economist in charge of a food safety agency as to have a toxicologist or a forester in charge of a competition regulator. Such a bargain can work either through long tenure in particular parts of the state structure (as has traditionally been the German approach, after a period of switching jobs at an early stage in the career), or through shorter-term political appointment of subject experts (as in the US civil service system, where political appointees increasingly need to be credible with the 'policy networks' they have to work with in office (see Peters 2004: 139)). And *Fachkompetenz*-type skills can be defined in more than one way, notably in terms of policy subject-domain (transport, energy, agriculture, etc.) or of elements of the policy process (finance, accountancy, engineering).[11]

The *Fachkompetenz* approach to competency in PSBs is deep-seated and reflects the specialist expertise and technical ability that Max Weber thought lay at the heart of the development of modern bureaucracy. That sort of competency bargain is much in evidence, even in state traditions that have traditionally downplayed *Fachkompetenzen*. No major government system can do without strong elements of this sort of competency, whether appointment to public service works through depoliticized merit, party-spoils or some mixture of the two, such as the German party-book bureaucracy. In recent years, it has come out in new ways with the development of specialized, expert semi-independent regulatory agencies for utilities and competition law

---

[11] Some similarities with this sort of differentiated understanding of *Fachkompetenz* seems to have been at the heart of the 2004 UK proposals for 'professional skills in government'.

in many developing and developed countries over the last decade or two, partly following the US regulatory tradition (see e.g. Majone 1997; Moran 2003). Part of the rationale for the development of such bodies as a key part of the state's economic and industrial policy machinery across many countries, which once had a very different approach to the management of industrial and economic policy, is the assumption that technical expertise in fields such as law and economics is necessary for credible decision-making over stand-ard-setting and rule enforcement.

But equally, the *Fachkompetenz* approach to public service competencies often brings its discontents. Its implication, already noted, that members of the public service are highly sector- or process-specific can serve to buttress the already strong tendencies to balkanization in state bureaucracies and impede the kind of lateral thinking across different parts of the bureaucracy that can produce major policy or process innovations. Moreover, stressing technical competencies of a traditional kind may undervalue generic or portable skills in management or policy analysis, and the potential benefits of being looked at through fresh eyes that can often apply when people from a 'minority tribe', not socialized in the immemorial technical folkways of a particular domain, hold leadership positions in well-established organizations.[12]

Some of those criticisms of the *Fachkompetenz* approach to public service competencies were voiced by a number of our German interviewees, and they are of long standing. Such arguments against the technocratic form of competency bargain were prominent in the French attempts after the Sec-ond World War to introduce a 'generalist' form of training for senior civil servants to offset the divisions within the bureaucratic structure that were introduced by the Napoleonic system of *grands corps*. The same reaction against the *Fachkompetenzen* bargain is also found in the attempts to introduce (often with very limited success) some form of senior executive service structure as a go-anywhere corps at the top of the government structure in the USA and many other countries, including Australia and the UK (Hede 1991).

Indeed, discontent with a *Fachkompetenz*-centred view of public service competency, resonating with politicians' frustration with what they saw (or were encouraged to see, by consultants with product to sell) as avoidably poor leadership and management styles in public servants, was reflected in the 1990s in a new managerial language of competency introduced by human resources (HR) consultants into debates and procedures for managing top

---

[12] Some of our German interviewees also condemned the invocation of *Fachkompetenzen* by bureaucrats to counter politicians' ideas with what was presented as a detached expert view.

civil servants in several countries, as was noted at the outset.[13] Those competency frameworks tended to focus on behavioural skills associated with leadership and corporate management rather than subject-specific expertise. But the *Fachkompetenz* view of civil service competency remains important, and indeed those who instinctively distrust the Moonie-type language of modern management-speak[14] saw the new competency frameworks as part of a conspiracy to downgrade civil servants' traditional skills and knowledge in favour of a more plastic and politicized approach to selection and appraisal, producing pliable 'organization men' (and women) at the expense of subject expertise.

5.3. GO-BETWEENS AND BROKERS: BOUNDARY-SPANNING COMPETENCY BARGAINS

A second strain of skills and knowledge, often not fully separable from the first, puts the emphasis not on the public servants' technical skills or knowledge, but rather on their ability to straddle and bring together different 'worlds', acting as facilitators, brokers, spies, diplomats, or go-betweens rather than operating within a chain of command. Diplomacy—the ability to understand different 'worlds', languages, or worldviews, the capacity to be an *interlocuteur valable*, and to work effectively in a context where rules are precarious and direct orders cannot formally be given by one person or unit to another—is one of the oldest skills required in any state bureaucracy. It can be romanticized into Kiplingesque or Lawrence-of-Arabia-type portrayals of 'the great game' of foreign relations. But skills of a closely similar kind—of boundary-spanning, deal-making, the ability to understand and work across different 'worlds' within and beyond government–have often been argued to be a major requisite for effective public service in domains that are far from the traditional high-politics world of foreign relations. Such skills may be particularly valuable in complex systems of governance that comprise different levels of government and a variety of different providers, where there are limited possibilities for any one actor to dictate to the others. It is 'people,' rather than technical skills, that are central to this kind of competency, but they are the sort of skills that enable effective functioning across disparate parties in anarchic or semi-anarchic contexts.

---

[13] See Lodge and Hood (2003), Hood and Lodge (2004), Lodge and Hood (2005).
[14] Such as Protherough and Pick (2003) who see modern management language as a 'psychological plague' sweeping through society.

For example, Desmond Keeling (1972), in a reflective book that anticipated much of the 'public management' boom of the 1980s and 1990s, argued that 'diplomacy', the ability to negotiate without resorting to authority as a trump card, was one of the central arts of management in government. Bill Mackenzie (1975)—perhaps appropriately, a student of government who built his own career on his ability to understand and cross professional, ethnic, and cultural divides in Britain—wrote in a somewhat similar vein about the facility to move among different 'acceptance worlds' in the context of the ramified structure of modern executive government and 'policy communities'. And a similar theme was taken up in the 1990s with the development of ideas about 'knowing who rather than knowing how' as a key to public service leadership by Patricia Ingraham (2001) and others. Among our British interviewees, one claimed that British civil servants were often ineffective in industrial sponsorship because they simply did not have enough personal knowledge of the personalities in each domain (UK21), and another reflected on diplomatic skills in discussing the art of persuading third parties without exercising authority in a hierarchical sense:

the old civil service [skill] of telling people, I know you don't like this thing, but in order to get the public off your back and [to ensure that] you won't be forced into a more extreme position, let's have this one. (UK8)

Similarly, a German civil servant engaged in a complex process of policy development argued that as society becomes more differentiated and 'wicked issues'[15] are said to be proliferating, public servants' capacity to negotiate becomes more important:

We are doing classic negotiated solutions here. That has nothing to do with traditional understandings of administration and project management. There you have a clear goal and end result. In negotiated processes, there are neither predefined goals ... nor predefined ends nor predefined results ... everything is part of the process. (D18)

Competency of this kind can come in numerous forms. One of the ways in which British civil servants used to hone their knowledge of different 'accept-ance worlds' was through a relatively unpredictable system of career postings that could move them to unexpected corners and frontiers of the adminis-trative system in something that approximated to a 'skills casino'. Such boundary-spanning abilities can also be obtained through the recruitment of 'poachers' to act as gamekeepers, or by recruiting people in other ways who can work across boundaries. And spanning competencies arise in many other conditions as well. For instance, public servants are likely to need the ability to

---

[15] That is, polyvalent and non-linear problems involving basic value conflicts (see Church-man 1967).

span the different 'estates' in the 'corporate states' where government has been centrally concerned with bringing together business and labour organizations, or other key organizations. They are likely to need the ability to span parties in a coalition government structure. And they are likely to need the ability to span levels of government in federal government structures, whether for dramatic exercises in policy entrepreneurship or simply for keeping the lines of communication open.[16] So the boundary-spanning bargain is by no means an exotic case.

5.4. INDIVIDUAL MAKING-IT-HAPPEN SKILLS: DELIVERY- TYPE COMPETENCY BARGAINS

In contrast to 'wonkish' and 'spanning' competencies, individual executive ability—the skill of being able to make things happen within a government organization in a desired way, rather than just following rules or routines—is at the heart of some public service competency bargains. For example, the ability of individual managers to run organizations or manage projects was central to the PSB represented by the US city-manager movement that developed from the 1880s. What is valued here is not so much technical knowledge of subjects like law or economics, nor the ability and disposition 'to speak truth to power and power to truth' in the high echelons of government, but the ability of an individual to make things happen on their own or by working on others in ways that are not fully prescribed in some manual. In Charlotte Brontë's great novel *Shirley* (1994: 273) it is remarked of one of the characters that 'she was far better informed, better read, a deeper thinker than [another character], but of administrative energy, of executive ability, she had none.' In delivery-type competency bargains, it is precisely that 'administrative energy... executive ability' that is the most desired capability of public servants. Indeed, one of our UK interviewees put that sort of skill at the centre of the bargain for the job that interviewee did:

What my job is about is delivering the thing I am told to deliver. It is not my job to write the policy, to believe the policy, to care about the substance of policy... I am not committed to *what* I am delivering, I am committed to delivering. (UK7)

Indeed, several of our interviewees were at pains to point out that the sort of skills that bring success in organizing a delivery chain are very different from

---

[16] For instance, some German federal ministries aim to develop boundary-spanning skills by recruiting their staff from other levels of government and by sending their staff out to subordinate authorities (D3), and there were some moves in that direction in UK central government at the time of writing.

those that bring success in the world of policy advice. One British interviewee argued that:

The policy arm neither understands nor has a high regard for management and . . . in general it is much easier to set an organization a load of priorities and objectives that are unclear because in the world of policy, the way you advance is by being imprecise and unclear . . . In a world of management that does not work. (UK4)

Over the 'NPM' era of the last two decades or so, heavy stress has been placed on the importance of managerial or leadership skills in executive government—not just following rules or writing brilliant policy analyses, but also creatively finding ways to make public organizations deliver against targets in the services they provide. And that is certainly not the first time that such concerns about public service competencies have had strong political backing. For instance, after the disasters of the British Crimean War campaign in the mid-nineteenth century (when the UK, then supposedly at its zenith as an imperial super-state, nearly lost a war against a middle-sized power as a result of a lethal combination of malign chance and utter ineptitude in the civilian and military machine, particularly over matters of procurement), a strong Administrative Reform Association developed, with middle-class backing. In terms quite reminiscent of recent drives to improve the quality of public service management, that Association sought to improve the managerial competency of public servants, by means that included applying 'business efficiency' practices from the private sector (Mueller 1984: 213ff.).

Similarly, in the total wars of the twentieth century, the ability to deliver very concrete results—from aircraft components to meat and timber—came to be of particular importance in the UK civil service and many business people with those sorts of competencies were drawn in, particularly at the upper middle level of the bureaucracy, to run the relevant production, delivery, and allocation systems (Turner 1988: 205). Similar skills have been valued in peacetime contexts as well, including the US city-manager movement that developed from the 1880s (as already mentioned), the public corporation movement that was central to the development of public enterprise in the middle two quarters of the twentieth century, and the chief executives of the 'agencies' that became fashionable in the age of 'unbundled government' (Pollitt and Talbot 2004) in the last two decades.

Those who advocate this sort of competency bargain are often scornful of those who put the emphasis on technical skills and knowledge, rather than common sense, political judgement, and managerial drive. For instance, one British interviewee who strongly emphasized the individual 'deliverer' view of the competency bargain sardonically commented on a meeting of permanent secretaries he had attended in the 1980s:

In one meeting I noticed that the neighbour on my right was writing away like mad, and I did not understand what he was doing.... He was translating the agenda into classical Greek. And then I looked round the room and realized that at least half of the people would have been able to do the same. (UK20)

For this individual, and those who think like him, the central competency required for effective government is creative individual delivery skills rather than the skills of the wonk or the sage.

5.5. 'SAGES' WITH WISDOM, INTUITION, AND GENERALIZED RULERSHIP SKILLS: 'STATESPERSONS IN DISGUISE'—COMPETENCY-TYPE BARGAINS

No major executive government system can do without a strong element of each of the competency elements mentioned earlier. But in contrast to the sort of competency bargains that primarily value public servants' specific or technical knowledge within a specific field, their skills as negotiators or as individual deliverers, are those sorts of competency bargains in which the key qualities required are robust political judgement, steadiness under political fire, ability to read the runes and weigh the policy options, spot possibilities for making and breaking political coalitions, and find the pressure points that will produce responses from an apparently labyrinthine and fragmented structure of executive government.[17] The British civil servant's comment on 'the skill of government' quoted in our second epigraph relates to those sorts of qualities, and we had similar comments from several German interviewees, including one who described his skills in developing long-term policy as knowing 'which detours I have to take, because I know that the straight path will take me into fallen tree trunks' (D17).

The skill of the 'sage' in this sense is to give advice, rather than to rule directly or to do deals among groups, but the knowledge that the 'sage' commands tends to be tacit, intuitive, comprising the kind of 'common sense' and political judgment that comes from a mixture of innate qualities and experience, but cannot readily be taught in college classes. Indeed, the 'sage' provides just what the book-learned, college-crammed public servant with no practical skills in governing cannot provide, as in the quotation from Iago in *Othello* in the first epigraph, and a stress on 'sage' skills often involves a reaction against purely formal knowledge. In a comment on the traditional

---

[17] Max Weber has defined such knowledge as 'Dienstwissen'.

Chinese bureaucracy recruited through the famous literary examination system, Hsieh (1925: 179) points to the problem: 'By excellence in writing essays, one got ... an appointment [to the civil service]. But how many of the winners had learned anything about practical politics, or the art of governing?'[18] By contrast, the central quality of the 'sage' does not reside in paper qualifications or academic attainments, but consists of political 'nous'.

Perhaps the three central qualities of the 'sage' in this context are the ability to assess political positions, to identify and assess risks, and to identify 'heresthetics'. The former resides in the innate or learned ability to 'read' a political situation in the way that a capable military commander can 'read' a landscape'. One British civil servant told us that 'Civil servants live off jumbled half-messages ... [and] ... must use their intuition about what that [information] means in practice and what is off limits' (UK24), and several of our other interviewees said something similar. Richard Neustadt's *Presidential Power* (1960) was a book that deservedly became famous in the early 1960s because it made much of that kind of skill and encouraged would-be presidents to look for advisers who put the political needs of the president ahead of bureaucratic convenience, technical needs, or a supposed national interest. If 'pigthink' denotes a cast of mind that looks at everything from the political perspective of the holders of power (i.e. the viewpoint of the pigs in George Orwell's famous allegorical novel (1944) *Animal Farm*), it is a mindset that may not be attractive but is nevertheless the central quality that many politicians want from their top public servants.

The ability to identify and assess political risks intuitively is a second, central sage-type quality. Long before 'risk management' became the corporate buzzword that it is today, senior British civil servants traditionally used to describe one of their trademark skills as an ability to assess and handle political risks, typically in the form of having a 'nose', or intuitive sense, for what might cause political trouble for ministers and concentrating their activity on that, and some of our German interviewees said the same thing.[19] Advocates of 'rational' policy analysis often attack bureaucrats as excessively risk averse, tending to seek to avoid blame by over-inclusive legislation to capture that last 5 per cent of any social problem (see e.g. Breyer

---

[18] Similar criticisms of legally trained, but administratively inexperienced civil servants in late nineteenth-century Germany led to a change in legal training, with more stress on practical application in the later stages of the law degree (Röhl 1994: 133).

[19] One, describing the skills and abilities expected of political civil servants in the German federal civil service, saw them as a mixture of chain-of-delivery leadership skills ('the capability to manage the various parts [of the government machine], [to ensure] that they function, that the various political demands are transposed') and political sensitivity. 'Not just doing technical things, one needs to realize—"Ha! This could be politically sensitive."' (D13).

1993) and to cover their backs by elaborate procedures. But from a 'sage' perspective, political risk is unavoidable, and there is no well-understood rational means of dealing with it. In this vein, one of our German interviewees, unconsciously echoing Tversky and Kahneman's famous analysis of loss aversion (1991, 1992), argued that the 'rational' analysis of risk did not correspond with political reality:

> [Policy] must not be a flop. In this kind of bureaucracy, the mechanisms are harsh. For good initiatives one receives some praise ('OK, not bad, but could have been done better'), but when it *geht in die Hose* [20] ... it is a disaster. In politics, a good initiative appears once in the newspaper and if one is extremely successful then our industry has an additional growth rate of 0.2 per cent. Nobody notices it. A politician is remembered for ten years if there is a flop. That is why we are very risk averse here. (D16)

A third and related sage-like skill is the intuitive ability to find the points of leverage or heresthetics (in the term used by William Riker (1986) and Iain McLean (2001)) in any situation. That is the ability to form political coalitions along different dimensions of political cleavage, and to spot and exploit the possibility for realigning an established set of political forces by finding another dimension on which the groups will form into different coalitions. Such skills are not easily distinguishable from those belonging to elected politicians, and they are capabilities that can be argued to come more from experience and insight than from specific technical knowledge of the kind that is gained from orthodox academic study.

Most public service systems incorporate at least some elements of this kind of competency bargain. The 'mandarin' view of the public servant as a person with a background that gives them general skills in wise political counsel about ruling, rather than technical knowledge in the orthodox sense, partly approximates to this kind of bargain. As we noted in Chapter 2, that view is reflected in the Confucian tradition, as in Japan and in the bureaucratic tradition of China (arguably both of the imperial and of the communist era, at least until very recently), where the right to rule as a bureaucrat rests in general political 'soundness' or moral 'grit' as much as in any specific technical knowledge or attainments. The same can be found in the British 'Whitehall mandarin' variant of that tradition that is reflected in Sir Henry Taylor's (1993, orig. 1836) idea of *The Statesman* and developed in much of UK central government in the late nineteenth century.[21]

---

[20] 'Goes down the toilet', loosely translated.
[21] Although there have always been parts of the UK executive government structure (local government and many parts of central government, including the diplomatic service and particular departments and agencies such as the law officers) that emphasized *Fachkompetenzen*-type bargains.

Indeed, even in an age when 'delivery' was officially stressed as the watchword, many of our British interviewees tended to stress 'sage-like' qualities in reflecting on the competency bargain they worked within. One of them said:

The civil servant is normally in the business of influencing... politics is about influencing rather than exercise of formal powers. (UK8)

Others ruminated on the way competency was traditionally understood in the Whitehall mandarin bargain. One said:

Competency was primarily the ability to write well, being able to grasp a subject quickly (being bright counts [for] a lot)... write it for somebody... and that was about it... they [the opinion leaders in that system] undoubtedly valued a certain smoothness, a certain ability to deal with things without getting ruffled.... (UK9)

Others explained that the full 'sage' stage in the traditional Whitehall system was only reached after a period of apprenticeship.

The requirement on entry was intellectual capacity, never mind what discipline. An ability to absorb quite a wide range of information from a variety of sources, synthesize it and then help ministers work out what an appropriate policy response should be. (UK13)

People up to 35 were there to produce things on other people's behest. They were there to contribute their abstract intelligence rather than their experience to the analysis of the problems... the 40-to 50-year-olds were regarded as wiser heads and holders of knowledge and they therefore had to be a key part of the policy forming process. The 20- and early 30-year-olds were often silenced... they were there to listen and learn. (UK4)

I noticed going up the grades that... [at the higher levels] much more emphasis is [placed] on doing the right thing than doing things right. (UK7)

Sometimes these sorts of generalized rulership skills are recognized only when events prove their absence. For example, one British civil servant commented on an apparent crisis of 'sage-like' qualities in the upper ranks of the Treasury in the 1980s and 1990s:

There was a dissatisfaction in the Lawson [1983–9] and Howe [1979–83] era with the wisdom of the grey heads who were seen not to be wise at all... but actually to be narrow in their experience and unable to come up with fresh ideas about how to deal with underlying fundamental problems of the British economy and society. (UK4)

As we have already noted, a stress on sage-like general skills of rulership have often been tied up with an aristocratic ideal of government by 'gentlemen' in some form or another—notably family connections to the landed gentry, as in the older European tradition, members of the *Samurai* warrior-caste in Tokugawa, Japan, after the Meiji restoration, or a more meritocratic view of 'gentleness' for the Chinese Confucian tradition. But sage-like skills can be valued in other political contexts as well. The notion of intuitive political understanding and judgement as a central capability of senior public servants is also found in the communist state tradition, in the older traditions of spoils-system bureaucracy, and in newer forms of political-adviser positions to those in high office. Modernity may have weakened the older aristocratic form of the 'statespeople in disguise' form of competency bargain, but that bargain seems to have appeared in new forms in a post-aristocratic age.

5.6. MIXES AND COMBINATIONS

These four types of competency bargains represent differences of emphasis and they clearly overlap. As in Chapter 4, they can be thought of as circles on a Venn diagram rather than as wholly orthogonal qualities. For instance, diplomatic or go-between skills may in some cases depend wholly on the accident of birth or innate ability to empathize, but will often also depend on some degree of specific knowledge in the sense of mastery of different cultures and languages, technical or general, and hence will involve a hybrid of 'wonk' and 'go-between' competencies. And delivery skills start to merge with those of diplomacy as soon as public servants are involved in trying to broker deals among the numerous more or less autonomous players within a complex executive government structure, or even for a single organization, if bargaining with labour unions takes place at that level.

The 'sage's' ability to read the runes and find out the truth to speak to power may be based heavily on political flair and connections, but it will normally require some element of technical, diplomatic, or managerial experience as well. And the 'policy wonk' typically needs to be effectively plugged in to a cross-organizational network for his or her knowledge to be up to date, accurate, and effective. Triple hybrids are also commonly observable, for instance, in the perhaps increasing tendency, already noted, for top political appointees in the US federal civil service to supplement their sage-like qualities by being credible 'wonks' in their particular policy field, and to be able to work across policy community–government boundaries. Moreover, different competencies may be called for at different stages of a career, as we have already noted in comments from various UK interviewees who indicated a traditional process in which wonks gradually progressed into sages. Indeed, it is in the intersections among the four types we have described in this chapter where most of the interesting parts of competency bargains are likely to be found.

But that does not mean that all public service competency bargains necessarily come down to the same thing in practice. As the examples we have given earlier show, differences in emphasis among these four competency elements are certainly detectable at the level of the government system as a whole, both over time and between countries. The preference for 'sages' in many of the highest positions of the public service in some state traditions contrasts with the more technically specific competency requirements embodied in the traditional German *Juristenmonopol* and in the pre-1945 French system of recruiting specialists from the various *grandes écoles*. The other two variants of competency bargain discussed earlier seem to be rather less commonly found on a systemwide basis, but are readily encountered, at least for parts of other traditional state structures. And with current trends in governance—involving complex intergovernmental structures and policy regimes that cut across state, private, and third-sector forms, it is not surprising that much of the 'smart practice' contemporary public management literature tends to make much of leaders who can 'add value' by working across jurisdictional boundary lines (see Moore 1995; Bardach 1998).

Moreover, even within any one given state tradition at a single point in time, differences among these elements of the competency PSB will typically be detectable between subsets of the public service or even within those subsets. For instance, one UK interviewee suggested that permanent secretaries (official heads of departments) offered skills of different kinds, with some offering primarily delivery or managerial skills and others offering the skills of the wonk or the sage:

Permanent secretaries fall into two categories...those who are fascinated by policy and really would like to be ministers...[and those] who are shepherds of their sheep. (UK16)

More generally, as we have already noted, the 'statespeople in disguise' tradition of competency PSB in central government in Britain is only part of a larger public service picture in which it is balanced by equally strong emphasis on the *Fachkompetenzen* PSB within the local government service, which was traditionally much larger than central government and delivered most public services on the ground. In the German case, while *Fachkompetenzen* formed the traditional basis of the competency bargain for most public servants, the group of politically appointed top public servants in 'posts of confidence' operated under competency bargains that were more 'sage-like' or 'deliverer-like' than 'wonk-like', focusing largely on political judgement and political management skills. And the 'deliverer' type of managerial bargain reflected in the US city-manager tradition contrasts with different competency bargains for public servants in other US city-government structures and other parts of the public service.

5.7. TRENDS AND CHANGES OVER TIME

Apart from using the distinctions made earlier to identify subsets of competency bargains within different parts of the executive government structure, we can also use those distinctions to identify changes over time. Over recent decades, more stress has overtly been placed on the 'delivery' variant of competency bargain in many political systems—a rhetorical development that has been discussed by innumerable commentators, with a million reasons being adduced for why a shift to a more managerial approach to public service should have occurred when and where it did (see e.g. Hood and Jackson 1991). Indeed, if we are to take that pervasive rhetoric, and the major outpourings of the academic and practitioner NPM industry over the last decade or more, at face value, we might conclude that the competency-bargain story of that era is in essence one of replacement of older *Fachkompetenzen* or 'statespeople in disguise' competency bargains, with an older emphasis on wonks and sages being swept away by delivery-type bargains adapted for a new managerial age.

Some of our UK interviewees certainly saw change in those terms, as reflected in the following comments:

More and more you are looking for people who can actually manage their departments. (UK1)

A big change is that No 10 sees the job of the top of the civil service...as that of managers. They have to manage things, turn the screw on the system and make it hit more targets...[even though] they went in because they were 'thoughtful chaps' [rather than managers]. (UK6)

Some of the [competency demands]...have changed. Thirty years ago...the explicit focus on management and leadership was probably less and there was more focus on policy and the substance of policy skills. (UK11)

In the 1950s and 1960s, the Permanent Secretary was above all the policy adviser to the minister, spent most of the time discussing policy-type issues with the minister, whereas by the 1990s that was at most one-third of their time; most of the time was managerial....When I started [civil servants] produced extremely polished papers in the prose style and, by today's standards...terribly mannered. There was...more emphasis on pure policy advice to ministers...who generally did not have much of a clue as to what they wanted to do. [But later] ministers...had a clearer idea of the direction where they wanted to go...officials [were] more in the business of helping ministers to achieve the broad goals they have set out. (UK13)

There is a difference between the modern and old-fashioned White Papers. With the old-fashioned ones you had a degree of analysis and description. You would take pride in how they were produced and certainly ask the question of how long the (White) Papers would stand the test of time and feel some responsibility towards that. With the modern White Paper it is impossible to take that degree of personal involvement. (UK23)

But not all saw the changes in quite such simple terms, and even for the UK, which is often taken as one of the leading 'NPM' countries, there are some complications to add to such accounts, in at least two ways. First, the rhetorical slant of reform documents did not necessarily reflect what was wanted from public servants in practice. Most commentators base their analyses more on the first than the second, but many of our bureaucratic interviewees in the UK told us that, in spite of their constant drumbeat about the need for public servants to be 'deliverers' above all else, elected politicians still needed traditional 'statesmen in disguise' competencies from public servants to get them out of trouble when the inevitable political crises struck.

Second, even in the UK, the traffic in competency bargains does not seem to have been all one-way. While the 'statespeople in disguise' element of the competency bargain for many upper-level civil servants seems to have shifted to some extent towards a greater emphasis on managerial skills and ability (particularly for the new group of executive agency CEOs that developed after 1988, but also for the regular departmental civil service), the 'statespeople in disguise' element was the central competency of a new group of political-appointee 'political adviser' that civil servants developed from the 1970s, when their position was first formalized. Indeed, one British political adviser described the adviser's key skills to us in terms that thirty years earlier could have been a standard account of regular senior civil service skills:

... making sure ministers got lively interesting advice, that they knew where advice was coming from, put it into context, smoothing it with other departments. (UK2)

Moreover, while there was more emphasis on generalist-managerial skills and abilities in some organizations where domain-specific technical knowledge and qualifications had traditionally been required for the topmost positions, concern with *Fachkompetenzen* by no means disappeared, even in the departmental civil service. In some cases, there has not so much been a decline in the stress on 'wonkishness' as a change in the sort of 'wonks' required. And indeed, in other parts of the bureaucratic forest, the competency traffic moved in the opposite direction from wonk or sage to 'deliverer'. The most important instance of that reverse flow, as already mentioned, lay in the quasi-independent economic regulators that developed from the 1980s to replace the older era of publicly owned industries, departmental sponsorship, and substantial ministerial intervention in matters of business competition.

In the German case, none of our interviewees saw change on the scale that was cited by the UK interviewees quoted earlier. Some thought that contemporary changes simply intensified the demand for lawyers, especially in matters relating to the EU and the development of regulation, such as consumer protection. Indeed, some saw no significant change at all. One senior German civil servant (D1), questioned about 'managerial competency', retorted scornfully:

These are just words. I can hardly see any change.

But not all our German interviewees saw a picture of no change. One (D9) pointed to the increased managerial and linking skills that modern politics demanded:

The divisions have to work together much more, set up *ad hoc* teams...that means you need more leadership skills to access the technical work.

Another, contrary to the views of those who saw an undiminished demand for lawyers in the bureaucracy, noted the relaxation of the 'lawyers' monopoly' in the civil service into a partnership between jurists and economists over a generation, and linked that development to a changing perception of the civil service's role and skills, noting that in his ministry there had been a notable change:

...away from a situation where lawyers decided everything, because they were the only ones capable of writing laws, to a situation where we are more a service provider for the *Wirtschaft*. (D17)

Like many other hasty obituaries, the death of the 'statesperson in disguise' form of public service competency bargain may have been exaggerated, even if the form of that kind of bargain is liable to shift. Rulers have always needed wonks, sages, deliverers, and go-betweens in the upper levels of their executive government structures. The risks and unpredictabilities of political life are always likely to produce some demand for sage-like competencies of some kind, especially when politicians see themselves as besieged by hostile media which can bring about their downfall through a few ill-judged words.[22] So, though the relative emphases and particular forms of the four competency bargains discussed here may certainly change, the basic mix seems unlikely to disappear altogether.

---

[22] As we noted in the preface, a wall poster in the British DTI in 2001 warned staff 'there are 152 political journalists noting your every word'.

6

Loyalty and Responsibility in Public Service Bargains: Judges, Partners, Executives, and Jesters

A cowed bureaucracy continues to promote with zeal what it supposes to be its masters' policies long after the masters have lost interest.

> (D. J. Enwright (1969), *Memoirs of a Mendicant Professor*, London, Chatto & Windus, p.146)

Ich hab hier bloß ein Amt und keine Meinung[1]

> (Wrangel in Friedrich V. Schiller, *Wallenstein*, 1799, fünfter Auftritt)

Like many court jesters before him . . . he [Paul Birch] was dependent on the tolerance of his masters. When Bob Ayling took over [at British Airways], Birch was summoned by the new strategy director and told, 'You've been taking the piss for the last year and it's got to stop.' Birch's plea that this was his job did not receive a sympathetic hearing. Nor did his pointing out to Ayling, 'You realise you can't sack me, because sacking me would show that you couldn't take it any more.' He was sacked.

> (B. Otto (2001), *Fools are Everywhere*, Chicago, Chicago University Press, p.267)

6.1. THE LOYALTY/RESPONSIBILITY DIMENSION OF PUBLIC SERVICE BARGAINS

At the most abstract level, all PSBs could be described as an exchange of some reward package in return for some bundle of skills and capabilities. But that is a bit like describing romantic love as the exchange of passion and affection for some specified set of desired properties possessed by the loved one (Edyvane 2003: 61–2). It might help enlighten the proverbial visitor from Mars, but it

---

[1] 'I just have an office, not an opinion.'

does not do justice to all the myriad complexities of such a relationship. And as we noted in Chapter 5, PSBs often require public servants to show properties of political or personal loyalty that are not normally included in conventional concepts of 'competency', and yet are often more important than skills or capabilities of a technical or managerial kind.[2]

Indeed, many kinds of public servants, from presidents to beat cops, are expected to take some sort of loyalty oath or declaration on assuming office.[3] And when political regimes change, there are invariably issues of political loyalty for public servants who worked under the old regime that demand some kind of loyalty bargain. Often such a bargain takes the form of an implicit, precarious, and usually contested type of amnesty, in which public servants who worked under the now-discredited old regime offer a born-again political loyalty to the new regime in exchange for a more or less explicit understanding that a veil will be placed over their previous activities in the 'bad old days'. So in this chapter, we explore what public servants obtain from the bargain in the way of trust, responsibility, or autonomy, and what they give up in the way of personal freedom or ability to 'play the field' politically.

These issues are certainly not fully separable from the matters of reward and competency discussed earlier, but they seem sufficiently important to merit discussion on their own. Indeed, loyalty and reward may come into conflict, as one German civil servant told us:

> The loyalty is immense. You can see it here—we all are civil servants but are continuously cutting our income, do so very loyally and even present it as if we thought this was appropriate. (D3)

The relationship between loyalty, competency, and reward is perhaps even more variable and problematic than the issues we have discussed in Chapters 4 and 5. As to reward, responsibility is sought and even longed for by some,[4] but dreaded and shunned by others as the very opposite of a reward—indeed,

---

[2] Perhaps we could, in principle, define loyalty in the sense of ability and disposition to commit as a behavioural competency, akin to faithfulness in dogs. Indeed, that is precisely the image used by one senior British civil servant (Sir Richard Mottram), who said the British civil service at the outset of the Labour government in 1997 was like 'a rather stupid dog' eager to please in exchange for affection: 'It wants to do what its master wants and it wants to be loyal to its master and above all it wants to be loved for doing that' (Public Administration Select Committee 2002: qs 340–51, 7 March 2002).

[3] As with the oath required of *Beamte* in Prussia from 1867, which committed them to *Treueeid, Diensteid* and *Verfassungseid* (loyalty to the king, the service, and the constitution).

[4] A view epitomized by Sancho Panza's remark in Cervantes' *Don Quixote*. 'It is good to have command, even if it is only of a flock of sheep.'

Table 6.1 Judges, jesters, delegates, and confidants: four elements of loyalty PSBs

'Jester' bargains	'Judge' bargains
'Irritating' loyalty	*Loyalty to the state and the law*
Acts as reality checker for rulers	Acts as semi-autonomous player with loyalty to some higher entity
'Executive' bargains	**'Partner' bargains**
Loyalty within a specified brief	*Loyalty as confidant and co-ruler*
Acts to pursue defined goals in some limited and revocable space of action	Acts as interlocutor and collaborator with rulers, with right to be heard

a punishment, a source of stress, blame, toil, and tears. In fact, a whole set of theories of blame avoidance and 'bureau-shaping' in political and bureaucratic behaviour have been built on precisely those sorts of attitudes.[5] The same can be said of loyalty. As with the married state, wholehearted loyalty or commitment to a single regime, party, or political leader is valued by some as part of self-actualization, since it enables them to accomplish as part of a team what they could not do alone. But it is seen by others as an irksome restraint that cramps their personal style and their freedom to give information to anyone they choose, publicly criticize government policy or behaviour, or make political alliances at will.[6]

In this chapter, following the same pattern as in Chapters 4 and 5, we pick out four kinds of responsibility/loyalty bargains, which emerged from the reflections of the public servants we interviewed. We term these four types: (*a*) judge-type bargains; (*b*) partnership-type bargains; (*c*) executive-type bargains; and (*d*) jester-type bargains, and summarize them in Table 6.1. As in Chapters 4 and 5, the terms we use to label these types are merely indicative, and we do not claim that these four types are either jointly exhaustive or mutually exclusive. But, as in Chapters 4 and 5, the four types to some extent follow the four worldviews identified by grid-group cultural theory. Judge-type bargains broadly seem to reflect something of a hierarchist worldview; while partnership-type bargains have more of an egalitarian flavour in relation to loyalty and responsibility; executive-type bargains seem closer to the individualist worldview; and jester-type bargains seem to reflect a form of fatalist way of life. Each of these four types is distinctive enough in comparative and historical perspective to merit some discussion.

---

[5] See for instance Dunleavy (1991), James (2003), Fiorina (1982, 1986), Ellis (1994), Hood (2002*b*).

[6] Still others see it as a precarious and uncertain existence coping with the vagaries of politics, constant intrigue and fear of 'cheating' on the relationship by politicians, as some German interviewees (D7, D8, D12) suggested to us.

6.2. 'JUDGE-TYPE' BARGAINS: AUTONOMY AND INDEPENDENCE

What we call a judge-type loyalty bargain is one where public servants are not expected simply to do the bidding of some superordinate or sovereign, but are loyal to some higher abstract entity partly or wholly interpreted by themselves—the department, the law, the constitution, the people at large, or perhaps even the deity. For example, at the time when this book was being drafted, a former US Deputy Secretary of Defence (Paul Wolfowitz) had been nominated to be head of the World Bank. The nomination was controversial in the light of the nominee's role in the 2003 Iraq war, and Wolfowitz was at pains to declare that he would be 'an international civil servant', implicitly of an autonomous kind, and not any kind of agent of the US President (*Financial Times* 1 April 2005, p.6).

The term 'judge-type' is just a broad label, since real judges in practice vary enormously in their degree of autonomy from direction from executive government, both over time and from one country to another. For instance, when judges are paid such a pittance that one in three is homeless, as Jon Quah found for Mongolia a decade or so ago,[7] they will need to be people of remarkable moral integrity for their independence from executive government to amount to much, whatever any constitution might say. But in using this label, we have in mind the liberal stereotype of the independent, autonomous dispenser of justice who is expected to operate without fear or favour, whose position as to reward and tenure is protected at least in some sense,[8] does not have a 'line manager' and is not an 'executive' in the ordinary sense.

It is not difficult to identify public servants whose loyalty bargain is broadly of such a type, but they come in various forms. In the case of the former West Germany, *Beamten* as a group traditionally had something approximating a 'judge-type' bargain, with their rights formally protected by the 1949 Basic Law, which in turn (Art. 33) declared their responsibility to uphold the constitution rather than just to serve the government of the day. The former East Germany had a rather different bargain, and there are numerous exceptions to the judge-type bargain in present-day Germany. But several German civil servants described their loyalty bargains to us in such terms:

---

[7] See Quah (2003*b*: 43). Judicial salaries in Mongolia in 1995 ranged from US$33 to US$51 per month.

[8] As in the provision of the 1701 English Act of Settlement, as mentioned in Chapter 4.

The loyalty is largely vis-à-vis the state and then at a lower level, loyalty is towards the institution that you are working for... belonging to the *Haus* (department) one is working for. Not through the minister—they come and go. (D3)

One is loyal towards the taxpayer and people in the country. Towards the Minister—only if one knows him and likes him.... (D2)

Another interviewee (D1), while expressing the loyalty-to-the-state view that 'We are *Staatsdiener*, we feel as such,' pointed out some of complications of loyalty to the *Haus* (department):

Every department has its own identity—it develops its identity over time... there were [political] leaders here who tried to impose their will [and] were not accepted by the *Haus*. When colleagues cannot identify with this [attempted imposition of political will], then it is artificial and temporary... We deliver when [it is] demanded. But it is not internalized, one works [only] on demand, one does not [actively] participate, and when the minister is gone... [it] all drains away. (D1)

In many state traditions, the judge-type loyalty bargain, or approximations to it, applies only to a subset of public servants. In the USA, types of public servant who have some form of judge-type loyalty include public and special prosecutors, auditors, and some kinds of regulators. The same goes for the UK, in which public servants with some kind of judge-type bargain are sometimes said to include the police, whose constitutional role as 'servants of the Crown' rather than of the government of the day has often been propounded in judge-type terms, mistakenly in the view of some commentators.[9] One former regulator (UK25) described to us a rancorous exchange with a minister who tried to cast him in the role of reporting or making recommendations rather than decisions:

'How could I possibly dare to take on one of Her Majesty's principal secretaries of State, a member of the Privy Council? I don't give a flying f*** about that. I was going to do my job.'

Moreover, as we shall see later, even 'regular' British central government civil servants have some 'judge-like' features that sit rather awkwardly with other parts of their loyalty bargain.

In the Japanese case, Article 9 of the 1889 Meiji constitution gave civil servants the power to make regulations without the approval of the Diet, and Gregory Kasza (1988: 12) suggests that provision reflected a distinctly 'judge-like' bargain for the higher civil service: 'The notion that the bureaucracy should be a mere servant of the non-bureaucratic political elite was not adopted even in theory by the Meiji founders, and was explicitly denied by their constitution.' Those powers were formally removed in the 1946

---

[9] For a classic exposition (and demolition) of the doctrine of 'constabulary independence', see Marshall (1965).

(Occupation) Constitution, which sought to move bureaucrats away from the traditional judge-type elements of their loyalty bargain. The extent to which there is a substantial element of the judge-type bargain in contemporary Japanese bureaucracy is debatable. Some scholars, such as Thomas Pempel (1974, 1978) in his original work and Chalmers Johnson (1982), accord a substantial degree of autonomy in the policy process to Japanese bureaucracy, while others, including Pempel (1982, 1992) in later work and particularly Mark Ramseyer and Frances Rosenbluth (1993), offer a more agency-type interpretation.

At the high end of judge-type autonomy are those public servants who exercise autonomous judgement on matters of high political salience, whose work cannot be directed by any political actor and who cannot be removed from office. One case in point, current at the time of writing, was the position of the Italian Central Bank Governor, Antonio Fazio, whose conduct in prohibiting the takeover of an Italian bank by a foreign owned firm led to explicit calls for his resignation by the Italian government (and strong criticism from the European Commission), yet was able to remain in office (notionally for life, in practice for a few months until his position became untenable) despite the total breakdown of his relationship with the elected government. A less dramatic case is that of the UK's Comptroller and Auditor General, who had indefinite tenure with no compulsory retiring age and who could be removed from office only by a vote in both houses of the legislature. Public servants who are independently elected (as in the case of some US judges and many state and local public servants whose equivalents are appointed officials in other countries) are, in the nature of things, their 'own boss' too, though the pressures of securing re-election or avoiding recall is likely to mean they work quite differently from appointees of the type given in the previous example.[10]

In other cases we find more diluted or hybrid kinds of judge-type bargains. For instance, in Germany, the 'judge-like' quality of the loyalty bargain for *Beamten* was cut across by the traditional 'political retirement' (*vorzeitiger Ruhestand*) rule dating from about 1848.[11] This rule, far from giving civil servants indefinite tenure of the kind associated with independent judiciaries, enabled elected governments to require civil servants above a certain rank to move into 'premature retirement' for political reasons, though those retirees retained the right to salary and privileges and indeed to return to public office at some future time (see Kugele 1976: 17–46). The rule represents a way of

---

[10] That is the argument used by such liberal luminaries as John Stuart Mill (1910: 335) against popular election of judges and other executive functionaries.

[11] The rule was enshrined in §20 of the 1852 Prussian *Disziplinarrecht*. The term *politischer Beamter* [political civil servant] seems to have become established rather later, in the 1870s and 1880s.

reconciling bureaucracy with democracy that is very different from the Whitehall 'serial monogamy' convention to be discussed shortly. It developed in the early stages of nineteenth-century German democratization as a bargain to reconcile increasingly legalized employment conditions in state service (and the desires of legislatures to provide civil servants with political rights), with the need of rulers to surround themselves with public servants they regarded as loyal to their interests rather than those of their opponents.[12] Albeit used more sparingly than the US spoils system, as we showed in Table 1.1, this rule means that the German bureaucracy involves at best a quasi-autonomous bureaucracy rather than a fully autonomous one.

There are other ways of diluting judge-type loyalty bargains as well. One is by appointment on relatively short fixed terms, where the need to secure re-appointment or find career openings after non-reappointment may have to be balanced against single-minded autonomy—unless the individuals involved are exceptionally high-minded, independently wealthy, or in their last job before a comfortable retirement. Further, to the extent that there is a hierarchy or career ladder for such 'judges', promotion or appointment to the higher positions often offer opportunities for the exertion of political influence. And even when such officials' tenure and pay is protected in some way, executive governments can often sap their autonomy in practice by changing the organizational or institutional structures they work in. For instance, statutory duties can be changed, organizational architecture altered, or individuals redeployed in a way that can sideline some of those 'judges' and promote others, without any formal assault on tenure or decisional autonomy.[13] Moreover, other ties could cut across the judge-type loyalty bargain when civil servants worked on a temporary basis for independent bodies, as one UK interviewee told us:

I used to be a [name of department] civil servant on loan to the regulator. That became untenable because I was seen as no longer loyal enough by the [name of department] and there was pressure to go back, [given] that [I was not seen as] looking after the [department's] interests effectively. (UK4)

Another interviewee (UK25) who had held a regulatory office that he interpreted in judge-type terms, told us that politicians and departmental civil servants had tried to deny his autonomous decision-making power and hampered his ability to function in judge-type mode by denial of crucial information.

---

[12] At first those civil servants perceived as politically untrustworthy were the monarchists, though later it was the liberal bureaucrats who were seen as prime candidates for political retirement (Kugele 1976: 21–4).

[13] For example, Ryan (2002: 447–8) suggests that after the People's National Party won government in Jamaica in 1972, Prime Minister Michael Manley sidelined traditional civil servants, particularly in the Ministry of Finance, by setting up new bodies staffed by individuals with closer political alignment to the new government.

The judge-type life in public service in practice rarely offers complete escape from political tightrope walking over questions of loyalty.

6.3. PARTNERSHIP-TYPE BARGAINS

At the opposite pole of loyalty from the judicial-type bargain come the various loyalty bargains in which public servants have no formal existence independent of those they serve, and in that sense have no sphere of autonomous action. We term such arrangements as partnership-type bargains, to mean that public servants work together with elected politicians but have no separate identity either in directing public organizations or in determining policy. Such arrangements mainly apply to what we earlier termed 'loyalists', whether 'personal' or 'serial'.

Traditionally, the Westminster-model civil service loyalty bargain seems to have been conceived as a 'partnership-type' bargain in these terms, and several of our British interviewees described what they saw as their loyalty bargain in that vein. One told us that 'as civil servants we have absolutely no independent *raison d'être*' (UK1), and several echoed Schaffer's account of the traditional Westminster PSB that we described in Chapter 1. That is, they argued that a key part of the 'partnership' loyalty bargain was some measure of anonymity, though, as we shall see later, many thought that side of the bargain was breaking down.

Civil servants by and large are anonymous and would not be expected to be 'outed,' so to speak . . . there is a connection between that and the impartiality rule. (UK13)

Some civil servants working within that sort of bargain likened the relationship to that of marriage. But if there is a parallel with any marriage contract, it would have to be a caricature or ideal that is far from the law and conventions of contemporary Western-type marriage, for at least three reasons. First, the serial–loyalty relationship is more like an arranged marriage than a spontaneously chosen partnership. Second, one of the partners to this relationship lacks independent 'personality' in a political sense, at least in the PSB implied in the 1985 'Armstrong memorandum' that we discussed in Chapter 3. The parallel would thus appear to be with the position of women in marriage before the advent of modern property and other rights for married women, in which women could not ordinarily own property or enter into contracts in their own right separately from their husbands, and had no political existence in the sense of rights to vote or run for public office. Considered like that, such a bargain would seem to exclude any personal political goals.

One former UK civil servant wryly made this point by telling us a story about interviewing someone for a job:

I remember interviewing somebody... who wanted to come into the department to make a difference to the world. I remember that being a bit unusual, actually... and that was seen as bizarre, and a good reason for [the department] not taking them further in the process. (UK9)

Third, as some observers and participants described the bargain, there was a further understanding (of a kind that is often associated with traditional forms of marriage) that there should be some trust and confidentiality between the partners, at least for the most intimate aspects of the relationship. Even if there is no affection, loyalty on one side is exchanged for respect on the other. In this case, the understanding is that the anonymous civil servant 'partners' do not speak openly against government activity or policy, however critical they might be in private, and do not reveal the political equivalent of the secrets of the bedchamber. Leaks, whistle-blowing, 'kiss-and-tell' memoirs or unofficial briefings against government count as 'cheating'.

Most systems of executive government contain partnership-type bargains in one form or another, although those partner-type bargains take more than one form. Traditionally in the UK, with its distinctive emphasis on a politically neutral or impartial civil service, the partnership-type bargain has approximated to (continue the marriage analogy) a combination of 'serial monogamy' with a convention of 'no discussion of exes'.

By 'serial monogamy' we mean that the partnership bargain implies the capacity and disposition to act as confidant to a succession of ministers and governments from different political parties, or with different political views and styles—and in confidential interviews, British civil servants often provide graphic examples of how much ministers vary in the way they work and the demands they make on their civil servants. In sharp contrast to one German civil servant we interviewed (D5), who felt unable to work under a political party with different policy preferences in their policy domain, loyalty is transferred from one 'partner' to another, whatever their political views and working approach may be.

We would be as loyal to [their opponents or rivals] tomorrow as we were to [our current ministers] today—what are we, we're harlots, aren't we? (UK19)

This 'serial monogamy' rule has not always been tightly observed. For instance, in the early part of the twentieth century it was not unusual for British civil servants to stay in political contact with ministers they had worked for after those ministers moved into opposition, to work more closely with other ministers than their own current secretary of state, and even to form close ties with backbenchers.[14] Our interviewees told us that serial monogamy operated more strictly than that today, and that when they met ministers they were formerly loyal to at social or ceremonial events, both sides observed an unwritten convention of not seeking or offering confidential information about current policy or practice. If that aspect of 'serial monogamy' was perhaps tightened up over the twentieth century, serial monogamy was slightly loosened in another way from the 1960s by a new convention allowing relations with the official opposition party at election times, when the civil service was, as it were, allowed to 'play the field' politically for some undefined period.[15] The monogamy metaphor also wears very thin when there is more than one 'partner' involved, particularly when the relevant Minister and Prime Minister are at odds with one another, creating a *menage à trois* rather than a dyad. It may also wear thin when new ministers appear at such frequent intervals that each relationship is so ephemeral as to suggest a metaphor rather different from marriage.

By 'no discussion of exes' (a convention that itself often evolves within marriages or similar relationships), we mean an understanding that civil servants do not provide information about what was done or proposed under a previous government to its successors, and in turn will throw a cloak of confidentiality over the doings of the current incumbent when working with a future partner, unless a minister specifically requests that his or her papers be shown to a successor. That part of the loyalty bargain seems to have become formalized in the 1920s (see Naylor 1984: 156). It might be thought of as a form of intergenerational bargain, in the sense that politicians are expected to appreciate that when their time comes to leave the scene, they will benefit from the same no-discussion-of-exes rule that may have worked against them when they took office. Another variant of the no-discussion-of-exes convention is the view that it excludes the publication of revelatory memoirs.[16]

---

[14] For example, Sir George Murray, permanent secretary of the Treasury, used official notepaper to write to the opposition peer and former Prime Minister Lord Rosebery, to undermine his own Chancellor's reforms in 1909 (O'Donnell 2005: 78). Sir Maurice Hankey, Cabinet Secretary, between 1916 and 1938, played an active role in editing the memoirs of David Lloyd George after Lloyd George lost office as prime minister (Naylor 1984: 203–9, especially 208). Winston Churchill in the early 1900s and in the 1930s received behind-the-scenes information and assistance over 'facts and arguments' from civil servants critical of their own government's policy stances (Theakston 2003: 156, 164).

[15] That period was often given as 28 days, but in practice it seemed (like so much else in British government), to be indefinite, and the degree of seriousness accorded to it appeared to depend on the anticipated closeness of the election result. In the 2005 British general election, the then Leader of the Opposition was reported to have begun talking with permanent secretaries four months before the election was held and three months before it was even officially called (*Financial Times* 5 January 2005).

[16] For example, the publication of a politically embarrassing memoir by Sir Christopher Meyer (former UK ambassador to the United States) in 2005 provoked intense condemnation both from affronted politicians and former Cabinet Secretaries.

One variable and apparently problematic aspect of a partnership-type public service loyalty bargain is the right of each party to have what Christopher Foster (1996, 1998) calls a 'conversation' with the other to put their point of view—the entitlement to be heard in private, offering a critical and perhaps unwelcome view of the minister's position, in return for loyal defence of that position in public (UK15). Some British civil servants we interviewed saw that 'conversational right' as a key part of their loyalty bargain; one declared:

> If that is what ministers want, however stupid it is, you have to make sure that we deliver it. *Although you must make sure they understand how stupid it is.* (UK8, our emphasis)

But other interviewees suggested that the notion of UK civil servants as having some sort of institutionally guaranteed right of access to ministers to express candid views about the folly of those ministers' proposed policies was a problematic and far from universal part of that particular loyalty bargain:

> There is absolutely no point in tackling ministers on some of their favourite topics and taking away their toys.... (UK3)

> If your minister insists on a stupid idea . . . rather than tilt in the wind when you know you will lose, you make sure that some safety valves are left through which ministers can make a more or less elegant retreat. (UK13)

> If a Permanent Secretary gets asked to do something that they think would be very unwise, with some ministers you know you can tell them, with others you know it is the end of your relationship.... (UK4)

Indeed, one senior civil servant (UK7) described three ways of handling this kind of problem within the British Westminster model. First, which this interviewee described as the 'Sir Humphrey' style,[17] consisted of apparently agreeing with ministers' views but in fact implementing rather different policies. A second consisted of open warfare between ministers and civil servants, a situation that is both rare and dangerous for civil servants in a parliamentary democracy, but certainly happens sometimes. And a third consisted of the situation where senior civil servants felt able to tell ministers that the course of action they were proposing was 'not sensible' (Whitehall-speak for 'completely insane') but nevertheless obeyed orders after their objections were overruled.

Such rules are subtle, demanding, tricky to work with, and increasingly difficult, according to many of our interviewees, as civil servants climbed

---

[17] Referring to the fictional Permanent Secretary in the *Yes Minister* TV series (Lynn and Jay 1981) who deviously seeks to outwit and undermine the egregious Jim Hacker.

up the ladder of promotion and found themselves exposed to awkward compromises between the constitutional niceties and accommodating ministers, especially when working in the minister's private office (UK4).[18] Many commentators see such rules as going against the grain of politics. They are not readily paralleled by corporate business practices and the conventions themselves seem to be precarious and often ambiguous and person-specific at the margin. Many civil servants in interviews saw the bargain as asymmetrical, in the sense that politicians were less committed to the arcane rules of the serial monogamy/no discussion of exes bargain than civil servants were. But politicians repeatedly pointed to failures on the part of civil servants to keep their side of the bargain, particularly by what they saw as pervasive leaking by their supposed partners for political reasons, and indeed the historical record is replete with evidence of 'cheating' through leaking.[19]

In turn, some civil service interviewees indicated that those ministers who publicly blamed their civil servants for shortcomings in their departments would be less likely to find the bureaucratic wagons drawn up in a tight circle around them when the going got tough for the minister in question. The implication was that withdrawal of 'love and respect' would be matched by a corresponding reduction in loyalty, while ministers who backed their civil servants when they made mistakes could expect to be rewarded by dog-like loyalty. For instance, remarkable personal loyalty was shown to one former Conservative minister, Michael Heseltine, who was known for supporting civil servants when they committed errors, after he resigned as Minister of Defence over the Westland affair in 1986.[20]

More commonly, as in the German and US cases, and in the growing class of temporary political advisors in the UK system itself, the partnership-type loyalty bargain has approximated more to that of a one-time monogamist, or at least a much less automatic pattern of serial monogamy than in the traditional UK case. In many cases it looks more like the traditional practice of suttee in Hindu marriage than serial monogamy, with the confidant likely to have to go on the funeral pyre on the political demise of their partner.

---

[18] Similar problems were reported to us by those acting as *persönlicher Referent* in the German federal bureaucracy (D14).

[19] For example, 'Jackie' Fisher (Admiral Sir John Fisher), First Lord of the Admiralty from 1909, leaked details of Cabinet discussions to the then editor of *The Observer* newspaper, to advance his position on naval policy (Gollin 1960: 34–92), and Percy James Grigg, who was private secretary to several Chancellors of the Exchequer in the 1920s, acknowledged in his memoirs that he had often discreetly passed 'leads' to the media (see Grigg 1948: 93).

[20] Heseltine's Permanent Secretary at the Ministry of Defence is said to have helped his former minister to write his resignation speech on ministry's premises after Heseltine had resigned, and Heseltine was said to believe the Permanent Secretary involved may even have damaged the chances of further promotion to Cabinet Secretary by doing so (Crick 1997: 288).

6.4. EXECUTIVE-TYPE BARGAINS

By an executive-type loyalty bargain, we mean a relationship in which bureaucrats are separately identifiable as individuals but are not free agents in any political sense. Unlike public servants working under partnership-type bargains as *éminences grises* or powers behind the throne, they have individual 'personality' in some formal sense. But their freedom is circumscribed. Unlike public servants working under judge-type loyalty bargains, they are expected to do the bidding of their superordinates, in one form or another.

Like the loyalty bargains already considered, executive-type bargains come in various forms, and at least three types can be distinguished. In one executive-type pattern, public servants work as general factotums following whatever orders of the day their superordinates may choose to issue. The obvious parallel is with the lines of command in a military hierarchy, with reports going up the line and orders of the day coming down to each level, though ultimately subject to a test of what counts as a lawful command within the laws of war.

Against that pattern of 'command and control' in the military sense,[21] a second executive-type pattern is that of public servants who work at arm's-length from their superordinates, with freedom to operate within their sphere unless the superordinate chooses to intervene or exercise a veto, as with those dog leads that can be reeled in at will. Prison managers in many government systems operate in this mode, exercising discretion over the running of the their prisons but sometimes finding themselves on a very short lead from the political centre in times of sensitivity over riots, escapes, suicides, and the like.

A third executive-type pattern is one in which public servants are set output targets reflecting some policy goal (such as reducing hospital waiting times or reducing road accidents) with some freedom in how they choose to meet those targets. The much-discussed executive agencies that were introduced into UK central government from the late 1980s were built around a bargain for the CEOs that was intended to be of that kind, and the targets and indicators approach to governance of public services reflects a similar idea. One senior UK civil servant described the framework documents that set out what the executive agencies were expected to do and expressed the bargain involved for their CEOs as follows:

It is your job to make [delivering on the framework documents] a success or not. If you completely screw it up, you will be sacked. If you partly deliver, your pay will suffer. Apart from that, I [the minister] will leave you alone to get on with it. (UK1)

---

[21] Or 'simple control' in the language of Henry Mintzberg (1993).

That sort of loyalty bargain has been much advocated by those who favour managerial approaches to public service, and we shall discuss it further in Chapter 9, but apart from whatever managerial benefits such a bargain has to offer, it also has the political attraction that such an executive can, in principle, serve as a flak catcher or lightning-rod to absorb the blame when public service delivery goes wrong.

We shall be discussing the blame-shifting issue further in Chapter 8, when we discuss cheating on PSBs. Here we will merely note that each side may have a different understanding of where the blame should be pinned in any situation where the contractual relationships among the various players are not spelt out for every contingency. We can also note that in most variants of the executive-type bargain, elected politicians are likely to want blame for failures to be attributed to public servants, but credit for successes going to politicians, while the 'executives' are likely to take the opposite asymmetric view of responsibility. We explore some of the strategic-action complications arising out of that in Chapters 7 and 8.

6.5. JESTER-TYPE BARGAINS: IRRITANTS AND REALITY CHECKERS

The three loyalty bargains discussed earlier—partners whose activity is not distinguishable from that of their political masters, executives operating as individuals on their own account but on a variable dog-lead basis, and judges making their own autonomous decisions—can all be more or less readily observed across executive government systems today. Rather more problematic is what we call the court jester-type loyalty bargain, in which certain individuals (normally from peripheral backgrounds of one kind or another and in a sense isolated at court in the same way as monarchs themselves) are given licence within some usually undefined limits to operate as jokers, mockers, wry commentators, irritants, or 'reality checkers' at the top level of the authority structure.

Royal jesters are said to go back at least to the days of the European Pharaohs (Willeford 1969: 154), and jesters were kept by popes and other holders of high ecclesiastical office in medieval and Renaissance Europe (Otto 2001: 53, 174). John Southworth (1998: 12), in his study of fools and jesters in the English court, sees humour as 'a human necessity' in institutions where supreme political power is exercised, and indeed the importance of the fool or jester as 'reality checker' was stressed by the great scholar Diderius Erasmus (1511). An example given by Southworth is the role of the court jester in telling the French king about the destruction of his navy by the English in 1340, when no one else in the court could summon up the courage to break this news: 'Entering the royal presence, he [the fool] was heard to mutter, "Those cowardly Englishmen, those chicken-hearted Britons!" "How so?" Philip asked. "Why, because they had not courage enough to jump into the sea like your own sailors, who went headlong from their ships, leaving them to the enemy who did not dare to follow them"' (Otto 2001: 11).

By its nature, a 'jester' PSB can apply only to a tiny minority of public servants. Those who are inclined to be critical of the competency of government officials might heartily agree with the title of Beatrice Otto's book (2001), *Fools Are Everywhere*, but that title is itself something of a jest. Though there have been various 'fool societies' (see e.g. Willeford 1969: 226), Otto shows that the role of jester has been very much a minority occupation, usually involving a single unusual individual, and the point of her title is that the court jester is a very widespread phenomenon (and not, as European scholars once thought, a role peculiar to a particular period of European history): 'The pre-conditions for the emergence of jesters are minimal—some courtlike institution in the form of a head honcho with a partly dependent entourage. No critical mass of courtiers or pomp is needed . . . This does not of course mean that every courtlike institution is bound to have a fool' (ibid. xvii).

The jester bargain involves an exchange—on the one hand, intimacy with the ruling group and licence to clown, mock, and criticize, and on the other hand some measure of restraint and loyalty. That restraint ('so far and no further') means keeping just on the right side of seriously threatening the status quo or the fundamentals of the authority structure. Court jesters do not seek to overthrow the rulers and institutions they mock (ibid. 168). But where exactly the line that cannot be crossed lies can never be known with certainty, and the successful jester thus tends constantly to live on the edge of punishment or extinction. Southworth (1998: 2–4) argues that the traditional court jester was outside the lines of competing court factions, and that a measure of independence was fundamental to the 'unwritten contract' (ibid. 4) between the fool and the monarch. If that 'contract' was breached, the monarch had the option of withdrawing royal favour from the fool (or having the fool whipped, banished, or killed), but equally the fool could refuse to play.[22]

Studies of fools and jesters are conventionally the province of historians, with the 'golden age' of jesters often said to have been from the twelfth to the

---

[22] In the extreme case 'their partnership may be so close as to allow an identification, even a voluntary exchange of roles, in which the fool becomes an *alter ego* of the king, and the king assumes his fool's identity in religious ritual or actual combat' (ibid. 5).

seventeenth century in Europe and for two millennia in China from 500 B C or so. So has the jester disappeared from the universe of contemporary PSBs, in a Weberian 'iron cage' of humourless modernity? There might be some reasons for thinking so. After all, those in high public office in the western countries do not have to look far in the arts, media, or political forums to find their persons, policies, and behaviour mocked and ridiculed to such an extent that they might think the role of jester had been 'outsourced', along with so much else in government, rendering such a role within the state structure redundant. One of our interviewees (D13) suggested that in such a climate, modern ministers needed to have 'love' rather than yet more ridicule heaped upon them from inside the government machine. But that kind of unofficial jesting lacks both the intimacy within the ruling group and the underlying personal loyalty that characterizes the traditional court jester, and it is those loyalty aspects that may create a continuing need for jester PSBs of some kind.

In analysing fools and jesters, historians have conventionally distinguished between 'innocents' and 'clever fools'. Innocents are those who speak the truth naively, like the small boy in Hans Anderson's story of the Emperor's New Clothes, while clever fools wrap up otherwise unpalatable truths in a humorous form. It seems doubtful if either type has altogether disappeared, and indeed instances of the 'clever fool' role can be found in the business world today as well as, and perhaps more than, that of the state. Firth and Leigh (1998) argue that modern corporate life has produced its own set of informal fools who parallel the court jesters of an earlier age, and have licence to operate outside the bounds imposed on everyone else. Otto (2001: 267ff.) notes several cases of jester-type figures in the courts of recent corporate leaders, and indeed, in 1995, perhaps in a moment of corporate madness, a major airline (British Airways) introduced an official 'court jester', Paul Birch. Birch, the subject of the second epigraph to this chapter, was expected 'to swan around, stick my nose in other people's business, and be a pain in the arse' (Otto 2001: 268).

Governments, no doubt fearing ridicule from the unofficial army of media jesters with which they are surrounded, have not employed officially named jesters for several centuries. But something approximating to the jester-type loyalty bargain can be detected in modern government, in several forms. One is that of those political appointees in the bureaucracy who work under an understanding that they will create upheaval, challenge received views and come up with left-field radical policy ideas.[23] For instance, a German polit-

---

[23] Indeed, combining the role of blue-skies thinker with that of count jester is not a new phenomenon. Jakob Paul von Gundling (1673–1731), who succeeded Gottfried Leibnitz as President of the Prussian Academy of Sciences, was both economic adviser and court jester to the Prussian King Friedrich Wilhelm I.

ician, reflecting on the political joke that 'parliamentary state secretaries are those who create work which would not exist without them and which they do badly' told us that 'my task is...to create upheaval' (D12).[24] Some UK political appointees described their loyalty bargain in similar terms, and a regular civil servant commented:

Your typical special adviser provided an alternative source of radical policy ideas, more radical than typically the officials would come up with...they had a challenge function. (UK13)

Something approximating to the jester role sometimes seemed to be found in the upper ranks of the regular civil service as well, against the backdrop of the tension and stress associated with the upper levels of executive government, with its endless showdowns, power-plays, loyalty displays, and high-stakes manoeuvring. Echoing Erasmus (we think unconsciously), one very senior former British civil servant told us that during his time in office he deliberately operated as a sort of part-time court jester 'to keep the jokes going' as a way of underpinning human relationships at the topmost levels of government, when feelings were running high between ministers and civil servants. Finally, something of the jester loyalty bargain may creep in with the official and unofficial hangers-on at the top levels of executive government—the astrologers, lifestyle gurus, personal trainers, drivers, and bodyguards who tend to surround the people at the top, and often gain some of the licence to criticize and *entrée* to the court that is traditionally associated with the jester role.

6.6. MIXES AND MATCHES

As with the dimensions of reward and competency bargains discussed in Chapters 4 and 5, the four loyalty types discussed here are often mixed and matched in practice. While each political system has its distinctive overall mix—with the 'judge-type' loyalty as part of the stereotype of the German bureaucracy and the 'partnership' bargain as part of the UK stereotype—in practice, every system of executive government seems to need some mix of judges, partners, executives, and jesters, and as soon as we probe below the surface, we find a rather more differentiated set of bargains than broad-brush 'national style' characterizations would suggest. And even in the business world, in spite of the 'agency' language that we discussed in Chapter 3, at least some aspects of some positions—notably the fiduciary obligations that

---

[24] Although to some extent these jester variants may have the potential to become future successors of their minister.

company directors have in company law—incorporate elements of the judge-type loyalty bargain.

Conventionally, the loyalty bargain applying to central government civil servants in the UK is portrayed as some mixture of the partnership and the executive types. In Chapter 3, we discussed the famous 1985 'Armstrong memorandum' declaring that serving the government of the day was the primary responsibility of civil servants; the head of the civil service in the early 2000s (Sir Andrew Turnbull) went on record to say that the primary job of civil servants was to 'deliver' for their political masters (*Financial Times*, 25 June 2002); and as we have already noted, overseas commentators, particularly Christoph Knill (1999), have tended to see the UK civil service as factotums doing the bidding of their principals, in contrast to the greater autonomy possessed by their counterparts in states like Germany.

However, the more closely we probed, the more hybrid the loyalty bargains of both Germany and the UK seemed to be. As we saw, the autonomy of German civil servants was alloyed both by a whole class of senior officials whose loyalty bargain was essentially of a partner, executive, or even jester kind, and by the potential effects of the political retirement rule. In the UK, the stereotype partnership bargain of the central civil service did not even traditionally apply to local government public servants; within central government, and as we have seen, there were a number of civil servants, including the new breed of regulators created in the 1980s and 1990s, whose loyalty bargain more closely resembled the judge-type form than any other. Moreover, even for the regular departmental civil servants, there were at least six aspects of a 'judge-type' loyalty bargain uneasily mixed with an executive-type or partnership-type bargain.

First, already referred to, was the convention that civil servants observed a period of 'political purdah' in the run-up to general elections, in which they offered information and advice to the official opposition party as well as to the party in government. A second was the role of three of the topmost public servants (the Cabinet Secretary, the Prime Minister's private secretary and the Queen's private secretary) in giving advice to the monarch on who to call for to form a government in the event of a hung parliament—a role that amounts to creating the government of the day, rather than just serving it. A third was the independent 'Accounting Officer' role, in which top civil servants (usually departmental heads) had independent responsibility for the lawful and economical spending of public money voted by Parliament, and could formally record their objections if ministers chose to spend in ways that Accounting Officers considered unlawful. This power was characterized by many of our interviewees as a 'nuclear weapon' that was seldom used and difficult to use because of the level of political fallout it could cause.

Fourth, beyond that independent role, the protection of merit principles of appointment to regular civil service positions was policed by the Civil Service Commissioners—who once had been regular civil servants working for the Commissioners as a mid-career posting, but in more recent times externally recruited public servants operating under more of a judge-type loyalty bargain.[25] Fifth were the conventions on handling of information, in the form of the 'no discussion of exes' rule that we referred to earlier, i.e. denial of information about dealings with ministers in previous governments to their political successors.[26] And a sixth was the role of senior civil servants, particularly the Cabinet Secretary, in policing tricky boundary lines between 'party' and 'government' activity—particularly over the dissemination of information and advertising (UK12, UK18).

When put together, those six elements seemed to amount to a greater 'judge-type' element in the UK civil service loyalty bargain than applied to their counterparts in Japan or the USA. But these 'judge-type' elements seemed to be precarious, and many of them were of more recent vintage than their common presentation as hallowed constitutional principles might suggest. For instance, the purdah rule in its modern form only dated from the 1960s, the Accounting Officer's 'nuclear weapon' in its current form only dated from the 1980s, and the modern role of the Civil Service Commissioners as quasi-independent regulators only dated from the 1990s. The 'boundary' rule between party and government work was also of fairly recent vintage. In the early years of the twentieth century, some officials like Tom Jones (Assistant Secretary to the War Cabinet and Deputy Secretary to the Cabinet from 1916 to 1930 and confidant to David Lloyd George and Stanley Baldwin) had no qualms about writing party-political speeches for their masters (see Naylor 1984: 129, 161). One senior civil servant remarked to us that the British civil service was good at instantly inventing supposedly time-honoured traditions, and many of these judge-like aspects of the loyalty bargain might be considered to be a case in point.[27]

Moreover, several of our interviewees said that civil servants were more aware of such 'judge-type' aspects of the loyalty bargain than were politicians. If this part of the loyalty bargain was asymmetrically understood, it was

[25] From 1996 the Commissioners replaced the Head of the Home Civil Service as the body to which civil servants could appeal when asked to do work they considered to be in conflict with the Civil Service Code.

[26] It is true that the no 'discussion of exes' rule might equally be considered an entailment of a particular view of the 'partner' bargain, rather than as something judge-like.

[27] Indeed, such 'long-standing conventions of recent creation' might be considered as another instance of the classic observation by Paul Flynn (Labour MP for Newport West): '[Under New Labour] only the future is certain. It's the past that keeps changing' (http://www.workskit.com/quotes/politics.shtlml, accessed June 2005).

precarious in conditions such as the advent of a new government whose ministers' views of the loyalty bargain are based on years in opposition rather than daily contact over a long period with civil servants, as applied to New Labour after 1997. Several of our UK interviewees thought there was a need to spell out more explicitly the terms of the PSB for that government, particularly in what came to be a touchy relationship between departmental civil servants on indefinite tenure, who saw the essence of their loyalty bargain as a mixture of partner and judge, and a new generation of political civil servants who were constituted as special advisers, served only during the tenure of their ministers and seemed to take a more active role in policy development than their counterparts in the previous Conservative government. One of our interviewees commented:

The administration was bringing in . . . special advisers and they were playing a role in the department that the department was not used to from non-elected officials. That caused resentment and forced the department to make explicit some pretty fundamental issues: what it meant to be a civil servant, what the relationship between minister and civil servant was meant to be, what the role of non-elected political advisers meant and where the lines were. . . . (UK9)

This problem—about how civil servants on different kinds of loyalty bargains related to one another—came to a head under the Blair government over the issue of special advisers giving direct instructions (or what amounted to direct instructions) to regular civil servants. After some spectacular public rows, notably over the role of a special adviser, Jo Moore, in the direction of other civil servants in the Department of Transport in 2002, which led to messy resignations, *exposés* of various kinds in the broadsheet press, and an inquiry by a parliamentary select committee (Public Administration Select Committee 2002), attempts were made to spell out the terms of the bargain applying to political advisers and to develop a code of conduct under which they were expected to work.[28]

Some of these judge-type elements in the British civil service had parallels in the German public service. For example, the *Haushaltsbeauftrage*, the nearest German equivalent to the British Accounting Officer, had draconian powers to veto expenditure proposals that were not lawful. And, beyond the issues of finance, civil servants faced with political requests that they thought inappropriate could, in principle, insist that their work be classed as *unter Weisung* (under instruction), with that term appearing on the front of their files. However, as in the British case, interviewees told us that both of these

[28] www.cabinetoffice.gov.uk/propriety_and_ethics/special-advisers/code.asp (accessed 9 April 2005)

'nuclear powers' were used very rarely, though their existence led to deals being struck in advance (D13). For instance,

I never had such an extreme case where I had to write on the file '*Auf Weisung*'. I have never experienced that.... I can't remember a case where the *Haushaltsbeauftragte* pulled the emergency brake. These things are discussed beforehand and sorted out there. (D14)

Very often my people have an idea what they would like to be done [describes activity] and we discuss it with those people from the *Haushalt* [budget]. Then [the *Haushaltsbeauftragte*] tells me, 'Mate, you can't do that'. If he is nice, he will also give me a hint how to fix it. And I won't even dare to start debating about it.... That is not a problem [with ministers]. (D11)

If these aspects of the loyalty bargain in the German federal civil service did not seem so very far away from that of their British equivalents, there were aspects of a partnership-type loyalty bargain too, even among the general civil servants. But the nature of the partnership bargain was different, in that it involved loyalty within party-political networks, sometimes but not always including the departmental minister. Interviewees (D13, D15) told us that civil servants in such networks produced 'non-papers'—that is, politically sensitive papers floating policy ideas that were circulated around a restricted group, but did not have the formal status of official papers and therefore did not appear in the official archive. Moreover, as in the UK case, ministerial *Leitungsstäbe* were increasing in numbers and involved recruitment of party activists and younger, more politically pliable, civil servants. Some people we talked to even saw a strong element of executive-type bargains in some federal ministries, displacing judge-type or partnership-type bargains:

These young *Referenten* are...file carriers...but they are incapable of joining a technical discussion.... 15–20 years ago it was different. One used experienced colleagues. Now one has these young people, partly taken from political parties. Some young [party name] from somewhere suddenly is *persönlicher Referent*...[They know] neither [policy] material, [this] department nor [government] bureaucracy. (D14)

Indeed, for some interviewees, some ministers were said to respond only to their 'old pals', rather than to the experts in the departments, to the point that civil servants saw themselves as 'slaves' whose main role was to display frenetic activity in response to ill-thought-out Friday-afternoon emails from those 'old pals'. That is a far cry from the high-flown judge-type bargain described by Knill (1999) and others who stress the autonomy of the German civil service, as noted earlier.

6.7. CHANGES OVER TIME: JUDGES AND OLD-STYLE CONFIDANTS AND JESTERS ON THE DEFENSIVE?

As with the reward and competency dimensions of PSBs that we discussed in Chapters 4 and 5, loyalty bargains are evidently not fixed and immutable. Patterns can and do shift, and we have shown that many of our interviewees identified changes they had seen or experienced. The question, as with reward and competency, is how far those shifts amount to trendless fluctuation, how far they follow cycles, and how far they follow an arrow-type pattern that adds up to a single 'big picture' of the type beloved by the more grandiose exponents of global public management trends.

Faced with such a question, most self-respecting academics would want to argue for some mixture of all three, and we are no exception. The jester-type bargain, perhaps appropriately, seems to be a 'wild card'. It is something that governments apparently can never quite live with, nor live without, for all the reasons we have already noted, but is not firmly institutionalized, at least in the way that it once was in classical China, medieval and Renaissance Europe, and other states of that time. Some of our interviewees mirrored the view expressed by a civil servant in Manfred Zach's novel on the Christian Demo-cratic Union (CDU)-state of Baden Württemberg in the 1970s and 1980s, who bemoaned the rise of rule-making jurists at the expense of the 'philosophically trained jester, who neither fears criticism nor hopes for promotion' (Zach 1997: 43).[29] In that sense, the pattern of change for the jester-type bargain seems to come somewhere between trendless fluctuation and an arrow-type change that began long ago.

For the judge-type bargain, we might conclude from the tone of the general commentary on the supposedly global rise of NPM that politicians and public service 'customers' want loyalty of the 'executive' kind, rather than 'judges' blocking their ideas and aspirations. We might therefore expect to find judge-type bargains becoming proportionately less salient over the last two decades or so, relative to a new form of 'executive' bargain. There were certainly instances where such a shift could be detected, but the traffic did not seem to be going in a single direction. Indeed, as the earlier discussion has shown, while the judge-type bargain has arguably come under more pressure at federal-government level in Germany (as a result of increasing use of political retirement to turn over senior civil servants after a change of party in

---

[29] Bemoaning the lack of jesters in the German ministerial bureaucracy, one senior civil servant, telling us about his hobby in staging 'Punch and Judy' shows for children, regretted that ministers had as yet failed to draw on this specific interest (D10).

government), the UK pattern is arguably the opposite. In the latter case, there has been a proliferation of 'judges' over the last two decades rather than the opposite (though their tenure is, for the most part, limited), and of a proliferation of judge-type functions in the hands of regular civil servants that traditionally were not there. That is not to deny that the emphasis on management has not increased, but rather only to point out that it is not the whole story and to suggest that what has often been portrayed as one of the exemplar cases of 'NPM' has exhibited a much more nuanced bureaucratic development than the managerial stereotype implies.

When it comes to partnership-type and executive-type loyalty bargains, we also see a mixed pattern. Along with some shift towards a 'judge-type' loyalty bargain in the UK has been a move in other parts of the bureaucratic forest to more executive-type forms of loyalty bargains. That change was formalized in the deals for heads of executive agencies from the late 1980s and informally developed, according to several of our interviewees, across much of the rest of central government in the late 1990s and 2000s. But those developments might be argued to have started much earlier, as we noted in Chapter 3, for instance over insurance company collapses and prison escapes. The new implicit bargain applying to civil servants with managerial or delivery responsibilities was seen as one in which they took personal responsibility for errors other than those caused by direct ministerial decisions, in exchange for their pay and perks, while ministers took direct credit for successes, whether or not caused by their own direct decisions.

From the perspective of our four types of loyalty bargains, it could be argued that what was going on was a shift from the traditional partnership-type bargain into an executive-type bargain for a number of senior civil servants. And at the same time, a new political top civil service, first formally institutionalized in the mid-1970s and still relatively small in number (less than a hundred) thirty years later, came into being to supplement—and rival—the traditional mandarins, with a new type of partnership-type bargain.[30] That new bargain differed from the one described by Schaffer in that it constituted a move from serial monogamy to a more restricted form, with a suttee-type fate in store for such confidants on the political demise of their ministers. That bargain required open political loyalty and offered access to the privy deliberations of ministers in exchange for lack of indefinite job

---

[30] The *Financial Times* reported the dismay of one permanent secretary with the (then) Cabinet Secretary, Sir Andrew Turnbull ('Andrew's allowed himself to be written out of the script. He's meant to see the prime minister once a week but almost every week Blair cancels'). The report also noted how Turnbull's predecessor, Sir Richard (later Lord) Wilson, would 'every morning...look at the prime minister's diary, find out what meetings were planned and then turn up, uninvited, saying he had come "to help"' (*Financial Times*, 16 May 2005, p. 2).

tenure. But the bargain amounted to another variant of the partnership-type, even if it was sometimes laced with some element of jester-type, as noted earlier.

How arrow-like these changes are, and how far the arrow is destined to travel, is debatable. Campbell and Wilson (1995) certainly argue that there is a long-term shift away from the old-type Whitehall partnership bargain, under the pressure of modern professional politics, and Maor (1999) also argues that the common thread of civil service changes in a number of parliamentary democracies is towards a different type of loyalty bargain (though Maor does not use those words). What remains to be seen is whether the currently small UK 'political civil service' and its new form of partnership-type loyalty bargain is destined to swell in a relatively short space of time to German proportions, or even US-type ones. But we postpone our discussion of that issue until Chapter 10.

7

———

Putting the Pieces Together

...les sucrins s'étaient confondus avec les maraîchers, le gros Portugal avec le grand Mongol, et le voisinage des pommes d'amour complètent l'anarchie, il en était résulté d'abominables mulets qui avaient le goût de citrouille....

(Gustave Flaubert (1910) *Bouvard et Pécuchet*, Paris, Conard, p. 40)[1]

7.1. INTRODUCTION

In Chapters 4, 5, and 6, we looked at three important dimensions of PSBs: reward, competency, and loyalty or responsibility. In this short chapter, we explore the ways in which these various dimensions link together into broader bargains of the type we discussed in Part I. Is there an infinite number of combinatorial possibilities among the types of sub-bargain that we discussed in Chapters 4, 5, and 6, or are there limits to the scope for a 'pick n' mix' approach?

In general, there does seem to be a large number of possible mixtures and much scope for creative blending. But there are some combinations that seem to be incompatible. The epigraph above reminds us that not all mixtures of types of melons will produce sweet and appetizing fruit. Similarly, on the kind of more sophisticated bicycle where there are two gear shifters (one for the crank-wheel that the pedals turn and the other on the bike's rear wheel), most positions of each shifter are compatible with most positions of the other, but selecting some extreme combinations is liable to make your chain fall off. PSBs seem to be a bit like that.

For example, what we have termed 'trustee-type' and 'agency-type' bargains at the macro level seem to be compatible with most of the bargains we

---

[1] 'In fact, as he had grown different species side by side, the sweet melons were mixed up with watermelons, large Portuguese with Grand Mogul, and with the proximity of the tomatoes completing the anarchy, the result had been abominable hybrids tasting like pumpkins' (Flaubert 1976, transl. A. J. Krailsheimer, p. 47).

have described over reward, loyalty, and competency in the last few chapters, but there are some mixes that seem to be logically or practically problematic. And when we get down to the specific forms of trustee-type and agency-type bargains that we discussed in Chapters 2 and 3, there seem to be rather more 'barred combinations' of approaches to reward, competency, and loyalty or responsibility. For instance, what we termed a 'delegated agency bargain' in Chapter 3 seems in its nature particularly hard to reconcile with a jester-type speaking-truth-to-power loyalty bargain. And what we called a 'moralistic tutelary' form of trustee bargain will not mix with a wonk-type competency bargain. We shall explore this issue further in Section 7.2.

In this chapter, we look at the mixing and matching issue in two ways. First, we take a brief overall look at combinatorial possibilities and limits, focusing on the more problematic mixes. Second, we take a look at the two main cases explored in this book, namely Germany and the UK, to explore what their experience tells us about the scope and limits of a pick n' mix approach to PSBs. When we look at those two countries, we find more 'mixing and matching' of elements of different bargains in the UK than in Germany. But in the German case, the demise of the more agency-type PSB that existed in the bureaucracy of the former GDR after the reunification of the two Germanies meant in effect a return to Imperial Germany's dual-type PSB of 1871, albeit with some significant variations. In the British case, as we noted in Chapter 6, the recent so-called managerial age has ironically been associated with a formal strengthening of trustee-type PSB elements, and also with the creation of new kinds of civil servant (notably the 'econocrat' regulators of the 1980s) with a more trustee-type PSB, albeit with limited tenure.

7.2. ANYTHING GOES—OR BARRED COMBINATIONS?

We suggested earlier that many kinds of mixing and matching seem to be possible with the various elements of reward, competency, and loyalty/ responsibility bargains that we discussed in Chapters 4, 5, and 6. Indeed, adaptation and creative public service reform often seems to consist of finding new ways of mixing and matching among these types, and that seems to be the essential challenge facing many public service reformers today.

In Chapters 4, 5, and 6 we suggested that a loose linkage could be made between some of the varieties of reward, competency, and loyalty bargains that we drew out of our interviewees' responses and the four basic ways of life identified by grid-group cultural theory. Table 7.1 brings those analyses

Table 7.1   Reward, competency, and loyalty bargains in cultural theory perspective

Fatalist-type	**Hierarchist-type**
Reward: Lottery-type	Reward: Escalator-type
Competency: Sage-type	Competency: Wonk-type
Loyalty: Jester-type	Loyalty: Judge-type
Individualist-type	**Egalitarian-type**
Reward: Turkey race-type	Reward: *Noblesse oblige*-type
Competency: Individual deliverer-type	Competency: Boundary-spanner-type
Loyalty: Executive-type	Loyalty: Partner-type

together in summary form, identifying bundles of reward, competency, and loyalty bargains that loosely correspond with each of those ways of life.

Most cultural-theory analysis tends to lump all 'bureaucracy' indiscriminately into a common 'hierarchist' box, but in a more fine-grained analysis, we can find elements of all of the four ways of life in the world of PSBs, with predictable tensions among those different elements. Each of the four reward–competency–loyalty bundles in Table 7.1 has a certain coherence, and each has a recognizable place in the world of bureaucracy. Indeed, the 'hierarchist' type shown in Table 7.1 is by no means the only PSB bundle that we find in the world of traditional bureaucracy—strong elements of the egalitarian and fatalist bundles are often found in traditional PSBs as well. Similarly, one recognizable reform package for PSBs—much discussed in the age of NPM—consists of the individualist bundle shown in Table 7.1, with turkey-race rewards, individual-delivery competency, and an executive-type loyalty bargain. But that is not the only vision of 'modernity' either. The egalitarian-type package—with some variant of a *noblesse oblige* reward bargain, a stress on boundary-spanning competency and a stress on partnership rather than autonomy—also comprises a coherent public service vision, while in the growing world of autonomous regulators and econocrats, it is the hierarchist style that tends to be stressed. As cultural theorists expect, we do not see a single traditional pattern or a single 'modern' one, and nor can we expect to see a once-and-for-all move from one of these bundles to another.

But there are clearly hybrids as well, and once we penetrate beyond first-order stereotypes, no public service system seems to fit within any one of these four bundles of bargains. The traditional stereotype of the (West) German approach is that of the 'hierarchist' type in Table 7.1, and that certainly seems to apply to the competency component of the PSB. But we find on closer inspection that the traditional German PSB seems to have mixed hierarchism with other elements for reward and loyalty—with fatalism in the case of reward and with egalitarianism in the case of loyalty. The traditional stereo-type of the British approach is perhaps the 'clubland' image, with its over-tones of egalitarianism at least among an elite of 'sound' Oxbridge males, and the loyalty element of the traditional British PSB does seem to have stressed 'partnership' in egalitarian style. But in the traditional reward bargain, egali-tarianism was mixed with elements of both the hierarchist and fatalist ap-proaches, and in the traditional competency bargain just as much emphasis seems to have been laid on the fatalist and individualist approaches as on the egalitarian boundary-crossing one. We might conclude that no single cultural way of life dominated in the traditional PSBs of either of these major states in the upper echelons of their bureaucracies. And the changes that our inter-viewees commented on do not suggest that either state is moving towards a new PSB that will reflect only one of the four bundles in Table 7.1. Variety and hybridity in that sense seems to be a common feature of PSBs.

At the same time, there are some PSB combinations that do seem to be problematic, like the melon hybrids or bicycle-gear combinations we referred to earlier. Three such problematic combinations can be used to illustrate this point. First is the combination of an individualist hyper-competitive 'turkey race' reward bargain with a hierarchist 'judge-type' loyalty and responsibility bargain. The more public servants are expected to be independent in their judgements of policy, the more difficult it is to reward them in the form of a competition with other public servants on terms set by a third party. That is why 'performance pay' is so hard to incorporate into judicial salaries[2] and why the fixity of judicial salaries is sometimes even written into constitutions, as already noted. Indeed, a pure individualist turkey-race reward bargain is not likely to fit with a strong emphasis on either an egalitarian (boundary-spanning) or fatalist (sage) approach to competency either. Where there are no clear yardsticks to evaluate performance, such a bargain will tend to mutate into some form of lottery.

Second, while the individualist 'delivery-type' competency bargain can potentially link with all four types of reward bargains shown in Table 7.1, it seems inherently hard to combine such a competency bargain with either the egalitarian (partner-type) or the fatalist (jester-type) loyalty bargains, and it may even be difficult to combine with some aspects of a judge-type loyalty bargain. And indeed the conflicts we discussed in Chapter 6 over the PSB applying to political advisers in the UK precisely involved a combination of power-behind-the-throne 'partner-type' loyalty bargains with a de facto em-phasis on delivery competency.

---

[2] Though Sweden, perhaps contrary to stereotype, briefly flirted with such an idea at the height of the NPM era in the early 1990s (Hood and Peters 1994: 18).

Third, the jester approach to loyalty and responsibility seems, in its pure form, to link most easily to the fatalist sage-like competency bargains and lottery approach to reward, as illustrated in Table 7.1. While the jester approach to loyalty can be combined with hierarchist or egalitarian approaches to reward and competency, it seems very hard in its pure form to combine with the individualist 'delivery' type of competency bargain. That is because the jester approach to loyalty and responsibility involves 'speaking truth to power' (to use a phrase popularized by the late Aaron Wildavsky (1979)) rather than project management. However, as we noted in Chapter 6, the jester approach to loyalty and responsibility seems to occur mainly in adulterated, rather than pure, forms.

When we move to the broader kinds of bargains of the trustee and agency type that we introduced in Chapters 2 and 3, there seems considerable scope for mixing and matching reward, competency, and loyalty bargains. Competency approaches seem to be widely 'mixable' and lottery, escalator, and *noblesse oblige* approaches to reward could, in principle, be adopted for most types of agency and trustee PSBs. But even at this broader level of analysis, some combinations seem to be more problematic than others. The agency-type PSB, while apparently compatible with most of the reward and competency bargains summarized in Table 7.1, seems harder to reconcile with 'judge' and 'jester' approaches to loyalty and responsibility. Similarly, the trustee-type PSB does not seem easy to reconcile with most forms of the 'executive' loyalty bargain or the turkey-race approach rewards bargain. In other words, 'judge' forms of loyalty seem in their nature to presuppose some form of 'trustee' bargain, while a 'turkey race' approach to reward tends in its nature to presuppose some form of 'agency' bargain.

Moreover, when we consider the variants within agency and trustee-type bargains that were discussed earlier, we find more combinations that are problematic, because some of those subtypes are defined in ways that tie them to particular approaches to competency. Table 7.2 gives a summary indication of the scope and limits of combining different reward, competency, and loyalty bargains with the various forms of agency and trustee-type PSBs. For instance, by their nature, technocratic forms of trustee-type PSBs have only one form of competency bargain that fits, which is that of the 'wonk'. Serial-loyalist forms of agency PSB may also be hard to combine with the 'turkey race' form of reward bargain, because the latter requires judgements to be made about winners and losers and the terms of the 'race', and such judgements may effectively turn serial-loyalist agency bargains into personal-loyalist ones. The personal loyalist form of agency PSB seems to be compatible with most of the competency and reward bargains discussed earlier, though a turkey-race approach to reward requires there to be several

Table 7.2 Sub-types of agency and trustee bargain and approaches to reward, competency, and loyalty/responsibility

Type of bargain	Approach to reward	Approach to competency	Approach to loyalty/responsibility
Consociational	Best fitted for *noblesse oblige* or 'escalator' forms in its basic logic	Fits most types but has some element of 'spanner' in its basic logic	Fits most types
Selective representational	Fits most types	Fits most types	Fits most types
Moralistic trustee	Best fitted for *noblesse oblige* or 'escalator' forms	Tends to emphasize 'sage' in its basic logic	Fits several types, but 'executive' may be problematic
Technocratic trustee	Best fitted for *noblesse oblige* or 'escalator' forms	Implies 'wonk' competency in its basic logic	Best fitted for 'judge' form
Complex delegated agency	Fits most types, though 'turkey race' may be problematic given multiple principals	Tends to emphasize some element of 'spanner' and 'delivery' rather than 'sage' in its basic logic	Tends to emphasize 'executive' in its basic logic
Simple delegated agency	Well fitted for turkey race approach but can operate with other types	Tends to emphasize 'delivery' rather than 'sage' in its basic logic	Tends to emphasize 'executive' in its basic logic
Personal loyalist	Turkey race approach likely to be problematic where the number of such loyalists is small	Fits most types	Tends to emphasize 'partnership' or 'jester' in its basic logic rather than 'judge' or 'executive'
Serial loyalist	Arguably fits most types but extreme forms of 'lottery' and 'turkey race' may undermine 'serialism'	Fits most types	Tends to emphasize 'partnership' or 'jester' in its basic logic rather than 'judge' or 'executive'

such agents per principal. But the personal loyalist type of agency PSB largely precludes judge-type or executive-type loyalty/responsibility bargains, and seems to be largely compatible with 'partnership' or 'jester' forms.

In short, while there seems to be a lot of scope for creative mixing and matching of approaches to reward, competency, and loyalty to form different types of PSB, it is not quite a case of 'anything goes'. Some forms of hybridization will lead to the sort of results produced by indiscriminate mixing of melons or bicycle gears. Some of the barred combinations we have noted arise from incompatible logics of organization. But even combinations of bargains that do not obviously involve such clashing logics can turn out to be problematic through mismatches that develop in practice. After all, as we shall see shortly, it only took alterations to the competency and loyalty parts of the traditional German PSB in the 1930s to turn what had been seen as the paradigm case of a 'trustee-type' bargain into an agency one. And in Chapter 9, we shall argue that some recent or contemporary attempts to institutionalize public service 'managerialism' in the form of simple delegated agency bargains have been problematic precisely because of the difficulty of firmly combining the reward, competency, and loyalty elements in the bottom left-hand quadrant of Table 7.1. In particular, the executive form of loyalty bargain that is at the heart of the managerial vision seems to have been precarious, with key conditions needed to underpin that form of loyalty bargain either left out from the start or unintentionally removed by a fatal mixture of central 'oversight creep', covert political interference, and institutional 'blame games'.[3] In Chapter 10, we will return to the issue of whether the ability to mix and match PSBs might grow further in the future as thinking about public services moves out of traditional tramlines.

7.3. CHANGE AND STABILITY: MIXING AND MATCHING PUBLIC SERVICE BARGAINS IN TWO STATE TRADITIONS

Having looked at the possibilities for mixing and matching different elements across different types of PSBs, we now turn to the two cases explored in most detail in this study, looking at the mixtures of reward, loyalty, and competency bargain in Germany and the UK since the nineteenth century. We will

---

[3] Thereby producing functional disruption, the term used by Sieber (1981: 57–79) for the unintentional removal of a critical element needed to make a complex system work. The paradigm example used by Scott (1998) in his account of the failures of 'high modernism' in social intervention is that of unintentional destruction of forest ecosystems by the creation of monoculture.

first sketch the broad outline, proceed to look at each case in slightly more detail, and then analyse the two systems in a more schematic way.

Beginning with the 'helicopter' perspective: in the case of Germany, we see the development of a fairly uniform bargain—or rather set of bargains—across the public service, in all of the forms of the German state over the last century or so. That contrasts with the bargains specific to particular parts of the public service that we find in the UK (local government, police, civil service, as well as differences among the component countries in the UK). In Germany over the course of a century, there have been at least three abrupt PSB changes linked to regime change, with a pattern of change that looks like a circle over that period. In the UK over that period, we see more of a 'water on stone' style of PSB change, with steady erosion or reshaping rather than dramatic break points, and a pattern of change that looks more 'arrow-like' than 'circle-like' (McFarland 1991). And there is a common factor in that both countries, as member states of the EU, have seen another layer of EU governance, with its own different and distinctive form of PSB applying to the Brussels bureaucracy, added to the nation–state level of governance. Both countries have experienced major stresses and strains with their PSBs over the past twenty-five years or so, though the creaks and groans coming from the British civil service variant are those that have attracted the most attention from commentators, as we have already noted.

In the German case, a major shift from an agency type of PSB to a more trustee-type form occurred during the first half of the nineteenth century and particularly after 1848. The move from absolutism to 'bourgeois democracy' or constitutional monarchy turned the focus of politics away from state managerialism to the *Rechtsstaat*. The creation of the German empire in 1871 consolidated and generalized this PSB pattern but did not alter it significantly. The civil bureaucracy conceived itself as a group of judge-type interpreters of the law, rather than state managers, but the device of 'political retirement' invented in 1848, as discussed in Chapter 6, allowed government to choose its 'trustees' to some extent, and the development of a 'political civil service' introduced a form of agency bargain alongside the trustee-type one. The late nineteenth-century German military and diplomatic corps had their own forms of trustee-type bargain, as we have already noted, with the former conceiving itself as a 'state within the state'.

Under the Weimar Republic and the Nazi regime, that extreme trustee form of military PSB was challenged (though arguably it survived in part up to 1945), and under the Nazi regime, a move to an agency form of PSB developed in the civil bureaucracy as well—a trend that had already begun during Weimar with its growth in 'party-book' bureaucracy. Key stages in the move from 'trustee' to 'agency' bargains were the emasculation of the administrative courts,[4] the granting of 'secret police' status to Nazi gangs in 1933 and the wholesale takeover of police forces by 1936. Elements of the older PSB may have lingered to some degree, in line with the idea already discussed of the Nazi state as a 'dual state' combining arbitrary rule with some rule-of-law elements (see Fraenkel 1941; Broszat 1969). After the Second World War, the West German state created in 1949 in effect adopted a constitutionally entrenched variant of the 1848 style of trustee-type PSB for the civil bureaucracy, though the proportion of 'political' civil servants with an agency-type PSB tended to grow over time. The Eastern German state, on the other hand, developed its own form of agency-type PSB for civil and military bureaucrats alike, plus the central and regional party officials that formed a key part of the state apparatus, especially the regional party secretaries responsible for the delivery of targets, like their counterparts in the Soviet Union (see Scherzer 1997, orig. 1988).

Unification of the two Germanies in 1990 was in PSB terms something of a replay of 1871, in the sense that it was the trustee-type bargain espoused by West Germany in 1949 that became generalized across the unified state. But that trustee-type bargain was being nibbled away at some of the edges, for instance, in the creation of 'probationary periods' for *Beamte* in higher leadership positions, which was seen by many of our interviewees as creating the basis for a more politicized and therefore perhaps more agency-PSB style of civil service. Moreover, the route into the supposedly trustee-type regular civil service positions at the higher level seemed to lie increasingly through a successful period as a young political civil servant operating as a personal assistant to a minister. These trends were even more pronounced at the local levels of government. While the German cartel office was perhaps an archetype of an economic regulator operating under a judge-type loyalty bargain, there was no marked trend to the creation of new business regulators of this type, in contrast to developments in the UK from the 1980s.[5]

In the case of the UK, we see a more complex, if perhaps less dramatic, pattern. In the nineteenth century, different PSBs developed for different parts of the public service. As we noted in Chapter 6, the police, created in their modern form in the mid-nineteenth century (but harking back to older English ideas about the 'office of constable'), laid claim to a form of

---

[4] Through the *Führerprinzip* (introduced in 1934) that placed obedience to the *Führer* above the status of the law.

[5] Indeed, the regulatory authority for post and telecommunications that was created in Germany on privatization in the 1990s is claimed by Döhler (2002) to operate more on agency than trustee-type lines, and at the time of writing was about to take on the character of a 'complex delegated agency' bargain with the addition of energy and railway regulation to its portfolio.

'trustee-type' bargain, rather than an agency one of following the orders of elected local authorities. The local government service, sharply separate from the civil service that ran the national government, developed a PSB that had some trustee-type elements, in that local public servants in many cases had direct statutory duties laid on them. That local government PSB had a strong agency element as well, but of a 'complex' form, in that local government officers were conceived as serving the council as a whole and not just the majority party. In the case of the civil service, the response to democratization in the nineteenth century was to evolve a distinctive form of serial-loyalist agency bargain, but with those serial loyalists selected by a Chinese-type examination system that was designed to prevent the development of a US-style spoils system (Mueller 1984).

As in Germany, the pre-First World War military and intelligence corps conceived its PSB in 'trustee' terms, rather than in clear agency terms, and that PSB also became attenuated though it did not entirely disappear (elements of it came dramatically to the surface in the politics of the war against Iraq in 2003). The different countries of the UK also manifested very different kinds of PSB. For instance, the police in Ireland, in contrast to those of Great Britain, formed a military-type corps quartered in barracks and self-consciously 'selective representational' in the form of its trustee bargain (i.e. it was drawn almost exclusively from the Irish protestant minority—a pattern that continued in Northern Ireland for seventy years or so after the twenty-six counties of southern Ireland formed an independent breakaway state in 1922). Scotland was largely governed by a set of boards or quangos up to the late 1930s, instead of by Whitehall-style departments, and that too in many cases led to a form of trustee-type bargain rather than the 'agency' form identified by Bernard Schaffer. The same applied even more dramatically to Northern Ireland following the imposition of 'direct rule' from London after 1972.

Change to this set of UK bargains came piecemeal, rather than in sudden break points. Periodic moves have been made to produce a more agency-type police PSB in Great Britain, but even in the managerial 1990s attempts to introduce performance pay (in a very mild form of 'turkey-race' pattern of reward) were resisted. In Northern Ireland, a more dramatic attempt to change the police PSB took place in the late 1990s (following the 1998 'Good Friday agreement' between the British and Irish governments), with the intention of shifting that PSB from a selective representational form of trustee bargain to a consociational one. The age of state enterprise from the early years of the twentieth century saw the creation of a new corps of enterprise managers operating under delegated agency bargains of a complex or simple type. In the civil service, the last quarter or so of the twentieth century saw new forms of PSB introduced alongside the traditional 'agency' form identified by Schaffer.

The creation of executive agencies within central government from the late 1980s (conceived as delivery organizations with some degree of managerial autonomy from day-to-day control from departments and ministers) was reflected in a new corps of higher civil servants operating on a delegated agency form of PSB. Those public servants running some state agencies, notably the Health and Safety Executive created out of an older set of safety regulators in 1974, found themselves operating in a 'complex delegated' form of agency bargain with the creation of elected assemblies in Scotland and Wales in 1999. The creation of a new set of industry regulators to oversee the privatized utilities in the 1980s and 1990s was reflected in a small but significant corps of higher civil servants operating as 'technocratic trustees'; and in the early 1970s, a new breed of political civil servants was formally recognized, operating with a form of 'personal loyalist' PSB.

In the case of the 'regular' civil service notionally operating on the traditional form of 'agency' PSB, schizophrenic pressures seem to have developed in the final decades of the twentieth century. On the one hand, a strong drumbeat from reformers and politicians dissatisfied with the traditional form and operating style of the civil service produced pressure for generalizing the delegated agency form of PSB applied to the chief executives of the executive agencies created from the late 1980s. On the other hand, as we argued in Chapter 6, some of the 'judge-type' features of the Whitehall civil service were formally strengthened at just the time when the 'managerial mood' for public service reform was said to be at its height. How these contradictory pressures would play out was by no means resolved at the time of writing.

Table 7.3 summarizes this pattern. What we see by looking over time and across different parts of the states and their public services is that both countries display a variable and dynamic pattern of PSBs, and not a single one as their stereotypes suggest. Both states, when examined across their public services and across the comparatively short time span of a century and a half, are virtually all over the map of different PSB types identified in this book, although as we suggested earlier, the long-term historical dynamic does not seem to be the same for both of these cases.

Turning from this broad-brush perspective to a closer look at what has happened to the PSB at central government level in both states over the last decade or two in terms of reward, competency, and loyalty, we see some important changes as well as continuity in both states. In terms of reward, the formal structure in Germany at the time of writing remained one dominated by the traditional escalator and pyramid approach, though the system was

Table 7.3   Some different PSBs over time: Germany and the UK

Type	Subtype	Germany	UK
TRUSTEE TYPE	Consociational	The Brussels-bureaucracy EU component of public service that formed part of the governance of both states, with its unofficial nationalities quotas	
		In a weak form, the legal obligation for the federal civil service to be drawn from the regions of Germany	Aspiration for the Northern Ireland police force after 2001
	Selective representational	Military 'state within state' prior to Weimar Republic	Royal Irish Police and Royal Ulster Constabulary under Protestant ascendancy
	Moral exemplar		Some 'sleaze-buster' offices and similar functions
	Technocratic trustee	19th century *Beamte* bargain generalized in 1871	Expert regulators created especially since the 1980s
AGENCY TYPE	Complex delegated agency	*Bundesnetzagentur*	Health and Safety Executive
	Simple delegated agency	GDR regional party bureaucrats in managing targets	Heads of executive agencies—begun in early 1970s, generalized from late 1980s
	Personal loyalist	The traditional political civil service after 1848; strong elements of this PSB in the Nazi and GDR states	Political advisers (political civil service) formalized in the 1970s
	Serial loyalist	Elements of such a PSB in the Nazi and GDR states, uneasily mixed with personal loyalist PSB	The traditional Whitehall bargain of the later nineteenth century as discussed by Schaffer

beginning to introduce elements of performance-related pay. But there was a widespread perception among our interviewees that traditional escalator careers were being undermined by cutbacks that in effect stopped the escalator, by increasing the length of service needed to earn automatic increments, and by a growing number of young civil servants who took a short and fast route to the top via a political-civil servant stage as political adviser to a minister. Was this perception any more than another instance of the perennial complaint by middle-aged bureaucrats everywhere that they are being unfairly overtaken by young upstarts? It is hard to tell, because of the lack of historical data on the age of section heads at appointment in the German bureaucracy, though it seems likely that the comprehensive change in the governing coalition in 1998 presented unusual opportunities for rapid advancement by young civil servants with the right political connections.

In the UK case, the modest element of performance pay originally introduced in the 1980s developed into a pattern increasingly dominated by the 'turkey race' approach (although uncertainty about the rules of the 'race' also introduced strong elements of a lottery), with larger proportions of total reward being constituted by a variable performance-pay element and with civil servants at the upper levels being rated relative to one another rather than against some absolute standard of performance.[6] And at the same time, the *noblesse oblige* pattern that had once dominated the UK civil service pay pattern in the union-dominated 1970s seemed to be being left far behind from the mid-1980s as senior civil service salaries rose both above those of the ministers they served and relative to the increases obtained by the lower grades—to the point where their German counterparts at the time of writing could only dream of salaries approaching those of top UK civil servants.

When it came to the competency element of the bargain, much was talked in both countries from at least the 1960s (and arguably much further back than that, e.g. after the First World War in the UK) about the need for more relative emphasis on managerial competency. The stereotype narrative of the rise of NPM might lead us to expect a decisive shift in the competency dimension of PSBs from traditional 'policy wonk' and 'sage' approaches to those of 'deliverer' and 'spanner'. Indeed, the managerial-type competency frameworks that both countries produced in the 1990s might lead one to think that such an approach to competency had become dominant in the PSB

---

[6] In the UK senior civil service, the pot of money available to be distributed as performance bonuses amounted to some 4 per cent of the total senior civil service wage bill in 2004, but was intended to rise to 10 per cent by 2008. For permanent secretaries (departmental heads), the bonus component amounted to between 4.4 and 10.5 per cent of their salaries in 2004 (Review Body on Top Salaries 2005)

of both states. But our interviewees in many cases led us to think that the story
was not as simple as that. 'Spanners' and 'deliverers' were not competencies
that were wholly new to the public service over the past fifteen years, and
the bottom had by no means dropped out of the bureaucratic market for
'wonks' and 'sages', though new types of wonk and sage competencies,
notably in presentation, had certainly emerged. Moreover, in the UK over
that period there had been a notable professionalization of many aspects of
human resources across the public sector, producing individuals at the middle
level of the public service whose own competencies—ironically perhaps—
were often more those of the 'wonk' or 'sage' variety than those of the
'deliverer'.

As for the loyalty/responsibility element of the bargain, there were signs of
non-trivial change in both systems. In the UK, as we discussed in Chapter 6,
some substantive new PSBs were introduced for parts of the higher civil
service that involved both 'executive' and 'judge' elements of loyalty and
responsibility, in the form of new regulators operating at arm's length from
ministers and new agency CEOs with direct responsibility for 'operational'
matters. The latter in particular made it possible for ministers to redefine
their role in managing the public services from direct operational responsibility to a role analogous to that of the chairman of a football club who fires
the club manager when the team plays badly, producing some high-profile
sackings of 'failed' agency CEOs. These dismissals might seem to have been an
instance of Voltaire's famous remark (in *Candide*) 'ici on tue de temps en
temps un amiral pour encourager les autres', but only if that remark is taken
as ironic.[7] For the 'regular' departmental bureaucracy, as already noted, there
were schizophrenic pressures on reward and loyalty, with continuing pressure
for a move towards a more 'executive' type bargain on the one hand, and on
the other, a formal strengthening of 'judge' type elements.

In the German case, we might perhaps have expected a period of consolidation and stability over the past fifteen years or so after the major change
of the absorption of the former PSBs of the GDR into the West German
model that was generalized for the new state.[8] But from the West German
perspective, that period also witnessed the only complete change in coalition
government since 1945 (in 1998), producing a purge of some of the 'judges',

---

[7] Because the effect seems just as likely to have discouraged rather than encouraged the
others, because such dismissals were often less about keeping managers on their toes than
getting ministers out of a political hole, and because, like children learning to smoke, one
satisfactory experience of firing a CEO on an 'executive' bargain may have encouraged ministers
to repeat the exercise rather than removing the need to fire others.

[8] Though many of our interviewees, looking at developments from a West German perspective, perceived stability rather than change in such arrangements.

a tendency for careers to be built on the basis of being a 'partner' in loyalty/responsibility terms before becoming a 'judge', and some tightening of the screw by politicians in other ways, as we have already noted.

These changes are summarized in Table 7.4. What they seem to have amounted to for the UK PSB is a set of senior public servants who were better paid than their counterparts of a generation before, less secure and more diverse in loyalty/responsibility terms, and more inclined to talk in 'managementese' in a way that at least gave an impression of greater instrumentalism. In the German case, senior public servants were, in reward terms, keeping up with the comfortable standards of their predecessors (but not with the British Joneses across the North Sea, at least in gross salary terms), were 'talking the talk' of a more managerial approach to competency without necessarily 'walking the walk', and in loyalty/responsibility terms, were widely perceived to be witnessing increasing politicization that had the effect of weakening the 'judge-like' element of the loyalty/responsibility bargain.

7.3. CONCLUSION

In this chapter we have tried to 'put the pieces together' of our PSB analysis in three main ways. First, we have tried to show how PSB analysis can be used as a mapping tool. We can represent particular PSB arrangements as a vector of

Table 7.4 Some recent changes in reward, competency, and loyalty/responsibility elements of PSBs in the central bureaucracies of Germany and the UK

	Germany	UK
Reward	Broadly following the former West German pyramid/escalator style	Richer at the top and moving away from '*noblesse oblige*' style
Competency	'Bolting on' of some 'deliverer' element onto previous 'wonk-based' West German competency frameworks	Much talk of more emphasis on 'deliverer' competencies in the departmental civil service, but with new forms of 'wonk' and 'sage' competencies too
Loyalty and responsibility	Broadly moving to West German model on unification, but with more creative political interference into the judge-type element (e.g. by new probation rules for top positions) and with a tendency for the route to the 'judge-type' element to lie through that of 'partner'	Broadly, more 'executive' style with 'public hangings' of agency CEOs, but also some moves formally to strengthen the 'judge-type' elements of loyalty and responsibility for departmental civil servants

the types and dimensions we laid out in Chapters 1–6, and also describe changes over time as moves from one combination of PSB bargains to another. If we look back during the era of 'democratization' (with its numerous lurches and lapses) in the European countries over the past 150 years or so, and across different elements of the public service, we find that most of the squares on the PSB map have been, or are being traversed by, advanced democracies over that period. For developing and transitional countries we can expect the same to apply with at least equal force.

Second, we have suggested that, while creative mixing and matching is the essence of change in PSBs, there are some kinds of combinations that are likely to prove as problematic to the public service reformer as a barred combination of gears is to the cyclist or of the unfortunate mixes produced by Flaubert's melon-growers in the epigraph. But both of those analogies may be limited or even misleading, in so far as the barred combinations are probably more likely to result from surreptitious cheating and pulling and hauling at the extremities rather than from a deliberate, perhaps inept, selection or official adoption of a combination that will not work. Indeed, it is often likely to be the difference between pious official hopes and actual practice, or between different views of what the 'real' PSB is that is likely to lead to such an outcome.

Third, using the analytic approach we developed in Chapters 1–6, we have turned from a dimensional and classificatory style of analysis to a more holistic or *Gestalt*-type analysis of particular countries, showing how the two main cases in this study, Britain and Germany, figure and compare in their long-term and more recent PSB dynamics. The two countries adopted somewhat different styles of PSBs in the first wave of democratization in the nineteenth century, and those differences have by no means disappeared in the current age of digital technology, globalization, and professional politics. Germany has shown more dramatic long-term shifts in its various PSBs, and those shifts have up to now been associated with major regime changes, while the UK has produced more noticeable shifts in the decade and a half since German unification, without regime change in the ordinary sense.

Analysing PSBs in this way raises several questions that we pursue further in Part III of the book. First, what are the different ways that PSBs can rise or fall, and what, if anything, can keep them in existence, given that in most cases few or any of their dimensions are entrenched constitutionally and that they must operate in a political world in which it is often said that only losers play by the rules? Second, how serious in practice is the 'barred combinations' problem that we discussed in Section 7.2, and more particularly, is it a problem for the 'managerial' approach to public service reform—in which public servants operate in some sort of delegated-bargain style of PSB within a particular set of reward, competency, and loyalty expectations—that has been so favoured by public service reformers over the past generation? And third, whatever the past experience of the kind we have explored in Section 7.2 for Germany and the UK, are there good reasons to believe that different public service systems will tend to converge on a common type of PSB for the information age of the twenty-first century?

Part III

Blame, Change, and Cheating

8

How Public Service Bargains Change and Fall

L'honnêtcté n'a pas besoin de règles.[1]

> (Albert Camus (1969, orig. 1942), *Le Mythe de Sisyphe*, Paris, Gallimard, pp. 93–4)

We kicked them, thumped them and beat them.

> (British civil service interviewee (UK20), recounting his experience of reform)

Here is a bunch of interlopers...they won't be here for long...we don't have to bother.

> (Perception of civil service attitudes to his government by an Indo-Trinidadian politician (TT2))

Wherever there are agreements or bargains, there is the possibility of breakdown for a variety of reasons. Those reasons include sudden changes in habitat or environment that overtake the original compact, longer-term changes that do not necessarily involve any single 'big bang' event, and processes of cheating, 'creative compliance', and a range of other strategic responses by one or more of the parties.

Those various forces of breakdown are hard to separate in practice. And perceptions vary too, dependent on worldviews, attitudes, and beliefs. As we saw at several points in Chapters 5, 6, and 7, what one observer might see as cheating, another might see as habitat change or normal behaviour. But the general point is that PSBs are not necessarily stable or self-reinforcing. Like any other sort of agreement, from marriages to international treaties, they can break down or become degraded in several ways. This chapter explores some of the ways in which those bargains can weaken or collapse, focusing the analysis particularly on the way that PSBs can break down as a result of cheating by one or more of the parties.

---

[1] 'Integrity needs no rules'.

8.1. SUDDEN HABITAT CHANGES

One way that PSBs can break down is as a result of sudden changes in habitat, in what Nelson Polsby (1984) and others call 'acute' patterns of change. Sudden habitat changes mean particular events that disrupt a system of rule of which a PSB is an integral part. It has often been remarked that at the level of their standard operating routines, bureaucracies can continue to function much as before after revolutions, military defeats, critical election outcomes, and other forms of 'regime change'. But that does not necessarily apply to the political terms of engagement of the bureaucracy, and such events can bring about a change in PSB at the top. One example is the development of the Weimar Republic in the post-First World War Germany and another is the defeat of the Nazi regime in 1945 that led to a constitutionally entrenched element of autonomy in the PSB in the 1949 Basic Law for the then West Germany, as discussed earlier. But election results can produce sudden habitat changes too, as the following three examples may serve to show.

First, a case of 'acute' habitat change precipitated by an election result, as discussed earlier in this book, is the electoral defeat of the Japanese LDP in 1993 after nearly forty years of rule by a single party with multiple factions. That critical election may have partially disrupted the traditional 'Meiji' PSB, in which senior civil servants took the initiative in making policy proposals and drafting laws while politicians had the last word. But it certainly disrupted a more particular type of PSB that had grown up from the 1950s, in which civil servants were expected to negotiate only with factions and policy organizations within the ruling LDP, and to pay no attention to other political parties (see Hori 2003). Though the LDP was out of government for only eight months after 1993, and the changes evidently did not affect all ministries to the same extent, the 1993 election outcome seems to have been an important force in edging Japan away from a PSB that involved an exclusive relationship between the bureaucracy and a single political party, and towards something more like an agency bargain of the Schafferian type.[2]

A second example is the case of regime change in Hong Kong at the end of the twentieth century. When Hong Kong moved from 156 years of British colonial rule to the new status of a 'special administrative region' of the People's Republic of China in 1997, little ostensibly changed in the role and status of the civil service, since the 'Basic Law' that had been drawn up in 1984 (to govern

---

[2] A key feature in this change seems to have been LDP anger at the way the 1994 budget was handled by the Ministry of Finance under the Ozawa/Hosekawa government when the LDP was briefly in opposition (see Suleiman 2003: 248–9).

the 'one-country two-systems' regime after the return of Hong Kong to China) protected the status of the Hong Kong civil service for fifty years. But in another sense, this regime change served to alter the PSB of the Hong Kong civil service away from one that mixed elements of agency with trusteeship to a new form of trusteeship, in which senior civil servants, in effect, had to act as 'Ministers', defending their policies and answering questions in the Legislative Council. This situation arose because of the political constraints placed on the government of the Special Region of Hong Kong by the Beijing government, which was reluctant to countenance a fully elected legislature with strong powers in Hong Kong or a Ministerial system of the conventional parliamentary-government type. The upshot was the emergence of a new 'political civil service' elite in the early years of the twenty-first century, enjoying much higher pay but more limited tenure than their colonial-era predecessors, to fill the gap left by the absence of ministers in the regime (see Lee 2003).

A third example is that of two critical election results in Trinidad and Tobago, which seem to have produced PSB changes that were somewhere between sudden 'acute' change and more long-term processes of habitat change. One was the 1986 election that disturbed the twenty-year pattern of rule by Eric Williams's People's National Movement party since Trinidad's independence in 1966 by bringing a non-People's National Movement coalition government to power. The other was the 1995 election that produced the largely Indo-Trinidadian United Nation Congress government under Basdeo Panday. Those two elections, and particularly the latter, seem to have heralded some change away from the PSB that had characterized Trinidad since independence (comprising a career-tenure corps dominated by Afro-Trinidadians under what was claimed to be a merit appointment system), and towards a different kind of PSB with increased representation of Indo-Trinidadians in the bureaucracy and a different approach to career tenure.[3]

8.2. LONGER-TERM HABITAT CHANGES

As that last example shows, 'acute' and 'incubated' habitat changes that cause PSBs to break down can be hard to distinguish at the margin, since that 1995 election result in Trinidad arguably reflected social changes and increasing

---

[3] It needs to be added that these changes came after 'structural adjustment' reforms affecting the Trinidadian public service in the late 1980s, severely curtailing career expectations for many bureaucrats. One Trinidadian public servant (TT4) told us that this experience caused many bureaucrats to 'start recognizing that security of tenure may well become a thing of the past. So it made sense that you come in, spend some short time, get some decent wages, build your CV and move on'—a far cry from the traditional concept of the career PSB.

discussion of the potential problems of ethnic imbalances in the public sector that had been building up for some time through processes of increased education and social mobilization. The habitat changes noted by Harold Nicolson and Anton Graf Monts, which we discussed at the outset of this book, may be another example of that kind. Nevertheless, some changes to PSBs seem to reflect longer-term changes, ('incubated' changes, in Polsby's (1984) language) with a cumulative build-up of tension or dissatisfaction, but no single big-bang event in the form of a critical election or other form of regime change. Incubated change producing PSB breakdown may include long-term agenda shifts (e.g. in the conduct of economic policy), changes in technology, shifts in levels of corruption, or styles of rent-seeking.

For example, Sergvey Braguinsky, and Grigory Yavlinsky (2000) argue that the 'bargain' applying to enterprise managers in the Soviet Union changed dramatically as a long-term consequence of Stalin's death in 1953. During the Stalin years, when over ten million people were continuously held in labour camps (Ibid: 37), Soviet enterprise managers are claimed by Braguinsky and Yavlinsky to have been far less secure than their counterparts in Western private firms. But the elimination of terror in the years after Stalin's death steadily changed the rules of the game between 'principals' and 'agents' in that system (Ibid: 46, 83, 191). Managers obtained a progressively stronger position relative to the target-setting apparatus (representing the political 'principal'), were able to cheat with greater impunity and to affiliate themselves with the parallel economy that the central authorities were obliged to tolerate.

It also seems to be a long-terms patten of change of this type that Colin Campbell and Graham Wilson (1995), in their well-known 'End of Whitehall' thesis, have in mind as what has undermined the Schafferian PSB in the UK. The argument is that long-term changes in the way that politics works have meant that elected politicians now place less value than they used to on the traditional policy skills and competencies of the Whitehall mandarinate, meaning that the traditional bargain started to become seriously asymmetrical in that it was valued more by civil servants than by politicians. So the claim is that it is not any one election or government—whether Margaret Thatcher's New Right government of the 1980s or Tony Blair's New Labour government of the 1990s and 2000s—that caused the change, but rather a slow long-term change in the way that electoral politics works that has created steadily building pressures for politicians to break the traditional PSB.

Several of our British civil service interviewees echoed that view, even if they were not familiar with Campbell and Wilson's book. For instance, one civil service interviewee (UK13) thought that long-term shifts in the economic policy agenda meant a shift in what governments wanted the bureaucracy to do. A second said that 'the claim to special skills [by 'grey heads'] in political insight coming with age and insight has broken down too' (UK4). A third bleakly observed:

The traditional relationship of creating the future between ministers and civil servants had become pretty creaky. And it was not clear to me . . . that . . . civil servants were in touch with the sort of future ministers wanted to create. . . . When Margaret Thatcher came in, in the 1979 election, they [the higher mandarinate] simply misunderstood what was happening. So trust was withdrawn . . . over a long period, and it took ages to see there was a problem. . . . The Thatcher era was destructive of quite a lot of the unspoken contract and took away some of the justification for assuming that you were in a policy-determining and successful partnership. . . . And [after Labour was elected in 1997] . . . distrust still rules, the incoming ministers were far from certain that [the higher civil servants] whom they were seeing were necessarily 'safe'. That old contract had gone. . . . (UK3)

The Whitehall 'Schafferian' bargain seems to be the most commonly discussed example of the erosion of a PSB arising from a long-term pattern of political change, but we found echoes of a similar process in the views of some German observers and interviewees. For example, Hans-Ulrich Derlien (2004) has commented on the steady development of the explicit 'party-book' approach to the federal bureaucracy since the 1950s, moving away from what had once been a more 'neutral' PSB to one that had greater overtones of political loyalism. Others have pointed to the tendency to increasingly appoint younger staff to 'confidant' positions—the so-called *Seiteneinsteiger*—as part of a long-term erosion of the older bargain, as noted in Chapter 7.

8.3. CHEATING AND STRATEGIC BEHAVIOUR

Habitat change prompting changes in PSBs can consist of relatively exogenous short- or long-term developments that alter demands for skills or competencies. Examples include changes between war and peace, a switch to new economic regimes, or even changes in the nature of the state, as in the case of the breakaway of what was then the Irish Free State from the UK in 1922, and the creation and then unification of the two Germanies in the second half of the twentieth century.

However, while habitat changes in nature can destroy the conditions that secure the survival of certain species, habitat changes of the kind explored earlier only affect PSBs through the action of various parties to the respective bargain. Quite apart from relatively exogenous factors such as war and peace, one of the familiar ways that any bargain can break down is if one or more of

Table 8.1   Public service bargains: cheat or deliver?

		Politicians	
		Deliver	*Cheat*
Public Servants	*Deliver*	'Cooperative equilibrium': high trust public service arrangements	Public servants fatalistic, but resigned or apathetic
	Cheat	Politicians distrust public servants, but feel unable to alter system	Low trust and unstable public service arrangements

Source: Adapted from Hood 2001: 20.

the parties choose to cheat or sees the other as cheating. We have already given various examples of 'cheating' in Part II of this book, and we might expect that to be a major source of breakdown in PSBs, regardless of changes of external habitat. Indeed, from a rational choice perspective it is possible to think of politicians and bureaucrats as engaged in one of those 'Prisoner's Dilemma'-type games—the well-known cooperation game in which each of two prisoners, accused of being partners in crime and held in separate cells, arc given the option of whether to stay silent or to go free by informing on the other.[4] An example of that kind of analysis is given in Table 8.1, in which each side has the option on whether to 'cheat' or 'deliver' on a PSB and in which the overall outcome will depend on who makes what move. If a PSB is considered as a Prisoner's Dilemma of this type, it will be supported if both sides 'deliver'. But it is not difficult to find reasons why each side would ideally like to be in a position in which it cheats on the bargain while the other side delivers, and therefore becomes the 'sucker'. If both sides follow that logic, the PSB is likely to head for collapse.

This sort of analysis is just the kind of abstraction that can give rational choice analysis a bad name. Objectors often say that such analysis misses all the interesting questions of who sees what as appropriate behaviour and the historical specificities of what counts as cheating in what circumstances. But nevertheless, it is common to hear complaints by politicians, civil servants, and others that in public service relationships important lines have been crossed, long-accepted understandings breached, or bargains reneged on by the other side.

Cheating can take various forms, and in a landmark analysis of cheating at work, Gerald Mars (1982) drew an important distinction between individu-

---

[4] The original story is ascribed to A. W. Tucker and was developed by Rapoport and Chammah in the mid-1960s (see Brams 1976: 81–3).

alized cheating—for example, when particular public servants individually 'leak' confidential information for profit or principle—and collective cheating, for example, when public servants or politicians operate as a group in behaviour that breaks earlier understandings. Often it is the collective form of cheating in the world of politics and bureaucracy that is most problematic, because it becomes hard to distinguish from the general political process. For instance, in Chapter 1 we mentioned the bargain under which the Chilean military accepted civilian rule after 1988, and a dramatic example of alleged cheating under that bargain came in May 1993. General (and ex-President) Augusto Pinochet put his troops on a high state of alert on the grounds that the civilian politicians had gone too far in investigating human rights abuses under his previous military regime. For their part, Chilean politicians accused the military of breaking the rules of the constitutional game by spying on government ministers.[5] As we noted in Chapter 6, major regime changes often involve delicate and often partly implicit understandings about drawing a line under behaviour in the previous regime, which can easily prompt perceptions of cheating when the lines become undrawn.

It is not difficult to find other examples of allegations of cheating on PSBs, both individual and collective. For example, when this chapter was being first drafted in 2004, several British newspapers were carrying stories about a 'war' between ministers and civil servants in the UK Home Office. A Labour junior minister (Beverly Hughes) blamed her civil servants for failure to follow formal procedures over the processing of immigration cases from Romania, claiming that she knew nothing about the problem. This ministerial line led to leaks to newspapers and the opposition parties from disgruntled civil servants that eventually caused the minister to resign.[6] In the previous year, following a case in which a weapons expert in the Ministry of Defence, Dr David Kelly, committed suicide over media stories about the doctoring of military intelligence reports before the 2003 Iraq war, a battle was raging in Whitehall over claims that politically appointed 'spinocrats' had overstepped their proper role relative to regular departmental civil servants in a way that undermined (so it was claimed) accepted understandings about demarcation lines and the terms of the traditional agency bargain. And whenever expected honours are denied, suggestions of cheating often surface, as in a 2005 case of serious conflict within the German Foreign Ministry over a ministerial decision no longer to publish the customary obituary in the internal newsletter

---

[5] After this event, a period of 'co-government' between the civilian government and the military is said to have ensured. See Wilde (1999).

[6] See Roy Hattersley, 'Yes and No, Minister', *The Guardian*, 2 April 2004, p. 26; 'Damned Lies and Targets', *Sunday Times*, 4 April 2004, p. 18.

for distinguished mandarins, following the death of a senior foreign office official who had been a Nazi at the outset of his service. Further, in both Germany and Britain we were told that politicians saw it as 'cheating' for regular civil servants to meet journalists in restaurants (D12, UK2).

Still, as already noted, what exactly counts as cheating can be hard to determine outside the contrived quasi-laboratory world of Prisoner's Dilemma-type games, where cheating is clear-cut and readily observable.[7] As we have already noted, for PSBs, cheating will often be a fuzzy and rhetorical concept, because who sees what as 'cheating' can be problematic and variable. In real-life social settings, a distinction is often made between 'honest graft' (or acceptable bending of the rules) and outright cheating, though the boundary line between the two is often very problematic. The notion that cheating has taken place may depend on bargains being recognized as applying to succeeding generations of politicians or bureaucrats, and, as the examples given in the previous paragraph show, may depend heavily on what is seen as the 'spirit' of agreements rather than the letter of the law (if there is any). For example, if elected politicians change the public service 'deal' in a regime change (as in the example we gave in Chapter 3 of what happened shortly after independence in Singapore, when Lee Kuan Yew's PAP government substantially cut the customary and lavish perks that the senior civil service had enjoyed under the previous colonial regime) is that cheating—or just democratic political change? What about the Nazi assault on the traditional German 'trustee bargain' after 1933? What if the new regime—or some of its prominent members at least—has apparently given undertakings that are later denied? If politicians go by the maxim (stated to us by one German interviewee (D12)) that 'As a politician, you are finished if you fully trust your civil servants', is that 'cheating' or just normal prudence? As in the case of marriage or other relationships, who has cheated on whom and how, on whose perception of what bargain, may depend on who you talk to. So we have to be as careful about reifying cheating as we do of reifying bargains.

8.4. VARIETIES OF CHEATING

There may be some 'universal' kinds of cheating, but much of what counts as cheating seems to be context-specific, depending on the character of the bargain. Each of the bargains we identified in Part I of this book lends itself to

---

[7] Even for the Prisoner's Dilemma it is possible to imagine complications. For instance, if the two prisoners are politicians or lawyers, they might be able to haggle over definitions of what exactly counts as 'giving information' about the other party.

Table 8.2 Examples of types of cheating in public service bargains

Type of bargain	Example of how public servants can cheat	Example of how other actors can cheat
B1a1 (representational-consociational)	Promotion of social divisions	Various forms of discrimination
B1a2 (representational-selective)	Failure to support ruling forces	Bypassing or sidelining favoured groups
B1b1 (tutelary-moralistic)	Failure to act as moral exemplar	Denial of moral or ethical authority
B1b2 (tutelary-technocratic)	Compromising on technical standards	Circumvention or denial of status
B2a1 (complex-delegated agency)	Playing the principals off against one another to evade control	Leaving it to the agent to resolve conflicts among principals
B2a2 (simple-delegated agency)	Evasion of blame or non-compliance with oversight regime	Covert interference in managerial space
B2b1 (serial loyalist-directed-agency)	Party political bias in loyalty	Party political bias in selection
B2b2 (personal loyalist-directed-agency)	Disloyalty to personal patron	Double crossing or blame shifting

Source: Adapted from Hood 2001: 19.

breakdown or degradation through some form of cheating, and Table 8.2 gives examples of characteristic forms of cheating corresponding to each of the types of bargain that we discussed in Chapters 2 and 3. What counts as cheating depends on what is taken to be the central or defining parts of a PSB and what is seen as a barred combination, in the terms we used in Chapter 7.

8.4.1. Trustee Bargains (B1)

We noted in Chapter 2 that the basic idea of a trustee bargain is one in which public servants seek to act in what they conceive to be the best interest of the beneficiaries in exchange for acceptance of their freedom of discretion from those beneficiaries. So trustees are to be judged on whether they put the interests of their beneficiaries ahead of their own, and whether they act with appropriate diligence and procedure, for instance, in consultation with experts.

The clearest form of 'cheating' under such a bargain therefore occurs when the supposed trustees in fact put their own interests ahead of that of the beneficiaries, as can happen in disasters or military defeats when members of emergency or medical services turn from their public duties to save themselves and their families. From the opposite side, the beneficiaries can cheat by not respecting the trustees' right to make autonomous decisions on their behalf and seeking to dictate to them, for example, when supposedly autonomous expert advisers or regulators are exposed to backdoor political pressure.

Both kinds of 'cheating' behaviour are frequently alleged. For instance, it became an article of faith with most of the early New Right public choice writers of the 1960s and 1970s that even (and perhaps especially) those civil servants who profess to operate as Confucian or Hegelian trustees of the general good will, in practice, cheat by putting their own self-interest first. And well before that, allegations that colonial civil servants in practice cheated widely on a supposedly trustee bargain to look after themselves or their own national or racial group were widespread during the post-Second World War struggles for independence.

Beyond that, the particular types of trustee bargains each imply more specific forms of cheating, as shown in Table 8.2. We have already suggested that some trustee bargains (of the B1a type in our earlier classification presented in Part I of this book) depend on the notion of the public service as providing an element of political or social representation in exchange for a degree of autonomy, and if that is the essence of the bargain, it can break down if representation becomes distorted or civil service autonomy is weakened.

If the 'consociational' variant (B1a1) of that B1a type of bargain is one in which civil servants from different ethnic, racial, gender, or linguistic groups offer support for the state that goes beyond their particular group in exchange for a share of administrative power, then cheating may take the form of ethnic or linguistic particularism by civil servants in practice. That is sometimes alleged for the multinational EU bureaucracy when the supposed bureaucratic 'glue' that helps hold the fissiparous political system together comes unstuck.[8] Alternatively, cheating under such a bargain may consist of other actors practising discrimination among groups within the bureaucracy or bypassing or downgrading the bureaucracy as a whole. And that consociational system may itself be threatened by gaming, as is said to have happened with the Indian quota system for 'scheduled castes' representation in the bureaucracy (Weiner 1984: 72; also Sowell 1990; Esman 1997).

In the more selective variant of the representative bargain (B1a2), as described in Chapter 2, public servants are intended to be representative of

---

[8] The 'Kinnock reforms' of the EU Commission bureaucracy under the Prodi Presidency are said by some to have had this effect, insofar as they produced more rotation of staff and the removal of fiefdoms from particular national groups.

a particular dominant or favoured group—such as the *bumiputras* in Malaysia or the Sinhalese in Sri Lanka. In this case, cheating can take forms that include failure to support the ruling regime in the selective-representation terms in which the bargain is conceived (e.g. a blue-blooded officer who undermines the monarchy or one of a favoured ethnic group who links up with the out-groups). Equally, cheating from rulers, politicians, or other actors can take forms such as the sidelining of the dominant groups entrenched in the civil or military service or bypassing their claims to authority.

For those trustee bargains that have been conceived as tutelary (the B1b stream), the personal qualities of civil servants are more important than their social representativeness in the exchange. In what we earlier termed the tutelary-moralistic bargain (B1b1), public servants are selected precisely because they are *not* representative of the mass of humanity. Rather, they are selected because they possess moral, religious, political, or intellectual qualities (but not specific skills of too utilitarian a kind) that make them stand out from society at large. As we have seen, the clearest example of this kind of bargain is the long Confucian tradition of 'scholar-gentry' in the public service.[9] If the quality that civil servants offer (in exchange for a degree of autonomy and social respect of their right to rule) is political zeal, religious purity or knightly integrity, or its modern-day equivalent, then cheating on the bargain will take forms such as bourgeois money-grubbing, self-serving compromises or intellectual sell-outs. As we saw in Chapter 4, one of the ways that approach has been modified in the traditional Japanese PSB is by the temporal compromise in which higher civil servants have traditionally ex-changed a relatively modest level of reward during public service for big-money rewards in life after the public service. But as we also noted in Chapter 4, even this compromise can be seen as 'cheating' by some critics.

The other type of 'tutelary bargain' (B1b2) is the technocratic variety, in which the primary quality civil servants offer, in exchange for a degree of autonomy or right to rule, their technical knowledge or judgement rather than their putative moral, political, or religious qualities, or literary/artistic accomplishment. This is the sort of 'tutelary bargain' that underlies offices such as independent regulators or central bankers, whose right to rule comes with their claims to technical expertise. In this case, cheating includes various ways in which technical or professional standards can be adulterated by political accommodation, personal self-interest, or other non-technical factors. In a sense, too, technical incompetence in forms such as failure to keep up with or

---

[9] An aristocracy of 'nature's gentlemen' rather than blue-blood, since office-holding was obtained through a supposedly meritocratic exam regime rather than heredity—in theory, at least.

abide by the latest developments in the field, can be considered as failure to abide by developing professional or scientific standards, by analogy with notions of medical competence, and the interpretation of that issue can be problematic, as we saw in discussion of competency in Chapter 5. And as with the other kind of tutelary bargain, tutelary-technocratic civil servants can be cheated against as well as cheating. As we noted in Chapter 6, they may be sidelined or bypassed in ways that undercut their autonomy, denied respect, authority, or the financial means they need to make a respectable living.[10]

8.4.2. Agency Bargains (B2)

As with trustee bargains, cheating over agency bargains can take various forms, some more palpable than others. As discussed in Chapter 3, the basic idea of an agency arrangement is one in which agents do the bidding of their principals in exchange for reward and respect from those principals. Accordingly, cheating will take place when agents disobey or distort the instructions of their principals, or where those principals fail to reward or respect their agents, give them impossible or contradictory instructions, blame them for their own failings, or secretly undermine them by deals with other parties. And again, claims about such supposedly cheating behaviour are commonplace. Much has been said, in fiction, political memoirs, and academic writing, about the ways that supposedly agent bureaucrats can seek to distort the wishes of their principals in ways that serve their own interest or power. For example, those agents may eagerly run with some instructions or reform initiatives that suit their interests for some reason or other (whether it be self-interest, political conviction, or simple 'do-ability') while they drag their feet on other goals that their political principals are equally or more keen to pursue. In Chapter 6, we quoted some of our interviewees' reflections in this vein on the management of ministers.

For public servants operating under forms of agency bargains that involve the formal delegation of decision-making powers from the principal to the agent, cheating on the part of the bureaucrats can take forms that include bypassing or capturing the principal, blaming the principal for their own faults, and gaming or data fabrication to manipulate information about their performance. Bypassing and capturing of the principal is often claimed to have been practised by state-owned eterprise managers in the Soviet Union after

---

[10] One interviewee describing the arrray of weapons available for politicians to use against independent public office holders out of line with goverment thinking, said: 'It depends what hurts. No reappointment, no gong [slang term for medals and honours], public criticism, refusal to state support, refusal to acknowledge ... jurisdiction' (UK25).

Stalin's death in 1953, when those managers secured a large degree of *de facto* control over the target setting process and 'the level of sanctions that any manager of an SOE had to face when caught cheating was considerably reduced' (Braguinsky and Yavlinsky 2000:83). And gaming and data fabrication itself figured large in the response of Soviet enterprise managers to the production targets set by the Gosplan regime in the USSR's planned economy, epitomized in a famous *Krokodil* cartoon about a nail factory that made only one enormous nail because its production target was set in tons (Nove 1980: 97). Cheating on the part of the politician 'principals', on the other hand, can include various forms of undermining the agent's ability to make decisions or take action within what is supposedly a delegated space, e.g. by secret backdoor interference.

In contrast, for 'directed' forms of agency bargain (B2b), the bureaucratic agent is expected to operate under orders of the day from the principal, rather than according to delegated powers. For 'serial loyalist' bargains of the Schafferian type (B2b1), in which public servants are expected to act as agents for the government of the day, whatever it is, party bias is the most commonly discussed form of cheating. Such cheating may take the form of permanent civil servants blocking policy initiatives that go against their own political preferences, or of politicians taking party or political affiliation into account when they take part in decisions over supposedly meritocratic promotions or top-level appointments. But there are other forms of cheating under such a bargain, including delay or lack or responsiveness to the orders issued by the politician principal. Several ministers in Harold Wilson's UK Labour government of the 1960s made much of such perceived 'cheating', and the same went for some ministers in Tony Blair's New Labour government elected in 1997. For their part, civil servants may see such delays as merely part of the deliberation and measured pace that responsible public service involves, and not cheating at all.

Similar forms of cheating may apply to the 'personal loyalist' variant of nondelegated agency bargains (B2b2), in which public servants act as agents only for a particular politician principal. Under such an arrangement, the main form of cheating consists of disloyalty to that politician, for example, in the form of embarrassing leaks or throwing off that particular political master in exchange for a chance of office under a successor.[11] Equally, for the politician principal, the main cheating response under this type of bargain is to pin blame on the loyalist agent for something the principal is responsible for.

In discussing cheating over agency forms of PSBs up to this point, we have focused on the dyadic relationship between the politician principal and the

---

[11] Though one British civil servant (UK18), in a quasi-theological reflection on dealings with often transient ministers, told us, 'You ... have a deal with an eternal Secretary of State, not just with the one who happens to have the job at the moment.'

bureaucratic agent. But there may be other parties who can cheat on such PSBs. For example, as we saw in Chapter 6, civil servants under a departmental minister may also have to relate to the prime minister and other ministers, backbenchers, and opposition politicians, and that creates fertile possibilities for allegations of cheating. Moreover, within the bureaucratic world, there will typically be public servants working on different types of bargain—such as personal loyalists and serial loyalists in the Whitehall system, or autonomous public servants in the form of independent regulators and agency bureaucrats in the US federal bureaucracy. Implicit or explicit understandings may also apply to the way that these various actors behave towards one another, and here too perceptions or accusations of cheating may come about, as we saw in Chapter 6 in discussing the loyalty and responsibility bargains of special advisers versus departmental civil servants in Whitehall.

Where the government system includes civil servants working on delegated and non-delegated agency bargains, there likewise has to be at least some understanding as to how those players are to relate to one another, and here too, claims of cheating are often made. For instance, agency heads operating under a delegated agency PSB sometimes feel their presumed autonomy to be undermined by what they see as spying, unreasonable demands for information or procedural controls coming from civil servants working under a non-delegated form of agency bargain. Indeed, one British civil servant from a specialist background claimed to have been treated as 'dispensable' in a way that would not have applied to a 'generalist':

Because I came to the civil service as a [name of specialism], I was not regarded as 'real'. I reckon they thought I was dispensable ... They were certainly not going to risk a decent civil servant for this [job]. (UK8)

In short, perceived cheating over agency PSBs does not begin and end with relationships between ministers and civil servants.

8.5. HOW CHEATING IS CHECKED

If the possibilities for cheating over PSBs are as extensive as the discussion in Section 8.4 has indicated, how can such cheating be limited or prevented? Rules, culture, and incentives are perhaps the most commonly discussed ways of keeping cheating in check for any kind of compact or bargains,[12] although those three approaches are hard to separate fully.

---

[12] As in the large literature on mechanisms of commitment, from security studies to political economy (see, e.g. Schelling 1960; Horn 1995; Levy and Spiller 1996).

The rules approach is to enshrine bargains in more or less formal compacts, meaning the bargain is written down and (so the presumption goes) violations can be more easily determined and understood. That means codifying, legislating, or constitutionalizing bargains, turning what had been implicit into black-letter law. In the German civil service code, even the requirement of 'collegiality'—in many systems an unwritten convention of bureaucratic behaviour—is written into legally binding codes of conduct (*Geschäftsordnung*). By contrast, the UK tradition was one of low formality and 'enactedness' of PSBs, but many British civil servants and public service reformers in the UK in the 1990s and 2000s favoured the rules approach as a way of dealing with perceived problems with the traditional Schafferian bargain that was described earlier in the book. The response to a greater lateral entry at mid-career by people who had not been socialized into the unwritten 'club government' rules about what was and was not 'done' in the bureaucracy was to write down the conventions and enshrine them in more explicit codes of ethics and the like. In an earlier study conducted by one of us (Hood et al. 1999: 71), a senior Cabinet Office civil servant was quoted as saying:

It used to be 'my word is my bond'. Now there are more what you might call 'uncouth businessmen' in the civil service and you have to write things down.

Indeed, at the time that New Labour replaced the Conservatives in 1997, it was the new government's declared position that it was not enough to prevent cheating on the bargain by writing down rules that had been traditionally been unwritten and learned through socialization. Rather, those rules needed to be given statutory form, as a civil service act, to enable the bargain to be justiciable—that is, enforceable in the courts. (At the time of writing, after eight years of New Labour rule, that act had yet to appear, though it had appeared in bill form and was still on the government's official agenda.)

The problem with the rules approach is that gaming within the rules can undermine the substance of bargains in at least three ways, all of which were brought out by our interviewees. First is the well-known phenomenon of 'creative compliance' (McBarnet and Whelan 1991)—the Soviet nail factory problem—that undermines the intent or substance of rules while formally observing them.[13] The second is disputation over the precise meaning or application of rules to particular cases—the approach of the 'barrack-room lawyer'. Given the open-texturedness of ordinary language (or even its stilted legal form), such disputation can also destroy agreements or bargains in practice. The third is the temptation offered by codification of established

---

[13] An argument made by Jean-Jacques Rousseau (1993: 154) in his claim that 'prudence is never so ready to conceive new precautions as knavery is to elude them'.

conventions for further alteration, rendering them unstable when the opposite is intended. So merely writing down the rules in the 'ethics code' approach is likely to be of most value when non-compliance with bargains is produced by ignorance of what the rules are rather than by incentives not to comply. And even the establishment of rules in statutory form—which makes them open to enforcement in the courts—is likely to be of most value when one or both of the parties have more incentive to seek remedies at law than to condone violation of the agreement. The production of rules without widely shared attitudes and beliefs that underpin them may have negative effects on substantive compliance.[14]

Accordingly, a second mechanism that can keep cheating in check is the presence of a culture—a common outlook and set of values—that underpins the formal rules or makes them unnecessary. And the idea of culture as a solution to compliance problems has been much canvassed in many fields, from the corporate-culture passion-for-excellence ideas of the 1980s (such as Peters and Waterman 1982), to related ideas about 'safety culture', 'compliance cultures', and other types of cultural solutions to cheating problems. Miller (2000), whose analysis of cheating between employer and employee has already been referred to, argues that 'professionalism' is a key mechanism for keeping cheating in check. and John Brehm and Scott Gates (1997) reach a similar conclusion in their analysis of shirking and sabotage. Indeed, Hugh Heclo and the late Aaron Wildavsky (1974) once declared that the mechanism that kept top British civil servants under control—true to the implicit PSB—was not formally enacted rules or oversight from ministers or parliament, but rather shared attitudes and beliefs, reinforced by continuous interaction and mutual rating within a small elite group in the centre of London, whose careers extended over thirty years or more.[15] The creation of a distinctive public service culture—by means like closed-career structures, location within a closed world (either in the capital city or by regular rotation among postings), recruitment from aliens or minorities without strong roots in majority cultures—has been historically common as an attempt to overcome the cheating problem in PSBs.

But culture considered as a solution to cheating problems is a bit like those handy instant management solutions that amount to saying 'if you can solve your problems, you can solve your problems.' Indeed, it often seems to be canvassed just at the point where immanent understandings about how things are done are starting to weaken as a regulatory mechanism. If there are multiple cultures rather than a single monoculture, views of what counts as

---

[14] A point made by one of our senior interviewees (UK19) as well as by numerous academic writers such as Levy and Spiller (1996), Brehm and Gates (1997), and O'Neill (2002).

[15] Finer (1950: 68) had made the same point long over twenty years earlier.

cheating are likely to vary and the force of culture in checking cheating may be accordingly weaker. And many of the features that have traditionally been created by structures designed to breed compliance with unwritten rules into the bone of public servants—namely social homogeneity, monasticism, unworldliness, and a scepticism with the nostrums of private business—are precisely those that have been most heavily criticized by reformers looking for more gung-ho, politically responsive, culturally diverse, and socially heterogeneous bureaucracies.

A third mechanism that can keep cheating in check, not fully separable from rules and culture, is the existence of incentives for compliance that help embed the PSB in some way. The parallel is with those mechanisms identified by anthropologists that eliminate social deviance other than by shared attitudes and beliefs *simpliciter*. Perhaps the best-known such mechanism, heavily borrowed by political scientists for theories of pluralist democracy after the Second World War, is the way that cross-cutting cleavages can limit conflict (see Mackenzie 1975), and a parallel with that mechanism may sometimes operate to reinforce PSBs, where career, family, or social lines cut across the public service and other parties to the bargain.

For example, where the political and bureaucratic elites are heavily intermarried, there are likely to be more built-in checks against cheating than in conditions where these elites are socially segregated. And if senior civil servants may go on to become politicians after—or in the middle of—working in the civil service, as many have traditionally done in countries like France or Japan, they may have an incentive to comply with conventions about the relationship of politicians and civil service in a way that does not apply when there is no such career path. We might expect such an incentive to be strongest in cases where politicians may find themselves back in the civil service after politics, as in France. Where such 'reinforcing' mechanisms operate less strongly on PSBs, we might expect such bargains to be more brittle and precarious, with little to back them up when strain and conflict starts to appear. Cases in point might include countries like the UK, where ties of that kind between the civil service and politicians have traditionally been weaker than in France, consociational bargains where the social groups that the public service is intended to bring together have no other cross-cutting links, or societies like the Soviet case discussed earlier, where the removal of the sort of heavy duty sanctions for cheating represented by millions of people in labour camps, leaves little behind to underpin the bargain.[16]

---

[16] Germany is perhaps an intermediate case between France and the UK, in that top bureaucrats seldom go into electoral politics, even though it is common for other types of civil servants (such as teachers) to do so.

Such mechanisms tend to be immanent and cannot be developed out of nothing. But at least they can help identify conditions in which PSBs are more or less likely to 'stick'. And indeed, a particularly testing case for devising cheat-proof PSBs is the particular form of agency bargain (focused on delivery of 'results') that was much advocated in the era of NPM and indeed for some formed the centrepiece of the NPM approach. In Chapter 9, we concentrate on that particular form of PSB, looking at how it fits into the general array of PSBs discussed earlier in this book, examining its particular features, and exploring the 'cheating' opportunities that it presents to the various parties involved.

8.7. SUMMARY AND CONCLUSION

Like everything else, PSBs are not 'for ever'. They rise and fall for various reasons. Sudden events may bring them down, they may become outworn as a result of longer-term changes in behaviour, or they may weaken or collapse as a result of cheating. This chapter has concentrated on the cheating problem, because cheating is perhaps the central issue in the analysis of PSBs.

We have shown that cheating problems are potentially pervasive. The conditions needed to sustain PSBs can be quite demanding. As the quotations in our epigraphs remind us, making a PSB cheat-proof is not just a matter of spelling out the rules, but requires the presence of particular social conditions that cannot be readily engineered at will.

The same thing goes for the remaking of PSBs, which has been the ambition of the much-discussed NPM reform approach in the recent past, and we turn to such attempts to reshape PSBs in Chapter 9. The declared aim has been to get away from 'grubby politics' undermining the performance capacity that effective professional management can bring to public service. The recipe for a new PSB along these lines has tended to prescribe a clearer division of responsibilities between managers and politicians, with managers and politicians agreeing to abide by a set of arrangements about target-setting and transparency. But as we will see in Chapter 9, that implied NPM bargain is far from cheat-proof or problem-free.

9

Public Service Managerialism and Public Service Bargains: Control, Blame Avoidance, and Cheating

Last week's salad.

(How one senior UK public servant, formerly an agency enthusiast and executive agency CEO, described the UK's executive agency approach in an interview in 2003 (UK 3))

9.1. INTRODUCTION

As we have already noted, 'managerial' reforms in executive government systems have had so much academic attention over recent decades that a person would need to be a public administration Rip Van Winkle, asleep for at least twenty years, to have missed all the discussion of the so-called NPM.[1] The part of that discussion that matters for our analysis here is the implicit idea of a new kind of PSB that lay behind the doctrines advanced by the NPM reformers of the 1980s and 1990s.[2] The idea was that government could be improved by the development of a new form of agency bargain that gave at least some civil servants more of the sort of discretionary power to manage staff and budgets that private-sector managers have traditionally possessed. And the quid pro quo was that those civil servants would take direct responsibility for failure when things went wrong and submit to *ex post* controls in the form of measured performance targets and arm's-length monitoring (Thompson 1993).

---

[1] If there are any Rip Van Winkles among our readers, they might like to compare Barzelay (2001), Pollitt and Bouckaert (2004), and Suleiman (2003) as examples of rather different normative and analytic takes on NPM.

[2] And indeed their predecessors, such as those who led the movement for city-managers in the USA a century before.

That sort of bargain, the reformers claimed, would make for better government than existing kinds of PSBs, because such an arrangement would focus senior public servants more firmly on getting 'results' rather than following 'rules-based, process-driven' routines (Osborne and Gaebler 1992). Explicit targets and performance indicators agreed with politicians and legislators would help those managers prioritize and focus their activity rather like their private-sector counterparts, instead of finding themselves expected to do dozens of different things at once without any indication of their relative priority. And a managerial bargain conceived in such terms was itself often presented as a cure to the problem of 'cheating' by bureaucratic agents and elected politicians under other kinds of bargains in some of the forms we discussed in Chapter 8. In particular, explicit targets and performance agreements would produce clearer standards of failure and success, which would make more difficult the commonly observed public-sector 'blame games' in the form of mutual buck-passing and blame-shuffling among different office-holders over blurred areas of responsibility.

Indeed, in some ways the sort of 'new PSB' that the NPM advocates argued for could be considered a political dream ticket. Such a bargain could benefit blame-averse elected politicians by enabling them to shift the responsibility for delivery failures onto civil servants, and at the same time to gain political points from a much-publicized posture of championing better management of public services. Assuming the role of 'target-setter' offers those politicians a golden opportunity to use managers as political 'lightning rods' (Ellis 1994), to be fired and/or dragged blinking into the media spotlight to take the rap for blunders and poor performance, when the going gets tough over the nitty-gritty of policy delivery.

But such a bargain could potentially benefit public service managers too, by enabling them to gain more status, recognition, and discretionary power, and to get away from the 'double-bind' approach traditionally used by those at the centre of government to control those down the line. The double-bind approach, classically expounded by Andrew Dunsire (1978), takes the form of unacknowledged contradictory objectives, such as clearing cases rapidly to limit waiting time and accurate processing to limit errors. Those contradictory objectives are permanently held in tension without open discussion of the trade-offs among them, with the balance adjusted according to the political dictates of the moment. Since the double-bind approach makes it possible to condemn public service managers whatever they do, a new bargain built around clear targets for service delivery might seem to offer a better deal for those managers, if it meant more transparency, more coherent oversight, and less micro-management from the centre.

Nor are blame-averse politicians and managers fed up with schizophrenic control by politicians, the only players who could, in principle, benefit from a new bargain along those lines. Public service users could benefit, not just from the better-managed public services that were expected to result from this new PSB, but also from clearer specification of what service standards were being aimed for, in the form of the targets set for managers. For central agency staff such as budget overseers, a new approach based on a few key targets may seem to offer the prospect of freeing themselves up from the detail (and the potential for blame) of approving specific management decisions, to concentrate on more strategic activity in setting and monitoring the targets.[3] And for lobbyists and political activists, the cardinal potential advantage of a new PSB based on transparent targets and performance agreements is that it pins down the elected politicians, not just the bureaucrats, to the pursuit of specific goals. Everyone, one might think, could win from such a new managerial bargain—to the point that it might seem a mystery as to why such a bargain had not been thought of years before.

In practice, of course, nothing is ever that new; life is never that simple; administrative reforms without losers are vanishingly rare; and not every country or government system presented both motive and opportunity for moving towards a new managerial bargain of that type, as we shall see later. Nevertheless, a major academic and consultancy industry has grown up around NPM, and the idea has gained its defenders and detractors, its assessors and reframers, its obituarists and chroniclers of all persuasions. The 'death' of NPM and its replacement by other at least equally ill-defined and all-encompassing notions—such as 'governance' and the 'third way'—has often been proclaimed. But despite the frequency with which the last rites have been said over it, the putative corpse has a uncanny habit of coming back to life for another round of books and conferences. It is not the business of this chapter, or this book, to go over that much-trodden ground in detail again. Rather, our aim in this chapter is to look at the idea of public-sector 'managerialism' from the angle of PSBs. Precisely, what sort of bargain does a 'managerial' approach to public service imply? What exactly are its entailments for reward, competency, and loyalty? And what are its implications for 'cheating' over PSBs, as discussed in Chapter 8?

In this chapter, we argue three things. First, we argue that the managerial vision of public service provision over recent decades links to a recurring vision of 'rational control' in government. Second, we examine the bargain that such a vision implies and argue that, though most of the NPM discussion

---

[3] Such an argument is central to Patrick Dunleavy's (1991) well-known bureau-shaping interpretation of the shift to public-service managerialism in the 1980s and 1990s.

has focused on only one side of the bargain—the changes expected in the behaviour of public servants—the managerial vision depends on a bargain or reciprocal exchange agreement restricting the behaviour of *both* elected politicians and public servants to make it work. Third and relatedly, we argue that any such bargain is extremely vulnerable to cheating—or at best 'creative compliance'—by the various parties. And such cheating may help to explain the paradox we noted in Chapter 1—that while governments and government-watchers talk endlessly about an apparently relentless drive to managerialism, the outcome tends to fall far short of the lofty rhetoric.

9.2. RATIONAL CONTROL OVER BUREAUCRACY AND THE MANAGERIAL VISION OF PUBLIC SERVICE

Each commentator has their own favourite interpretation of NPM, but most would agree that it is one of the many reform movements that aim to change the way that the organizations and individuals providing public services are controlled.[4] And the approach to control favoured by those who have a 'managerialist' vision of public service provision resembles the operation of a thermostat.[5] It means specifying targets or settings for public servants to meet in ways that are somewhat detached from all the messy operational details of the implementation process. Control that is exercised in this way is 'output-oriented' and involves specifying the desired outputs with some degree of precision, normally (but not necessarily) expressed in numbers. In that way, it is roughly analogous to setting a thermostat to a preferred temperature setting, as distinct from controlling inputs directly, for instance, by opening or closing windows or turning radiators on or off.

More precisely, this approach to control is like the way we use thermostats to control our heaters or fridges or air conditioners, because the mechanism that registers the desired outputs or outcomes is linked to 'negative feedback mechanisms'; in the jargon of cybernetics, the science of general control systems. The equivalent of the temperature settings on the thermostat are specifications of the sorts of policy outputs governments want public servants to deliver—what proportion of crimes they want to be cleared up, what proportion of school students they want to be able to achieve

---

[4] For different ways of conceiving control systems in public and other organizations see, e.g. Beer (1966), Beck Jørgensen and Larsen (1987), Hood (1998*b*).

[5] One of us has used this metaphor before in previous work; see Hood (2002*a*).

specified standards of numeracy or literacy at particular levels, what proportion of patients of a particular type they want to be treated within a particular time.

In this vision of control over bureaucracy, those who set the thermostat are normally expected to be the elected politicians, such as legislatures, ministers, or presidents. However, such settings could in principle be formally decided by the voters at large through processes of direct democracy, and even under representative democracy, those settings may be heavily influenced by mass public opinion, as in Christopher Wlezien's explicit model (1995) of public opinion as a 'policy thermostat' controlling executive government through the elected politicians. As with a thermostat, the policy settings thus selected need to be linked with more or less elaborate monitoring systems (like temperature-sensitive bimetallic strips on a real thermostat) that compare the actual state of the system with the settings selected. And as with a thermostat, there have to be negative feedback systems (like the valves or switches that control the input to heat exchanges on a real thermostat) to make managers bring their outputs into line with the policy settings that have been chosen, if their actual outputs do not correspond with those specified.

The metaphor of the thermostat to represent control over policy delivery in a democracy has its limits, in at least two ways. One is that there are good reasons for supposing that politicians or legislators will not normally be concerned with only one overriding objective for any given policy domain to the exclusion of all others, and in that sense, their problem is not exactly like that facing a person setting a thermostat for a preferred room temperature. We therefore have to imagine a more complex kind of thermostat in which there are multiple settings, not just for heat, but also for fuel mix or type of heat exchanger, for instance. Nor does the thermostat metaphor easily capture one of the distinctive (though far from novel) elements of control over public servants in the managerial era, notably through comparisons on league tables.[6] For that too, we would need to imagine a complicated kind of thermostat that compared the performance of each heating element or exchanger in a system relative to all the others.

However, the notion that control over public services should approximate to a 'thermostatic' process is a recurring feature of visions of more rational public management. In the NPM era, the notion that politicians should concentrate on deciding policy settings or targets to hold others accountable for on matters of delivery has been a drumbeat or leitmotif of many

---

[6] An idea that goes back at least to Jeremy Bentham's early nineteenth-century 'tabular-comparison' principle for public management, but has been much advocated and applied in the NPM era.

reformers. An early and much-discussed example was New Zealand's 'output contract' reforms of the late 1980s, which distinguished the 'outputs' for which managers were responsible from the 'outcomes' that ministers were responsible for (see Schick 1996). In the 1990s and 2000s, this sort of approach became more widespread with the development of more targets and performance indicators in several government systems.

Other examples of such developments include the 1993 US Government Performance and Results Act, the 1990s executive agency reforms in UK central government (with framework agreements and explicit performance indicators) and the later extension of targets across all of the governments in the UK since 1998, the development of performance indicators in the Netherlands, and the French budgetary law of 2004. The broad thrust of the 'thermostatic' approach to control was championed in an American public management best-seller of the early 1990s, David Osborne and Ted Gaebler's *Reinventing Government* (1992), which used the older metaphor of separating 'steering' from 'rowing' in government. And several judicious and long-established commentators on public service reforms have argued that this approach to control is the central feature of the 'managerial' reforms in the recent past, particularly in the Anglo-American countries. Cases in point include Philip Giddings' analysis (1994: 11) of the UK agency reforms of the 1990s, Donald Savoie's comparison (1995) of public service reforms in three countries in the 1980s, and Robert Behn's analysis (2001) of changes in performance accountability in the USA.

While the novelty of this approach was played up both by its advocates and by many of the NPM commentators, not everyone would share that perception. Indeed, three decades ago, Charles Sisson (1976: 255–60), an early and distinguished British 'managerialism sceptic', argued, 'The characteristic of the last few years is a growth of the *mythology* of management. There has been a deliberate and persistent propagation of the idea that management is a new conception... and an attempt to persuade people... that analytical procedures of a kind which have always held an important place at middle executive levels have now been introduced as a startling novelty from the top....'

The idea of steering public sector organizations by specifying output targets in the form of some *numéraire* in advance and holding managers to account for their performance relative to those targets *ex post* can also be found in the long history of attempts to produce 'rational' public expenditure control, by involving central agencies only in setting and monitoring output targets, but not in detailed oversight and authorization (see Wildavsky 1966, 1971; Parry, Hood, and James 1997: 404).

Similar ideas can be found in the theory and practice of public enterprise management, not only in the long history of quantitative target-setting in the former Soviet economies and in war-production systems like the British aircraft production regime in the Second World War (see Devons 1950) but also in the peacetime operation of mixed economies, particularly in the target-setting ideas developed in the French *Contrats du Plan* for public enterprises in the 1960s. Analogous ideas, too, can be found both in public utility regulation and in control systems in large business firms (see Thompson 1993). So while many of the underlying ideas and practices associated with the 'thermostat' approach to controlling public providers were far from new, those doctrines were skilfully repackaged and re-spun by public sector reformers in the 1980s and 1990s to appeal to a range of different constituencies within executive government, as was argued earlier.

9.3. THE PUBLIC SERVICE BARGAIN DIMENSION OF THE THERMOSTATIC CONTROL APPROACH

From the analytical perspective of this book, the key question is, what sort of PSB does such an approach to control imply or entail? Is it a go-anywhere approach that can be fitted onto any of the types of PSB we have discussed earlier in this book? Or does it amount to a unique hybrid of those types? Or neither?

The first possibility seems the least plausible. This thermostat approach to controlling public servants is hard to reconcile with the trustee form of PSB in any of its forms, because in most versions of the managerial approach, the targets or settings on the thermostat come from elected politicians, whereas the central element of the trustee bargain is that public servants, within some range at least, work for goals that are not set at will by the government or legislature of the day. That is why we categorized the mix of turkey-race rewards with judge-type loyalty as an apparently barred combination in Chapter 7. Only if we cast elected politicians in the role of a settlor of a trust could we reconcile the managerial-control model with a trustee bargain—but to do that is to remove the key difference between the trustee and the agency model. So it is not surprising that the greatest resistance to, or difficulties with, the managerial-control model seem to have come from states with a trustee-type PSB tradition, or from types of public servant who have a trustee-type conception of their PSB.

Accordingly, the thermostat approach to controlling public servants seems to imply an agency-type conception of PSB—that the role of public servants is to use managerial or other competencies to meet targets set by their principals. But evidently it does not exactly fit the sort of agency arrangement that we called 'directed agency bargains' (B2b), in which public servants respond to orders of the day from their principals. After all, as we noted earlier, a central feature of the thermostat approach is 'indirect steering' by elected politicians. That means that the sort of PSB needed for thermostat-type control is some variant of the 'delegated' form of agency-type bargain (B2a), in which principals set the goals but not on an orders-of-the-day basis. Even then, the complex type of delegated agency bargain (B2a1), where there are multiple principals (or multiple agents, or both) is likely to be more problematic for the thermostat approach to control, unless the various principals can easily agree on what the settings should be. So the thermostat approach to control that lies behind the 'managerialist' conception of the public service is a public management model compatible with only some of the PSBs that have been discussed in this book.

But if the 'thermostatic control' approach means adopting PSBs of the simple delegated agency type, as described in Chapter 3, such a move is likely to be more easily achievable from some PSB starting points than others. And if we look carefully at the PSB starting points from which different political systems entered the recent age of public management reform, we can see—in detective-story style—why some of those bargains created both motive and opportunity for substantial change, while others created neither and yet others one but not the other (see also Hood 1996).

In the first group are those where the pre-existing serial-loyalist bargain cramped politicians' style and where a compact political coalition could readily obtain the legislative power to change it. Australia and New Zealand are arguably the prime cases of that type, since in both of those cases, the Public Service Acts had been interpreted to give iron tenure for top public servants even when there was bad 'chemistry' between them and their political masters. In both cases, politicians took the chance to legislate that tenure away in the 1980s.

In the neither-motive-nor-opportunity class are cases like the USA, where elected politicians already had very strong control over public servants by the 1980s. After all, patronage appointments extended far lower down the federal bureaucracy than in most European states, and there was micro-management capacity in the hands of Congressional committees that was not matched by European legislatures (see Hood et al. 2004). But even if there had been strong political motivations for tightening political control, powers to change were divided and there was no common interest among different fractions of the political class.

In the motive-but-not opportunity class are semi-trustee PSB cases such as that of West Germany, where the status of the German civil service entrenched in the 1949 West German Basic Law made it much harder for politicians to embark on changes to the contractual terms of civil servants that had been made elsewhere; however, much they might have wished to do so, and forced them to take a more roundabout way to shape the civil service to their ends. In the final category, of opportunity but not motive, are cases such as that of the Japanese civil service during the long reign of the LDP up to 1993, in which politicians had the concentrated legislative power to effect changes in civil service status but had no motive for doing so, as long as the civil service fitted in smoothly to the LDP regime. And we might possibly put the Swedish case in the same category, insofar as a form of delegated agency bargain already existed in Sweden long before the current managerial era, even though other managerial features (particularly over reward) were added during that era.

In short, except in major political crisis and constitutional breakdown, it will be harder to move to simple delegated agency–type PSBs (B2a2) from a trustee-type PSB point of departure than from other agency-type bargains (with the possible exception of the complex delegated agency–type B2a1). Nor do all agency-type bargains seem to constitute points of departure from which it is equally easy to get to B2a2. Directed agency bargains of the personal-loyalist type (B2b2) tend to be deeply rooted in the party systems they are embedded in, because of the political patronage they involve. And complex delegated agency PSBs (B2a1) are likely to be rooted in jurisdictional complexities that no one group of politicians can readily change on their own.

As was illustrated in the examples from Australia and New Zealand given earlier, that leaves the serial loyalist-directed agency bargain (B2b1) as the most likely or normal point of departure for adoption of the B2a2 PSB that is assumed by the thermostat approach to control. Such a PSB might be adopted from other starting points in conditions of major systemic crisis, but the B2b1 type of bargain combines politician incentives to shift blame onto public servants for operational foul-ups with the ability to effect such changes from a single point, without upsetting deep-seated constitutional or quasi-constitutional arrangements or entrenched systems of patronage. That would explain why the 'managerial' approach to public service reform has so often been heavily associated with the 'Anglo-Saxon' countries. But it would also account for the exceptions to that rule—notably the move towards forms of the delegated agency bargain in political systems outside the 'Anglo-Saxon' cultural group, such as the Netherlands and some of the Scandinavian countries, and the lack of substantial movement towards a delegated agency bargain in the USA, because of the lack of motive and opportunity to move in that direction in that governmental system.

However, the PSB implied by the thermostatic-control approach to public sector managerialism is not just any old 'delegated agency' type. Generally, it seems to require a tricky mix of individualism with hierarchism or egalitarianism, for instance, in the combination of individualized targets and rewards with observance of collective rules about provision and sharing of information. And more specifically, it seems to require some special features associated with reward, competency, and loyalty—the dimensions of PSBs that we discussed in Part II. The managerial variant of the delegated agency type of PSB has a more obvious fit with the 'turkey race' form of reward bargain than with the *noblesse oblige* or 'escalator' form, though it may well be perceived as the 'lottery' form. Evidently, it fits more closely with the 'delivery' form of competency bargain than with the 'wonk' or 'sage' form discussed in Chapter 5, though it may interlink with 'boundary spanner' forms for some forms of management. And when it comes to the loyalty and responsibility dimension of PSBs, the managerial variant of delegated agency bargain evidently fits with the 'executive' form that we discussed in Chapter 6.

But the delegation in this case follows a special pattern. While elected politicians—legislators, ministers, or other elected officials—are expected to steer indirectly rather than directly through the settings they select for the policy 'thermostat', that indirect steering is expected to take a particular form. The expectation is that the targets—the settings on the thermostat—are transparently set and altered, precluding the traditional double-bind approach to controlling bureaucracies that was described earlier. The published targets are assumed to be the ones that really matter, rather than cosmetics or smokescreens to hide deeper but unacknowledged goals. While elements of *ex ante* authorization, changes in targets, or even wholesale suspension of indirect steering in an emergency are not precluded by the 'thermostat' approach, the implicit bargain is that there will not be continuous ad hoc or unacknowledged interventions by politicians (or their staffers) on points of detail. And if the implied assumption is that performance targets represent some kind of 'deal' between managers and politicians, there may well be an expectation on the part of the managers that the targets have to be explicitly accepted by both sides, rather than being unilaterally imposed without discussion.

The thermostat approach to control also implies a specific executive-type loyalty/responsibility bargain relating to the provision and use of performance information. Managers are obliged to cooperate with the monitoring regime that their principal sets up to gather information and assess their performance against targets, or against other players in a league table. Such information may be drawn from third parties or by 'unobtrusive' forms of observation, but managers themselves often have to provide some of it, like taxpayers obliged to furnish details about their income to the tax authorities, within some specified timescale and level of accuracy and detail. Over performance details at least, the bargain excludes a '5th Amendment' approach.

This aspect of the loyalty and responsibility bargain is also potentially problematic. Managers often expect there to be some limit to the scale and scope of performance information that can fairly be demanded from them, to leave them with enough time and resources for their 'real work'. What counts as 'honest reporting' on the part of managers may also be disputed and problematic. It is common to find reporting systems in which managers doctor or even make up the numbers they think the 'centre' wants to receive, in the belief that such licence will be helpful, for example, in the reporting of nuclear accidents in the former Soviet Union. And the information provision part of the bargain may also be problematic where the principal delegates the role of monitoring the managers to numerous monitoring agents, since the managers may expect the monitoring agents to coordinate their demands for information and not make contradictory demands, or ask for slightly different variations of information already provided to several other overseers. That is often a sore point in managerial bargains in practice.

Third, the thermostat approach to control implies a specific bargain about how both parties behave in seeking to achieve the targets. There has to be an understanding that managers will make an active effort to reach the targets, rather than ignoring them. There has to be an understanding about the bounds within which those active efforts are to take place—for instance, that the means chosen for reaching the targets will be lawful and that they will preclude espionage and deliberate sabotage of rivals' efforts. And there has to be an understanding that managers will take responsibility for the achievement of results relative to targets. That is, managers under such a bargain have to be able to gain credit when targets are reached, and they have to be willing to take the blame and run the associated career risks (e.g. over contract renewal, salary, and performance bonuses) when targets are missed.

In short, the 'thermostatic' approach to rational control over bureaucracy implies a PSB between senior public servants and elected politicians about their respective exposure to risk and blame, coupled with their responsibilities and rewards. In that bargain, managers accept career risk, personal blame, and obligations to provide performance information in exchange for some decision autonomy and—in most versions—a managerial level of pay and perks. Politicians for their part undertake to steer managers only by transparent and achievable preset objectives in exchange for avoidance of formal blame for operational failures. And managers in particular may interpret that PSB to have implications for the activity of other actors, notably auditors, central agencies, and evaluators. Those specific features of the PSB implied by the thermostatic vision of control over bureaucracy are far from unproblematic. Each of them opens up substantial scope for cheating, misunderstandings, and mutual recrimination among the parties, which we explore in Section 9.4. And they involve restrictions on the behaviour of elected politicians

9.4. CHEATING AND THE MANAGERIAL FORM OF AGENCY BARGAIN

We earlier described the sort of 'new PSB' envisaged by managerialist reformers as potentially attractive to several kinds of players. But the realization of that win-win-win outcome is far from easy in the face of motives and opportunities to cheat, unless some or all of the immanent mechanisms for reinforcing bargains that we discussed in Chapter 8 are at work. As we noted in Chapter 8, cheating over PSBs can be asymmetric or one-way (one party cheats, others stick to the deal) or two-way (when all of the parties are cheating at once). And in the case of the managerial form of PSB, the cheating can be directed at the target-setting process, the information-gathering process, the incentives or sanctions regime, or all three.

As we have already noted, politician 'principals' have a strong incentive to cheat on any such bargain by efforts to ensure that credit for positive outcomes flows upwards to them while blame for negative outcomes flows downwards to other public managers. It is, after all, normal for elected politicians to make 'good news' announcements in person while leaving it to their 'managers' to take responsibility for reporting the bad news (see Ellis 1994: 3, 156, and *passim*). But NPM reformers wanted to have an agency bargain in which public service managers had real delegation, and could expect to take both credit and blame, dependent on their individual performance.

Nor is it only elected politicians who have an incentive to cheat on the managerial form of the agency bargain. Public servants on the other side of the bargain may also find ways to cheat on the 'blame game', by declining to take the blame when the going gets tough and seeking to pass it back to politicians. After all, when they are liable to be sacked by politicians anyway, the managers have little to lose by claiming that their politician principals have 'cheated' in some way, notably by denying them the resources or authority to perform their managerial tasks, by backdoor interference or other forms of undermining their position (see Hood 2002*b*). That incentive might be reduced by some of the anti-cheating mechanisms discussed in

Chapter 8, notably shared outlook and beliefs or overlapping social or kin ties between the various parties. But it could be argued that if such mechanisms were powerful enough, there would be no need to adopt managerial-type bargains at all.

Now if both politician principals and bureaucratic agents have incentives to cheat on the blame game, there is a potential for a Prisoner's Dilemma-type dynamic between them, of a somewhat more specific type than we discussed in Chapter 8. We illustrate the problem in Table 9.1. In cell (1), both sides stick to the delegation bargain through thick and thin, with both blame and credit delegated to quasi-autonomous managers along with some autonomous decision space. But, as we have already noted, politician principals have a strong electoral incentive to move to cell (2) in an attempt to dodge the blame for bad outcomes while attracting the credit for good outcomes. And for their part, the managerial agents have an equal incentive to move to cell (3), taking credit when the good times roll but finding ways of passing blame back to politicians when major failures occur. So in the absence of anti-cheating mechanisms, attempts by both parties to the managerial PSB to follow 'fair-weather' credit/blame strategies will trigger off a chain of move and counter-move that is likely to lead to cell (4), which involves conflict, deadlock, and blame sharing instead of the blame shifting which is a powerful political incentive for politicians to accept a managerial form of agency bargain.

Table 9.1 sets out the problem in very general terms. But since the specific form of delegated agency PSB that is at the heart of NPM ideas requires three particular sets of agreements, each of those three sub-bargains yields a specific

Table 9.1 Cheating on delegated agency bargains

		Principal	
		Delegate blame and credit	Delegate blame but not credit
Agent	Accept blame and credit	(1) **Symmetrical delegation** Outcome for principal: blame shift for negative outcomes, credit slippage for positive outcomes	(2) **Asymmetrical delegation 1** Outcome for principal: blame shift for negative outcomes, but no credit slippage for positive outcomes
	Accept credit but not blame	(3) **Asymmetrical delegation 2** Outcome for principal: credit slippage for positive outcomes, but reverse blame shift for negative outcomes	(4) **Incompatible delegation** Outcome for principal: conflict and deadlock over credit and especially blame, leading to probable blame sharing

type of cheating possibility. The first of those three deals, as we have seen, is that politicians agree to give up, and managers agree to accept discretion within a defined 'decision space', with politicians concentrating on arm's-length steering by setting general targets for managers to aim at. The second is that politicians impose, and managers agree to cooperate with, an information-gathering regime to register performance against agreed targets. The third is that success so measured is rewarded, and failure is punished through negative feedback mechanisms. Beguilingly rational as those three linked set of agreements may seem, each is vulnerable to cheating behaviour by one or both parties, and if any one of them succumbs to such cheating to any appreciable degree, the intended 'dream ticket' outcomes will not be realized, as shown in Table 9.2.

The implication that politicians will agree to concentrate on indirect steering by transparent output targets is vulnerable to politician cheating in at least three ways. One is unacknowledged or backdoor interference in operational details, a form of politician behaviour that is commonly observed in public organizations that formally operate on an arm's-length basis (see Christensen 1993; Hood 2000, 2001). Another, perhaps a variant of the first, is covert 'double bind' control by politicians and others, in which the supposedly transparent official targets turn out not to be the real standards by which agents are judged (see Behn 2001). A third is

Table 9.2 Specific aspects of managerial delegated agency bargains: some cheating opportunities

Specific sub-bargain or agreement	Politician cheating opportunity	Managers cheating opportunity
Agreement by politicians to avoid hands-on direction and concentrate on indirect steering by performance standards	Covert direct steering. Covert double-bind control (with covert goals or process rules contrasting with overt output targets)	Collusion with phoney performance standards
Agreement by politicians to impose and managers to cooperate with information gathering for performance monitoring	Creation of monitoring regimes with compliance demands that crowd out managers' discretionary decision space	Failure to cooperate with information gathering regime, e.g. by fabrication of performance data or creative categorization
Agreement by politicians and managers for success on published output targets to be rewarded and failure to be punished	Ignoring formal performance data or failure to develop transparent reward and sanctions regimes	Direct lobbying of politicians to short-circuit formal feedback mechanisms

politician cheating on the 'decision space' part of the bargain by fostering a multiplication of process rules and setting up overseers and progress chasers that reduce public managers' discretion to vanishing point by the compliance demands they generate (see Hood et al. 1999). In such circumstances, freedom to manage in government can approximate to the hoary old joke about freedom in Mussolini's Italy—whatever is not forbidden is compulsory.[7]

The second detailed agreement that is required by the delegated agency bargain—that politicians agree to impose, and managers to abide by, transparent information-gathering arrangements—is also highly vulnerable to cheating on both sides. Non-compliance and creative compliance by managers with such arrangements is familiar in the literature on managerial behaviour in planned economies, and analogous 'first-order' responses by bureaucracies to freedom of information and other transparency requirements have also been frequently observed (see Zifcak 1994; Hood and Rothstein 2001; Roberts 2005). When managers choose to game the system— either by outright data fabrication, as has happened in some UK health service cases, or by creative approaches to categorization of their activity—dramatic performance improvements can be registered on paper that somehow fail to match what is happening on the ground.

Such forms of managerial gaming have been much documented by historians of the Soviet Union (see, e.g. Dobb 1970; Berliner 1988). And similar responses can be found in the target regimes developed for public service management in the Western countries just as the Soviet targets system was collapsing. For instance, in response to targeting and performance regimes in the National Health Service in England in the early 2000s, managers cheated by fudging the performance data in several ways. One was marginal categorization calls that favoured managers, for instance, in classifying ambulance response times of between eight and nine minutes as within eight minutes. Another took the form of quantum recategorization, for instance, in putting beds into hospital hallways in order to meet a target that no patient ought to wait on a 'trolley' in Accident and Emergency departments for more than four hours before being admitted to a 'bed' (in effect, this ruse amounts to taking the wheels off a trolley (gurney) and calling it a bed). A third took the form of even more creative cheating, for instance, in seeking to meet a target that no patient ought to wait more than

---

[7] In addition, politicians and central overseers may cheat on what Richard Elmore (2000: 21) calls the reciprocity principle of accountability, namely that performance demands from the centre should be matched by provisions of capacity to meet such demands.

twelve months for a hospital admission by writing to patients on a waiting list to ask them when they were planning to take their vacations. When that information was obtained, the hospital concerned wrote back offering patients a date for their operation during the time that they had said they would be away (and if they declined the offer, they did not appear in the waiting list figures) (see Bevan and Hood, forthcoming). Such examples of hitting the target but missing the point would do credit to even the wiliest Soviet enterprise manager in the Gosplan[8] era, but they do not contribute to the 'dream ticket' outcome hoped for by NPM advocates.

The third detailed agreement that makes up the managerial form of delegated agency bargain—that success will be rewarded and failure punished—is also vulnerable to at least three common forms of cheating. The agents can cheat by bypassing the performance-recording regime and lobbying politicians directly over constituency interests, as Christopher Foster (1992) claims commonly occurred in the era of nationalized railways in the UK. Politicians can cheat by failing to reward or punish public managers according to their performance on published targets. They may simply ignore formal performance information (as has been commonly observed in the USA and UK over the Government Performance and Results Act (GPRA) and executive agency regimes (see Curristine 2002). They may blame their agents for inefficiencies created by their own activity (cf. Miller 2000: 313) or use covert political criteria rather than the published targets for rewarding or punishing their agents (see Maor 1999).

Nor can such forms of cheating be dismissed as a purely theoretical possibility. As was suggested earlier, there is plenty of historical and empirical evidence of such behaviour, both from the height of the public trading enterprise era of the mid-twentieth century, and from the later output-oriented late-twentieth century NPM vision of how to operate public services. Indeed, given the possible antidotes to cheating that were discussed earlier, such a bargain seems only likely to function without cheating in a subset of all politico-administrative cultures that is at least as atypical in the twenty-first century as was the military-bureaucratic Prussian administrative culture that Max Weber held to be the epitome of 'modern bureaucracy' a hundred years ago.

Indeed, the sharply limited supply of such cultures may account for the paradox of why, in spite of all the much-discussed rhetoric of 'managerialism' in public services over the past quarter of a century, real delegation of decision space to managers operating within a transparent performance

---

[8] The central planning organ of the Soviet state.

regime remains remarkably small, even in the Anglo-Saxon countries that are commonly said to have been the exemplars of that approach in the recent past (Hood 2000). Moreover, in the rare cases where politicians and their agents do not cheat on the demanding conditions of the bargain, managers may be led to act in a highly defensive way to avoid blame—concentrating on achieving audit-proof procedural correctness and tightly controlling potentially damaging information rather than bold and open initiatives (Hood 2002b). And that is, of course, exactly the opposite of what managerial regimes were ostensibly designed to achieve.

9.5. CONCLUSION

To judge by the outputs of the 'NPM industry', the unwary observer might conclude that something approximating the managerial PSB associated with thermostatic-type controls was becoming ever more widely established in modern public services. But that is just the sort of fallacy that might lead the same kind of observer, noticing the pervasive discussion and advertisement of diet and exercise programmes across all of the media in the West, to conclude that the populations of those countries must be becoming ever more lean and fit. In this chapter, we have argued that the thermostatic, arm's-length approach to controlling bureaucracies that lies at the heart of the vision of good governance espoused by contemporary 'managerialist' reformers, is not compatible with all types of PSBs discussed in this book, and indeed can be expected to develop only out of particular 'agency' types of PSB. We have argued that there was more than one type of 'old public management' PSB, not a single one, and the prospects of reaching the simple delegated agency bargain associated with the managerial recipe are much stronger from some starting points than from others.

Even when such a bargain does emerge, it is highly vulnerable to cheating by one or both of the major affected parties. The pervasive discussion of managerialism in contemporary executive government contains surprisingly little discussion of cheating or creative compliance on the part of the various players. The lack of discussion is curious given the relatively recent historical experience of such behaviour by enterprise managers in Soviet type economies and Braguinsky and Yavlinsky's (2000:28) ironic argument, discussed in the previous chapter, that lack of security for such managers caused by the terror regime of labour camps, was 'the condition sina qua non for the efficient functioning of the planned economy, that is for its functioning in accordance with the guidelines set forward by the planning authorities. And indeed, looking at public-sector managerialism from a PSB angle reveals a remarkably large range of cheating opportunities for those players, and that in turn helps us identify the demanding conditions needed to sustain the kind of bargain that 'managerialism' represents. Our analysis does not necessarily mean that the managerial type of delegated agency bargain is *peculiarly* prone to cheating compared with other types of PSB. After all, in Chapter 8, we identified forms of cheating that go with all the major types of bargain discussed in this book. But the analysis does suggest that there is nothing that makes the managerial variant of delegated agency PSB cheat-proof in the way that some of its advocates seem to have assumed. And as we have suggested earlier, the cheating problem may explain the paradox of how little, rather than how much, full-blown managerialism is observable even in the Anglo-Saxon countries in the 'NPM' era. Instead of being the global phenomenon that many have claimed (Aucoin 1990; Osborne and Gaebler 1992; OECD 1995) this type of bargain is likely to emerge and 'stick' only in some traditions and cultures, even if the 'talk' of managerialism goes far beyond that.

10

Conclusion

The [outcome]...was...dependent, not only on a very long process of change but also on some quite peculiar conditions and...a highly complicated bargain.

(Schaffer 1973: 252)

He [departmental head] admitted telling her [agency chief executive] the right colour for a public servant was grey and 'buying from a chain store is always the safer option...the Government did not want to see flashy displays of commercial-type managerialism'.

(*New Zealand Herald*, 5 July 2001)

Chapter 7 brought together the analysis of Parts I and II of the book, so this concluding chapter can be short. It is divided into three sections. Section 10.1 is a reprise. It summarizes what we have learned from our analysis of PSBs in this book, focusing particularly on the less obvious observations that come out of the analysis. Section 10.2 overlaps with Section 10.1, and briefly reflects on what the PSB analysis we have developed in this book can add to the prevailing literatures in public management, executive government, and administrative reform. Section 10.3, going beyond the analysis of our earlier chapters, discusses possible futures for PSBs.

10.1. WHAT WE LEARNED: PREDICTABLE OR SURPRISING?

In this book, we have shown that the idea of a PSB, conceived as an informal or semi-formal institution, can be used to analyse how bureaucracies fit into their political environment, particularly at the upper level. We have used this lens to look at differences over time, differences among countries, and differences among parts of the public service within countries. Parts I and II showed that PSBs do not come in any one single form, either for traditional or contemporary types of government. Part II drew heavily on interviews in Germany and Britain to bring out some of the variety and dimensionality of those bargains from the experience and viewpoint of public servants, and we explored the scope and apparent limits for mixing and matching different types of bargain over reward, competency, and loyalty. Part III concentrated on issues of change, cheating, and strategic behaviour. We began the book with observations made a century or so ago by Sir Harold Nicolson and Anton Graf Monts about the breakdown of the 'old diplomatic bargain' of pre-First World War Europe, and in Chapter 8, we identified some of the ways in which PSBs break down and some of the social mechanisms that sustain them. And in Chapter 9, we applied that analysis to one of the most discussed and controversial topics of contemporary bureaucracy, namely the idea of developing a 'managerial' public service. We explored the kind of PSB that is implied by that analysis and looked at the potential for 'cheating' that such a PSB creates.

Using the PSB lens has enabled us to see at least three things that we might not otherwise have been able to bring out. This first is that the idea of a PSB is a concept that turns out to 'travel' surprisingly well. Although it originated in the now rather obscure work of some talented 1960s British administrative historians, as we showed in Chapter 1, it is an idea that seems to be applicable across different state traditions and administrative cultures, once we accept that such bargains can take forms very different from those identified by Schaffer and Parris. The idea of a PSB resonated as readily with our German interviewees as with the British ones, even though the German state and bureaucratic tradition is often said to be very different from that of Whitehall and Westminster. As we showed in Part II, the ways those interviewees described their PSB worlds in terms of reward, competency, and loyalty seemed to link up to some extent with the worldviews identified by grid-group cultural theory, suggesting that PSBs and what counts as cheating on such bargains can be linked with cultural variety. But the general point is that those German interviewees were quick to seize on the notion of a PSB to describe a reciprocal relationship between *Staatsherr* and *Staatsdiener*, and to describe how they thought their positions in the state were changing. And though the German and British cases are the ones we have examined in detail in this book, the other examples we have mentioned in less detail suggests that the idea is capable of travelling more widely.

Secondly, and relatedly, Part III of this book showed there is rich scope for analysis of cheating and strategic behaviour around PSBs. The variety of types of PSBs is matched by an equivalent variety of types of cheating, and who sees what as cheating is variable too. Putting a cheating perspective to work in PSB analysis can help us to understand several things. One, as we showed in Chapter 8, is why PSBs break down through cheating, but also what the mechanisms are that prevent such breakdown, given that such bargains often prove surprisingly resilient. The other, as we showed in Chapter 9, is why ultra-managerialism in public services tends to be the exception rather than the rule, in spite of all the hype and endless discussion about a shift to 'managerialism' in public services that we discussed in Chapter 1. The opportunities for 'cheating' that a managerial-style PSB gives rise to are starting to be analysed, but up now until, most commentators on 'NPM-type' reforms have preferred to moralize in a general way about the presumed virtues or vices of copying business practice, or to speculate about the broader ideologies that drive such changes. That approach can blind us to the curious gap between commonly asserted aspirations to full-blown managerialism in public management and the relatively small extent to which the public-managerial Prometheus has actually been unbound, even in what are often said to be the NPM 'hot spots'. A cheating perspective on PSBs can help bring out that apparent disconnect between aspirations, received wisdom, and practice. Perhaps the 'managerial' delegated agency bargains of the contemporary age will prove to be as fragile as the 'jester' bargains were in earlier times and places (though there was probably never a 'jester boom' comparable to the boom in managerialism in contemporary government reform efforts).

Thirdly, PSBs are phenomena that can be understood at varying levels of detail and aggregation. We began by drawing some fairly coarse-grained distinctions in the branching-tree analysis of Part I of this book. However, the further down we delve, the more nuanced are the understandings (or misunderstandings) that emerge, as in the story of the ex-ambassadors' liquor allowance deal that figured in the epigraph to Chapter 4, or the subtle (and contested) understandings about dress codes highlighted in our second epigraph to this chapter. Other examples we have noted include the contested expectation in the German foreign service that senior staff would have obituaries in the departmental newsletter, even if they had a Nazi past (Chapter 6), or the long-standing unwritten understanding in the British case that up to seven years' service would be added to pension entitlements for senior civil servants for whom it was convenient to retire (or more usually, be retired) after their early fifties. When we probe the notion of PSBs down to these kinds of levels, we enter into a world of convention and subtle understandings, and the nature of the deals can rarely be read off any formal concordat, even in the most 'legalistic' state traditions. Often they turn out like those rules whose existence you only discover when you have broken them, as Tony Blair's government discovered during and after the 2003 Iraq war, when it was said to have broken a strongly felt but unwritten understanding that intelligence staff worked with a degree of autonomy in the advice they provided to government (Hutton 2004).

10.2. HOW A PUBLIC SERVICE BARGAIN PERSPECTIVE CAN REFINE AND MODIFY RECEIVED APPROACHES TO THE ANALYSIS OF EXECUTIVE GOVERNMENT

It would be ridiculous to claim that an understanding of PSBs can solve all the puzzles that students of executive government have been struggling to resolve for hundreds of years. Too many neologisms and minor conceptual tweaks in this field are presented as if they could make water run uphill or solve all the world's problems. But we do claim that the PSB perspective developed in this book, if used with appropriate care and sensitivity, can help to refine, modify, and improve several received approaches to the analysis of modern executive government and its reform. We touched on some of those approaches in Chapter 1, and here briefly pick out three kinds of analysis to which a PSB approach can potentially contribute.

10.2.1. Developing Established Comparative Approaches

First, a PSB perspective can fruitfully enhance existing comparative analysis of administrative reform. One very well-known, much-cited, and deservedly influential contemporary example of such analysis is Christopher Pollitt and Geert Bouckaert's account (2004) of 'four reform types' in cross-national analysis of public management reforms over two decades or so. What a PSB perspective can add to that type of analysis is a more economical way of describing past and present public management arrangements as exchange relationships (sometimes of a precarious kind), a way of describing the variety that exists within any national public service system, traditional or contemporary, and a way of looking at change, stasis, and 'barred combinations' from the perspective of the various parties to the PSB, following the kind of analysis we developed in Chapters 7, 8, and 9.

Another fairly well-known example of comparative analysis of administrative reform is Michael Barzelay's analysis of what he calls the 'benchmark' cases of Australia, New Zealand and the UK (Barzelay 2001, 2003). Barzelay's study offers a valuable comparative analysis of the similarities in what he calls the 'process dynamics' involved in those reforms, but a PSB perspective can also be fruitfully added to this kind of analysis. For instance, it can help us identify countervailing trends in public service relationships (such as the tendency, discussed in Chapter 6, to formalize and extend the 'judge-like' features of the Whitehall loyalty bargain during the *soi-disant* age of managerialism). And it can prompt us to examine the strategic-behaviour aspects of PSBs in a way that can explain some of the unintended effects of new managerial arrangements, as we showed in Chapter 9.

A further and probably better-known comparative analysis of public bureaucracy and administrative reform is offered by the comparative studies conducted by Joel Aberbach, Robert Putnam, Bert Rockman, and their colleagues in the 1970s and 1980s.[1] These studies divided bureaucrats in different countries into 'types', ranging from what they call 'classical' bureaucrats to more 'political' types, and pointed—not too surprisingly, perhaps—to a growth in the more 'political' types. In their later work, they focused on what they call 'Image IV' bureaucrats—those with strong links to both the political and administrative worlds—and pointed to the development of hybrids with particular party or personal political loyalties. This kind of analysis is very close to our PSB perspective, but the PSB perspective can arguably help take it a little further. For example, if we widen the focus beyond the small group of departmental elites and politicians that Aberbach and his colleagues concentrated on, we start to notice some of the possible counter-developments that swim against the apparently inexorable tide to 'politicality' identified in their analysis, for instance, in the form of independent economic regulators and sleaze-busters. Similarly, we can use the PSB perspective to link Aberbach et al.'s empirically observed types (originally drawn from the development of the US federal bureaucracy) with a strategic-action perspective that embraces gaming and cheating in a way that is not covered in their analysis.

10.2.2. Probing Beyond First-Approximation Analysis in Comparative Bureaucracy

Secondly, and relatedly, this type of analysis helps us to probe beyond first-approximation accounts of the differences and similarities among public service systems. For example, as we showed in Chapters 6 and 7, it can help us refine Christoph Knill's well-known distinction (1999, 2001) between instrumental and autonomous bureaucracies. That idea, building on a tradition of analysis comparing 'weak' and 'strong' states and 'classic' and 'civic culture' bureaucracies, is an important one, and as we said in Chapter 1, it is one of the ideas that led us to embark on our exploration of PSBs. But our analysis shows that Knill's beguilingly simple distinction can be no more than a first approximation, for two reasons.

---

[1] See Aberbach and Rockman (1988 and 2000), Aberbach et al. (1981), Campbell (1988).

Firstly, as we showed in Chapter 6, even the traditional Schafferian-type PSB in the UK was far from a purely 'instrumental' or 'agency' affair, in a number of quite significant ways. Further more, Knill has not fully followed the logic of his own analysis. In common with some earlier observers (notably Mayntz 1985), he notes the role of the political civil service, most of whom come from the 'technical' parts of the bureaucracy and are drawn into a bargain that is significantly different in terms of rewards, competency, and loyalty to the departmental leadership. But the implication of this insight, not followed up by Knill, is to understand the German federal bureaucracy as comprising multiple bargains, not a single one—including a powerful and growing group of federal bureaucrats whose 'bargain' is much less trustee-type and much more agency-type (indeed, arguably far more agency-type than that of the traditional Whitehall mandarins) than Knill's broad-brush picture of the German system suggests. And if there is indeed a multiple bargain of that type, Knill's explanation of the difference in the extent of reforms between the UK and Germany itself becomes more questionable.

Indeed, as we saw in Part III, some of the patterns in reward, competency, and loyalty bargains that emerged from our interviews in Germany and Britain seemed to show more than a passing resemblance to the worldviews identified in grid-group cultural theory, and it may well be that multiplicity of bargains within a single state may itself reflect the multiplicity and interplay of cultures that grid-group analysts expect to find within any complex society, rather than a single and unchanging culture. The issues that we discussed in Chapter 7 over the limits of mixing and matching different reward, competency, and reward bargains—for instance turkey-race rewards with judge-type loyalty—also turn on the possibility of mixing up distinct views of the public service world. PSBs, like cultural worldviews, seem to consist of multiple opposed views in dynamic tension, rather than a single dominant view, and the one is probably linked to the other.

10.2.3. Putting Principals and Agents in Perspective

Thirdly, as we briefly noted in Chapter 1 and explored further in Chapters 3 and 8, PSB analysis can refine and contribute to the now ubiquitous 'principal–agent' analysis of relationships between politicians and bureaucracies. That approach, as we noted at the outset, originated in its modern form in the theory of the firm in the 1960s and swiftly travelled into the world of public bureaucracy. Indeed, it has penetrated almost every other part of social science as well. Using a PSB perspective by no means requires us to abandon the sharp analytic tools of principal–agent analysis and the distinctive rigour that approach can bring to the study of strategic relationships among those parties. But differentiating trustee- and agency-type bargains can contribute to that vein of analysis in at least three ways. It can show how specific the 'agency' view of PSBs is, as compared with long-standing alternatives to which legal analogies can also be applied, notably the older Lockean analogy of government as a trust that we discussed in Chapter 2.

Further, a PSB approach can develop principal-agent analysis by helping identify some of the different sets of formal and informal 'rules of the game' within which cheating and strategic behaviour by public servants and other parties can take place. As we have shown, what counts as 'cheating' by one or more of the parties varies from one PSB to another. Cheating opportunities are not the same in all PSBs, as we showed in Chapter 8. And the development of PSBs—dependent (as our first epigraph argues) on long processes of change, 'peculiar conditions' and 'highly complicated' understandings—merit careful modelling of a kind that principal–agent analysis has not performed up to now.

Finally, and relatedly, without seeking to deny the importance of strategic and 'rational' action by the parties involved, which is the central feature of conventional principal–agent analysis in modern political economy, a PSB perspective enables us to explore the relationship between elected politicians and public servants in more dimensions than is allowed for by those analyses that aim to reduce that relationship to the legislative constraints on administrative action measured by the number of words in civil service statutes or constitutional provisions (Huber and Shipan 2002). Such analyses may be interesting, but as we showed at the outset of this book in Table 1.1, the volume and nature of those constitutional and legislative instruments seems to be only weakly related to such key features of political control as the dismissability of top public servants. Indeed, at the time of writing, a change of one word (from 'advise' to 'assist' in a 2005 Order in Council specifying the role of special advisers in the UK government)[2] was said to signify a major extension of political control over the bureaucracy in a way that would not be captured by Huber and Shipan's method of counting the number of words in a legal instrument to ascertain the strength of political control, but which lie at the heart of the relationship between political principals and agents.

---

[2] See http://www.cabinetoffice.gov.uk/propriety_and_ethics/publications/pdf/code_conduct_special_advisers.pdf (last accessed 27 July 2005).

10.3. THE FUTURE OF PUBLIC SERVICE BARGAINS

Our analysis of PSBs in this book has largely been concerned with the past and the present. But it is perhaps appropriate to conclude with some reflections on the future? We do not pretend to have Apollo's gift. Anyone trying to predict the future must be all too aware of the risk of repeating the kind of misjudgements shown by Irving Fisher, the unfortunate Yale economics professor who declared on the eve of the Great Crash of 1929 that stock prices would remain at a permanently high level.[3] But at least we can identify some possible alternative scenarios for the future of PSBs and consider the kind of conditions that would be needed to sustain them or bring them about. Accordingly, we consider four possible ways that PSBs might develop in the future. We call them 'stasis', 'convergence', 'divergence', and 'complication'.

10.3.1. Stasis: The Past as the Future

By 'stasis', we mean a future that closely resembles the past. If the future were to be like that, the NPM industry will continue to produce hype about public service reform, but underlying PSBs will continue to be varied and deeply rooted and will not change much in spite of all the ballyhoo. Such an outcome would go against the explicit or implicit expectations of some of the 'doomsters' that we referred to in Chapter 1, who see traditional PSBs, particularly of the Whitehall variety, as *in articulo mortis*. It would also surprise all those (normally of a more optimistic persuasion than the doomsters) who see a global march towards a new kind of public management, based on a delegated agency bargain that gives public managers more freedom to manage than in the putative bad old days of 'rules-based, process-driven' government.

Nevertheless, those who seek to look into the future should never write off stasis too hastily.[4] The past is often the best predictor of the future, especially for bureaucratic systems, which are frequently heavily embedded in political and wider social systems, and where the underlying dynamics often survive attempts at organizational rearrangement, as with the peculiar trustee bargain involving the European Commission, which has withstood various proposals to turn the Commission into some sort of agency-type civil service. The past

---

[3] Or perhaps slightly less spectacularly by Rudi Dornbusch of MIT, who declared in 1998, shortly before the dot.com crash of 2000, that 'this expansion will run forever' (see *Wall Street Journal*, 30 July 1998)

[4] As would be predicted by arguments focusing on 'path dependence' (see Pierson 2000; Arthur 1994; David 1985).

may involve more variety of practice than monochrome portrayals of the traditional world allow for, as we suggested in the discussion of the Whitehall loyalty bargain in Chapter 6 (see also Walker 2005).

Moreover, a few well-publicized upsets and deviations from a traditional pattern do not necessarily mean that a PSB will end up upside down in the ditch. Those upsets and deviations may instead lead to self-correction and negative feedback, as happened in New Zealand after the heady days of the managerial reforms of the 1980s. Several of the Whitehall people we interviewed argued in that vein, contrary to the end-of-era doomwatch predictions about the Schafferian bargain. Indeed, in just the opposite vein to some of the arrow-theory doomsters, some of the strongest critics of public service reforms in Whitehall argue that change tends to be superficial, taking the form of short-lived initiatives that are briefly pushed from the centre by a succession of attention-seeking careerists, but that never last long enough or gain enough real 'buy-in' to be properly followed through. Any such pattern of reform allows systems to revert to type as soon as pressure from the top is relaxed and it means that apparently radical attempts to change often get translated into a form that preserves the existing system. Many of our interviewees gave us graphic examples of those mechanisms at work.[5]

Nevertheless, the conditions for total stasis are demanding. After all, social systems can self-destruct as well as self-correct, and, as we have seen, PSBs can be self-disequilibrating through cheating and other mechanisms, as well as self-reinforcing. The pressures on at least some components of PSBs, even in states as legalistic and incrementalist in their traditional policy styles as Germany, are hard to dismiss as just the figments of fevered academic imaginations. And as we showed in Chapter 7, the PSBs of both Germany and the UK changed more in the twentieth century than the simple NPM view of history as an undifferentiated rules-based traditional form of public administration would allow for.

10.3.2. Convergence and Divergence: Closer Together or Further Apart?

If the future of PSBs is not to be simply a repeat of the past, it might take the form of convergence or divergence—bargains becoming more similar than they were in the past, or conversely becoming more different. The case for

---

[5] For instance, in our analysis of competency as a dimension of PSBs in Germany and the UK in the 1990s, we found a good deal of dynamic conservatism and even self-referentiality in the adoption of new and supposedly system-changing competency frameworks (see Hood and Lodge 2004, 2005).

convergence cannot be written off lightly either. For 'managerialists', the sort of bargain we explored in Chapter 9, in which elected politicians set the goals and professional managers work to deliver them within an agreement that gives those managers an autonomous decision space to exercise their skill and add public value, is a potentially go-anywhere 'best practice' recipe for better public service that deserves to drive out inferior alternative forms of PSB. And from a more *realpolitik* perspective, the similar pressures of modern professional politics, for instance, in the form of blame-avoidance imperatives on the part of politicians exposed to the media spotlight, might also lead to a more convergent effect on PSBs. After all, societies across the world now use common technologies and even common providers for many parts of their public services, such as payroll, waste disposal, power generation,[6] so why should the underlying bargains of the people involved in those services not also become more common?

However, those two visions of convergence are by no means the same. The optimistic high-minded managerial-revolution vision suggests a future of delegated agency bargains, while the more *realpolitik* vision might suggest a future of the personal-loyalist type of directed agency bargains rather than the delegated form implicit in the managerial form of thermostatic control.[7] And even if the doctrinal claims of those supporting a managerial form of PSB are well-founded, the cheating problems that beset the managerialist thermostatic-control bargain may prevent it from sweeping the world except on paper. That may account for why one of our UK interviewees, once a passionate advocate of that type of bargain, described it to us as 'last week's salad', as noted in the epigraph to Chapter 9. And there is no obvious reason why expectations of convergence over PSBs today should be more plausible than the unfulfilled expectations of a century ago of convergence over bureaucratic forms (see Silberman 1993: x).

Accordingly, divergence might be considered as a third possible future for PSBs. After all, divergence commonly happens in social systems. Empires can break up and the parts go their different ways. Originally unified institutions or movements can fragment into different sects or denominations. Indeed, Peter

---

[6] More than a decade ago, Patrick Dunleavy (1994) predicted the globalization of many kinds of public service production (into private corporations operating outsourced services in that case), and that prediction has proved accurate, with many of those trends evident across a range of public services.

[7] Following the *realpolitik* argument noted in Chapter 9 that underneath the convenient efficiency rhetoric and apparently unexceptionable managerial language, it is politicization of senior public servants—involving a move from trustee to agent and from delegated agent to personal loyalist—that has been a common trend across a number of parliamentary systems in recent decades.

Hall and David Soskice (2001) argue that is exactly what happened to different national styles of capitalism up to at least the mid-1990s, with each system developing its distinctive logic in an increasingly 'pure' form. The underlying social mechanism involved in divergence processes of this kind is some sort of feedback system in which a system responds to environmental pressure by developing those features that are distinctive to it, either because its response is to develop processes that are familiar, or for reasons of comparative advantage, or both.

For a divergence pattern to come about, there have to be differentiated responses to political crises, in which (for example) trustee-type public servants became ever more independent of elected politicians with each passing crisis, while in 'agency' PSB traditions the politicians responded to the same kind of crisis by tightening the screws of control still further on public servants. Such developments are certainly imaginable. But there do not seem to be many precedents for that sort of dynamic in the recent past, and our analysis of Germany and the UK does not suggest that the two systems are generally moving further apart in their PSBs as a result of variety-of-capitalism pressures. The sort of variety we noted in Table 1.1 seems unlikely to disappear, but it is not obvious that it has generally increased in the recent past or that it is set to do so in the future.

10.3.3. Complication or Multiplication: A World of Messier Hybrids

So a final possible future for PSBs, arguably coming somewhere between stasis and convergence, is one of a messier world in which such bargains become more multiple, differentiated, or complicated within each national system. That messiness could stem from a variety of possible causes, including changes in the international environment and immanent self-destruct pressures built into each bargain. For instance, it is not hard to see why politicians in countries with a trustee-type PSB tradition might want to add a subset of agency bargains, either for high-minded reasons or to produce new managerial cannon-fodder for those politicians to fire and blame when things go wrong in public service delivery. Similarly, politicians in countries with an agency-type PSB tradition may have good reason to add a subset of trustee bargains, for instance, to enhance commitment to particular policy stances or to compensate for falling trust and confidence in their own conduct. In Part II, we suggested that the various forms of reward, competency, and loyalty bargain could be conceived as the overlapping circles of a Venn diagram, and the effect of complexification pressures would be to add more of the circles and the segments to each national system. Or to use a more familiar if

perhaps hackneyed simile, the result would resemble the different architec-
tural styles that are often introduced as a building is developed, remodelled,
and added to over the centuries—with all the potential mismatches and
oddities that such a structure may create. Indeed, Stephen Skowronek's
seminal work on the development of the regulatory state in the USA (Skowronek 1982; see also Thelen 2003) highlights precisely such a pattern of
institutional 'overlap' through piecemeal development.

We certainly see some evidence of processes of complication or multiplication of PSBs at work in the cases we have investigated here—at the level of
the overall bargain as well as within the three particular components that we
discussed in Part II. As we noted in Chapter 7, the UK has notably moved
away from the sort of bargain described by Schaffer and Parris forty years ago,
not so much by dispensing with its central elements (or at least variants of
them) for much of the departmental top civil service, as by successively
adding and refining new categories of PSBs for different kinds of public
servants, notably political advisers, regulators, and agency managers. Similar
developments have occurred in other Westminster-model systems,[8] though
they seem less obvious in public service systems of the German type.

Now, complexification of this kind can produce various unexpected
effects. As with transplant surgery, the introduction of new parts taken
from elsewhere can result in rejection in some cases. Arguably, there are
some signs of that sort of mechanism at work, particularly in the case of the
UK. For instance, several quasi-trustee-type bargains adopted in the UK
over the last two decades or so have come to grief—such as the Parliamentary Commissioner for Standards, after displaying what some politicians
saw as an excess of zeal in pursuing ministers for wrongdoing, or some of the
regulators of the privatized industries in the 1980s, transformed into more
politically manageable committee structures a decade or so later. Something
similar may have happened to the much-hyped delegated-agency form of
PSB associated with the executive agency reforms of the 1980s, as we saw in
Chapter 9.

Such complexification might, in principle, turn into a variety of convergence, if the multiplication of PSBs into different subtypes within each
national system produced a number of domain-specific PSBs that were
similar across states while differing from the PSBs for other domains. Obvious

---

[8] For instance, in Trinidad, the bifurcation of the earlier PSB into permanent and limited-
contract civil servants could also be considered to be a complication of an earlier, simpler
model, and one that seems unlikely to be wound back in the near future, even though a similar
division in the UK after the Second World War (paralleling the division of the military into
'regulars' and temporary recruits) died out in the 1960s.

examples of a development of that kind can be found in realms such as competition regulation, central bank governance, or sleaze-busting watchdogs, each of which forms its own international 'club' in a way that can augment the pressures for sector-specific PSBs. But a world in which types of PSBs multiply within each state tradition is potentially a world in which the scope for conflict and misunderstandings among the players within executive government becomes greater, as with the mixing of melons and bicycle-gear problems that we discussed in Chapter 7. In such conditions, there may be no common understanding of what the dominant PSB is, or what amounts to cheating on what kind of bargain, and increased conflict and confusion ensues. We think there are signs of that kind of development as well, at least within the UK tradition.

10.3.4. Overall

None of these four possibilities can be dismissed lightly. There is a prima facie case for each of them, as we have seen. They all deserve to be on the PSB futurologist's radar screen somewhere. Indeed, each of them represents a mechanism well known to social theorists—dynamic conservatism, isomorphism, differentiation, complexification. Some of those mechanisms pull against one another and some can be combined, so some mixture of the four may come about. But from the perspective of the recent past, and particularly of the German and British cases we have examined in detail in this book, we think complication is on balance the most plausible future of PSBs for countries of that type—with all the prospects it may bring of the mixing-of-melons problem we discussed in Chapter 7. The twenty-first century equivalents Sir Harold Nicolson and Anton Graf Monts—and there are plenty of them—seem most likely to be experiencing messiness and 'complication' in the PSBs they have been used to.

Sources and Indicators for Table 1.1

Confidence in public service: World Values Survey, 1981/3, 1990/3, 1999/2000; Average of 'great deal' and quite a lot of confidence in civil service across three surveys (numbers for West Germany). High: 50% plus, Medium: 40–49%, Low: 0–39%. Average confidence scores: USA: 57.7; Germany (West): 36.1; UK: 46.3; Spain: 38.4; France 49.0; Japan 32.1; (Trinidad: n/a).

Top bureaucrats: US: 7,000 (SES); Germany: 1,504 (B-scale); UK: 4,450 (SCS); Spain: 10,111 (levels 28–30); France: 5,000 (Rouban 1999); Japan: 7,318 (7th grade/15th rank); Trinidad: 700 (executive group).

Dismissable civil servants: USA: 4,500 (Peters 2004: 128); Germany: 136, the actual number of actually dismissed civil servants in 1998 was 71 (Schroeter 2004: 71–2); UK: 76, number of political advisers in 2001; Spain: 2,603, number includes 585 political advisers (2003), 270 administrative posts (1996), and 1,748 level 30 bureaucrats (1997) (Parrado 2004: 227); France: 1,075, 500 departmental heads and administrative posts at discretion of prime minister, plus fluctuating number of Cabinet positions (here: 575 (2001)). Ratio of dismissable bureaucrats of total top bureaucrats includes political advisers.

Top public service pay in purchasing power parities: USA: 13,175 and 8,744 (SES max. and min., 2004); Germany: 9,753 and 4,131 (figures for B11, A15.9, 2004); UK: 4,763 and 16,012 ('range 10' and permanent secretary); Spain: 4,969 and 2,244 (General Director and level 28); France: 9,993 and 6,518 (directeurs d'administration (2004) and administrateurs et assimilés (2003)); Japan: 6,518 and 2,211 (designated and administrative class); Trinidad: 3,218 and 1,251 (Permanent Secretary to the Prime Minister and Senior Administrative Officer). Purchasing Power Parities based on: OECD conversion rates but for Trinidad, conversion into spending power in Berlin according to German foreign service calculator and subsequent conversion into PPP.

Average earning: Eurostat; Trinidad Statistical Office and personal communication; Japan Statistical Office; US Department of Labour–Bureau of Labour Statistics.

Sources: USA: Peters 2004, US Federal Budget, Office of Budget and Management; Germany: Federal Budget, Schroeter 2004, Bundesbesoldungsordnung; UK: Cabinet Office, Civil Service Yearbook; Spain: IGAE, Central de Personal, Parrado 2004: 227, personal communication; France: http://alize.finances.gouv.fr/budget/plf2005/jaunes/1001.pdf (last accessed 17 July 2005), Rapport au Premier Ministre (2004) La remuneration au mérite des directeurs d'administration centrale; Japan: www.gyoukaku.go.jp (Colignon and Usiu 2003: 10); Trinidad: personal communication, 15 June 2003.

APPENDIX 2

Interviewees Cited

The interview material for this book emerged from a series of interviews conducted for this book, as well as for an earlier study on civil service competency. Interviewees were drawn from a cross section of civil servants in central government. We provide here the codes for the interviews cited in the text. All interviews were conducted under Chatham House rules. Interviews in Germany were conducted in German and, as all other German sources, translated by us.

UK

1. Senior Manager, Inland Revenue, 20 November 2003.
2. Former Labour Special Adviser, 27 November 2003.
3. Chief Executive, DTI agency, 28 November 2003.
4. Chief Executive, Regulatory Agency, 30 November 2003.
5. Former Senior Official, Treasury, 4 December 2003.
6. Former Conservative Special Adviser, 4 December 2003.
7. Senior Official, Department of Culture, Media, and Sport, 10 December 2003.
8. Senior Official, Home Office, 12 January 2004.
9. Former Official, Department of Transport, 19 January 2004.
10. Former Conservative Special Adviser, 22 January 2004.
11. Senior Official, Department of Transport, 29 February 2004.
12. Former Senior Official, Government Information and Communication Service, 1 March 2004.
13. Senior Official, Department for Constitutional Affairs, 15 March 2004.
14. Official, Department of the Environment, 16 March 2004.
15. Former Secretary of State, 5 April 2004.
16. Former Secretary of State, 28 April 2004.
17. Former Secretary of State, 27 May 2004.
18. Former Senior Official, Cabinet Office, 3 June 2004.
19. Senior Official, Department of Work and Pensions, 25 June 2004.
20. Former Chief Executive of Agency, 13 July 2004.
21. Former Conservative Special Adviser, 13 July 2004.
22. Official, Department of Work and Pensions, 29 July 2004.
23. Official, Department of Trade and Industry, 7 August 2001.
24. Official, Department of Trade and Industry, 30 July 2001.
25. Former regulatory official, 21 September 2005.

Trinidad and Tobago

1. Senior Official, Department of Community Development, Culture and Gender Affair, 25 March 2004.
2. Senior Opposition Politician, 26 March 2004.
3. Senior Official, Department for Public Administration and Information, 29 March 2004.
4. Senior Officials, Office of Chief Personnel Officer, 31 March 2004.
5. Official, Department for Public Administration and Information, 29 March 2004.

Germany

1. Official, Bundesministerium für Wirtschaft und Arbeit, 5 August 2003.
2. Official, Bundesministerium für Wirtschaft und Arbeit, 6 August 2003.
3. Senior Official and colleagues, Bundesministerium des Inneren, 16 September 2003.
4. Officials, Bundesministerium für Wirtschaft und Arbeit, 17 September 2003.
5. Official, Bundesministerium der Justiz, 22 September 2003.
6. Senior Official, Bundesministerium für Wirtschaft und Arbeit, 22 September 2003.
7. Parliamentary Group Assistant (CDU), 23 September 2003.
8. Parliamentary Group Assistant (SPD), 24 September 2003.
9. Official, Bundesministerium für Wirtschaft und Arbeit, 25 September 2003.
10. Senior Official, Bundesministerium für Verbraucherschutz, Ernährung und Landwirtschaft, 7 September 2004.
11. Senior Official, Bundesministerium für Verkehr, Bau-und Wohnungswesen, 27 September 2004.
12. Parliamentary State Secretary, 27 September 2004.
13. Senior Official, Bundesministerium für Verbraucherschutz, Ernährung und Landwirtschaft, 28 September 2004.
14. Senior Official, Bundesministerium für Verbraucherschutz, Ernährung und Landwirtschaft, 28 September 2004.
15. Parliamentary State Secretary, 28 September 2004.
16. Senior Official, Bundesministerium für Wirtschaft, 9 July 2001.
17. Senior Official, Bundesministerium für Wirtschaft, 9 July 2001.
18. Senior Official and colleagues, Bundesministerium für Wirtschaft, 9 July 2001.
19. State Secretary, 5 July 2001.
20. Official and colleagues, Bundesministerium für Wirtschaft, 5 July 2001.
21. Official and colleagues, Bundesministerium für Wirtschaft, 3 July 2001.

References

Aberbach, J. D. and Rockman, B. A. (1988). 'Image IV Revisited: Executive and Political Roles', *Governance*, 1(1): 1–25.

—— —— (2000). *In the Web of Politics*. Washington, DC: Brookings Institution Press.

—— Putnam, R. D., and Rockman, B. A. (1981). *Bureaucrats and Politicians in Western Democracies*. Cambridge, MA: Harvard University Press, pp. 1–23.

Alesina, A. E., Roubini, N., and Cohen, G. D. (1997). *Political Cycles and the Macroeconomy*. Cambridge, MA: MIT Press.

Alt, J. and Chrystal, A. K. (1983). *Political Economy*. Berkeley, CA: University of California Press.

Arendt, H. (1964). *Eichmann in Jerusalem*, rev. edn. New York: Viking.

Armstrong, R. (1989). 'The Duties and Responsibilities of Civil Servants in Relation to Ministers', in G. Marshall (ed.), *Ministerial Responsibility*. Oxford: Oxford University Press.

Arthur, W. B. (1994). *Increasing Returns and Path Dependence in the Economy*. Ann Arbor, MI: University of Michigan Press.

Aucoin, P. (1990). 'Administrative Reform in Public Management', *Governance*, 3(2): 115–37.

Avineri, S. (1972). *Hegel's Theory of the Modern State*. Cambridge: Cambridge University Press.

Badie, B. and Birnbaum, P. (1979). *Sociologie de l'État*. Paris: Bernard Grasset.

Balogh, T. (1959). 'Apotheosis of the Dilettante', in H. Thomas (ed.), *The Establishment*. London: Ace Books.

Banfield, E. C. (1958). *The Moral Basis of a Backward Society*. Glencoe, IL: Free Press.

Bardach, E. (1998). *Getting Agencies to Work Together*. Washington, DC: Brookings Institution Press.

Barker, R. S. (1997). *Political Ideas in Modern Britain*. London: Routledge.

Barnard, C. (1938). *The Functions of the Executive*. Cambridge, MA: Harvard University Press.

Barro, R. J. and Gordon, D. (1983). 'Rules, Discretion, and Reputation in a Model of Monetary Policy', *Journal of Monetary Economics*, 12(1): 101–21.

Barry, B. (1975). 'The Consociational Model and Its Dangers', *European Journal of Political Research*, 3(4): 393–412.

Barzelay, M. (2001). *The New Public Management*. Berkeley, CA: University of California Press.

—— (2003). 'Introduction: The Process Dynamics of Public Management Policymaking', *International Journal of Public Management*, 6(3): 251–81.

Bates, R. H., Greif, A., Levi, M., Rosenthal, J. L., and Weingast, B. R. (1998). *Analytic Narratives*. Princeton, NJ: Princeton University Press.

Baumgartner, F. and Jones, B. (1993). *Agendas and Instability in American Politics*. Chicago: University of Chicago Press.

Beatson, J. (ed.) (2002). *Anson's Law of Contract*. Oxford: Oxford University Press.

Beck Jørgensen and Larsen (1987). 'Control: An Attempt at Forming a Theory', *Scandinavian Political Studies*, 10(4): 279–99.

Beer, S. (1966). *Decision and Control*. London: Wiley.

Behn, R. D. (2001). *Rethinking Democratic Accountability*. Washington, DC: Brookings Institution Press.

Bendor, J. and Moe, T. M. (1985). 'An Adaptive Model of Bureaucratic Politics', *American Political Science Review*, 79(3): 755–74.

—— Glazer, A., and Hammond, T. (2001). 'Theories of Delegation', *Annual Review of Political Science*, 4: 235–69.

Bentham, J. (1825/1962). 'The Rules of Reward', in J. Bowring (ed.), *The Works of Jeremy Bentham*. New York: Russell and Russell.

Berliner, J. S. (1988). *Soviet Industry from Stalin to Gorbachev*. Aldershot: Edward Elgar.

Bevan, G. and Hood, C. (forthcoming). 'What's Measured is What Matters: Targets and Gaming in the English Public Health Care System', *Public Administration*.

Blackett, P. M. S. (1962). 'Memories of Rutherford', in J. B. Birks (ed.), *Rutherford at Manchester*. London: Heywood.

Blau, P. M. (1964). *Exchange and Power in Social Life*. New York: Wiley.

Bogaards, M. (2000). 'The Uneasy Relationship between Empirical and Normative Types in Consociational Theory', *Journal of Theoretical Politics*, 12(4): 395–423.

Boston, J., Martin, J., Pallott, J., and Walsh, P. (1996). *Public Management: The New Zealand Model*. Melbourne/Victoria: Oxford University Press.

Boyatzis, R. E. (1982). *The Competent Manager*. New York: Wiley.

Bradley, I. (2004). *The Complete Annotated Gilbert and Sullivan*. Oxford: Oxford University Press.

Braguinsky, S. and Yavlinsky, G. (2000) *Incentives and Institutions: The Transition to a Market Economy in Russia*, Princeton, NJ: Princeton University Press.

Brams, S. J. (1976). *Paradoxes in Politics*. New York: Free Press.

Brehm, J. and Gates, S. (1997). *Working, Shirking, and Sabotage*. Ann Arbor, MI: University of Michigan Press.

Breyer, S. (1993). *Breaking the Vicious Cycle*. Cambridge, MA: Harvard University Press.

Bridges, E. (1950). *Portrait of a Profession*. Cambridge: Cambridge University Press.

Brontë, C. (1994/orig. 1848). *Shirley*. London: Penguin.

Broszat, M. (1969). *Der Staat Hitlers*. München: dtv.

Burn, E. H. (ed.) (1996). *Maudsley and Burn's Trusts and Trustees*, 5th edn. London: Butterworths.

Campbell, C. (1988). 'The Political Roles of Senior Government Officials in Advanced Democracies', *British Journal of Political Science*, 18: 243–72.

—— and Wilson, G. K. (1995). *The End of Whitehall: Death of a Paradigm?* Oxford: Blackwell.

Carpenter, D. (2001). *The Forging of Bureaucratic Autonomy*. Princeton, NJ: Princeton University Press.

Christensen, J. G. (1993) 'Corporatism, Administrative Regimes and the Mismanagement of Public Funds' *Scandinavian Political Studies* 16: 201–225.

Christensen, J. G. (1994). 'Denmark: Institutional Constraint and the Advancement of Individual Self-Interest in HPO', in C. Hood and B. G. Peters (eds.), *Rewards at the Top*. London: Sage, pp. 70–89.

—— (2003). 'Pay and Perquisites for Executives', in J. Pierre and B. G. Peters (eds.), *Handbook of Public Administration*. London: Sage.

Churchman, C. (1967). 'Wicked Problems', *Management Science*, 4(4): B141–2.

Coase, R. (1937). 'The Nature of the Firm', *Economica*, 4(15): 386–405.

Colignon, R. A. and Usui, C. (2003). *Amakudari*. Ithaca, NY: ILR Press/Cornell University Press.

Colomer, J. P. (1991). 'Transitions by Agreement: Modelling the Spanish Way', *American Political Science Review*, 85(4): 1283–302.

—— (1995). *Game Theory and the Transition to Democracy*. Aldershot, UK: Edward Elgar.

—— (2000). *Strategic Transitions*. Baltimore, MD: Johns Hopkins University Press.

Coser, L. A. (1974). *Greedy Institutions*. London: Collier Macmillan.

Crick, M. (1997). *Michael Heseltine: A Biography*. London: Hamish Hamilton.

Cumes, J. W. C. (1988). *A Bunch of Amateurs: The Tragedy of Government and Administration in Australia*. South Melbourne: Macmillan.

Curristine, T. (2002). 'Reforming Civil Service Accountability in the US and the UK: Two Highways Agencies Compared', D.Phil. thesis, University of Oxford.

David, P. (1985). 'Clio and the Economics of QWERTY', *American Economic Review*, 75: 332–7.

Davenport, D. (2002). 'The New Diplomacy', *Policy Review* No 116, December 2002. Available at http://www.policyreview.org/DEC02/davenport_print.html

Derlien, H. U. (2004). 'Germany: Village Life Becoming More Complicated', in C. Hood et al. (eds.), *Controlling Modern Government*. Cheltenham, UK: Edward Elgar, pp. 155–61.

Devons, E. (1950). *Planning in Practice: Essays in Aircraft Planning in Wartime*. Cambridge: Cambridge University Press.

Dickens, C. (1998/orig. 1857). *Little Dorrit*. London: Penguin.

Dixon, N. (1976). *On the Psychology of Military Incompetence*. London: Jonathan Cape.

Dobb, M. (1970). *Socialist Planning*. London: Lawrence and Wishart.

Döhler, M. (2002). 'Institutional Choice and Bureaucratic Autonomy in Germany', *West European Politics*, 25(1): 101–24.

Douglas, M. (1981). 'Cultural Bias', in M. Douglas (ed.), *In the Active Voice*. London: Routledge, pp. 183–254.

Dunleavy, P. J. (1994). 'The Globalization of Public Service Production: Can Government be "Best in World"', *Public Policy and Administration*, 9(2): 36–64.

Dunleavy, P. J. (1991). *Democracy, Bureaucracy and Public Choice*. Hemel Hempstead, UK: Harvester Wheatsheaf.

Dunsire, A. (1978). *Control in a Bureaucracy*. Oxford: Martin Robertson.

Eastaway, R. and Wyndham, J. (2000). *Why Do Buses Come in Threes? The Hidden Mathematics of Everyday Life*. London: Robson Books.

Edyvane, D. (2003). 'Against Unconditional Love', *Journal of Applied Philosophy*, 20(1): 59–75.

Eisenstadt, S. (1958). 'Bureaucracy and Bureaucratisation', *Current Sociology*, 7(2): 99–124.

Ellis, R. J. (1994). *Presidential Lightning Rods*. Lawrence, KS: University of Kansas Press.

Elmore, R. (2000). *Building a New Structure for School Leadership*, Washington, DC: The Albert Shanker Institute.

Elster, J. (2004). *Closing the Books: Transitional Justice in Historical Perspective*, Cambridge: Cambridge University Press.

Erasmus, D. (1511). *In Praise of Folly (Encomium Moriae)*. Available at http://www.ccel.org/e/erasmus/folly/folly.html, last accessed 15 July 2005.

Esman, M. J. (1997). 'Public Administration, Ethnic Conflict, and Economic Development', *Public Administration Review*, 57(6): 527–33.

Feaver, P. D. (2003). *Armed Servants*. Cambridge, MA: Harvard University Press.

Finer, S. E. (1950). *A Primer of Public Administration*. London: Frederick Walker.

—— (1962). *The Man on Horseback*. London: Pall Mall.

Fiorina, M. (1982). 'Legislative Choice of Regulatory Forms: Legal Process or Administrative Process?' *Public Choice*, 39(1): 33–66.

—— (1986). 'Legislator Uncertainty, Legislator Control and the Delegation of Legislative Power', *Journal of Law, Economics and Organization*, 2(1): 133–51.

Firth, D. and Leigh, A. (1998). *The Corporate Fool*. Oxford: Capstone Publishing.

Flanders, L. R. and Utterback, D. (1985). 'The Management Excellence Inventory: A Tool for Management', *Public Administration Review*, 45: 403–10.

Flaubert, G. (1976/orig.1910). *Bouvard and Pécuchet*, London: Penguin.

Foster, C. D. (1992). *Privatisation, Public Ownership and the Regulation of Natural Monopoly*. Oxford: Blackwell.

—— (1996). 'Reflections on the True Significance of the Scott Report for Government Accountability', *Public Administration*, 74(4): 567–92.

—— (1998). 'The Constitutional Role of the Civil Service: Would Legislation Help? Or The Haldane Relation: Can it, Should it be Reclaimed?' Paper presented at seminar in Oxford, 16 February 1998.

—— (2005). *British Government in Crisis*. Oxford: Hart.

Fraenkel, E. (1941). *The Dual State*. Oxford: Oxford University Press.

Franzese, R. (1999). 'Partially Independent Central Banks, Politically Responsive Governments, and Inflation', *American Journal of Political Science*, 43(3): 681–706.

Gentry, C. (1991). J. *Edgar Hoover: The Man and the Secrets*. London: Norton.

Giddings, P. (ed.) (1994). *Parliamentary Accountability*. London: Macmillan.

Gillis, J. R. (1971). *Prussian Bureaucracy in Crisis, 1840–1860*. Stanford, CA: Stanford University Press.

Gollin, A. (1960). *The Observer and J. L. Garvin* 1908–1914, London: Oxford Universty Press.

Gore, A. (1993). *From Red Tape to Results*. Report of the National Performance Review.

Graves, R. (1969). *Goodbye to All That*. London: Cassell.

Gregory, R. (1995). 'Accountability, Responsibility and Corruption: Managing the "Public Production Process"', in J. Boston (ed.), *The State under Contract*. Wellington: Bridget Williams Books.

Grigg, P. J. (1948). *Prejudice and Judgement*, London: Cape.

Gunn, L. (1972). 'Politicians and Officials: Who is Answerable?' *Political Quarterly*, 43(3): 253–60.

—— (1987). 'Perspectives on Public Management', in J. Kooiman and K. A. Eliassen (eds.), *Managing Public Organizations*. London: Sage.

Hall, P. A. (1983). 'Policy Innovation and the Structure of the State: The Politics-Administrative Nexus in France and Britain', *Annals of the AAPSS*, 466(3): 43–55.

—— and Soskice, D. (2001). 'An Introduction to Varieties of Capitalism', in P. A. Hall and D. Soskice (eds.), *Varieties of Capitalism: The Institutional Foundations of Comparative Advantage*. Oxford: Oxford University Press.

Hamley, E. (1866). *The Operations of War*, London: William Blackwood and Sons.

Hammond, T. and Knott, J. (1996). 'Who Controls the Bureaucracy? Presidential Power, Congressional Dominance, Legal Constraints, and Bureaucratic Autonomy in a Model of Multi-Institutional Policymaking', *Journal of Law, Economics and Organization*, 12(1): 121–68.

Hanbury, H. G. (1960). *The Principles of Agency*, 2nd edn. London: Stevens.

Hayward, J. E. S. (1983). *Governing France*. London: Weidenfeld & Nicolson.

Heclo, H. and Wildavsky, A. (1974). *The Private Government of Public Money*. London: Macmillan.

Hede, A. (1991). 'Trends in the Higher Civil Services of Anglo-American Systems', *Governance*, 4(4): 489–510.

Hegel, G. F. (1991/orig.1820). *Elements of the Philosophy of Right*. Cambridge: Cambridge University Press.

Heller, J. (1961). *Catch-22*. London: Vintage.

Helmke, G. and Levitsky, S. (2004). 'Informal Institutions and Comparative Politics: A Research Agenda', *Perspectives on Politics*, 2(4): 725–40.

Heper, M. (1992). 'The Strong State as a Problem for the Consolidation of Democracy', *Comparative Political Studies*, 25(2): 169–94.

Hintze, O. (1964). 'Der Staat als Betrieb und die Verfassungsreform', in G. Oestreich (ed.), *Soziologie und Geschichte*. Göttingen: Vandenhoeck & Ruprecht.

Hood, C. (1996). 'Exploring Variations in Public Management Reform of the 1980s', in H. Bekke, J. Perry, and T. Toonen (eds.), *Civil Service Systems in Comparative Perspective*. Bloomington, IN: Indiana University Press, pp. 268–87.

Hood, C. (1998*a*). 'Individualized Contracts for Top Public Servants: Copying Business, Path-Dependent Political Re-engineering—or Trobriand Cricket?', *Governance*, 11(4): 443–62.

—— (1998*b*). *The Art of the State*. Oxford: Clarendon Press.

—— (1999). 'British Public Administration: Dodo, Phoenix or Chameleon?' in J. E. S. Hayward, B. Barry, and A. Brown (eds.), *The British Study of Politics in the Twentieth Century*. Oxford: Oxford University Press and British Academy.

—— (2000). 'Paradoxes of Public-sector Managerialism, Old Public Management and Public Service Bargains', *International Public Management Journal*, 3: 1–22.

—— (2001). 'Public Service Bargains and Public Service Reform', in B. G Peters and J. Pierre (eds.), *Politicians, Bureaucrats and Administrative Reform*. London: Routledge.

—— (2002*a*). 'Control, Bargains, and Cheating: The Politics of Public-Service Reform', *Journal of Public Administration Research and Theory*, 12(3): 309–32.

—— (2002*b*). 'The Risk Game and the Blame Game', *Government and Opposition*, 37(1): 15–37.

—— and Jackson, M. (1991). *Administrative Argument*. Aldershot: Dartmouth.

Hood, C. and Lodge, M. (2005). Aesop with Variations: Civil Service Competency as a Case of German Tortoise and British Hare?', *Public Administration*, 83(4): 805–822.

—— and Lodge, M. (2004). 'Competency, Bureaucracy and the Orthodoxies of Public Management Reform: A Comparative Analysis', *Governance*, 17(3): 313–33.

—— and Peters, B. G. (1994). 'Understanding RHPOs', in C. Hood and B. G. Peters (eds.), *Rewards at the Top*. London: Sage.

—— —— (2003). 'The Top Pay Game and Good Governance: Where Immodest Theories Meet Slippery Facts', in C. Hood and B. G. Peters with G. Lee (eds.), *Reward for High Public Office: Asian and Pacific Rim States*. London: Routledge: 166–81.

—— and Rothstein, H. (2001). 'Blame-Shifters or Problem-Solvers', *Administration and Society*, 33(1): 21–53.

—— and Schuppert, G. F. (eds.) (1988). *Delivering Public Services in Western Europe*. London: Sage.

—— Scott, C., James, O., Jones, G. W., and Travers, A. J. (1999). *Regulation Inside Government*. Oxford: Oxford University Press.

—— and Peters, B. G. with Lee, G. O. (2003). 'Introduction', in C. Hood and B. G. Peters with G. O. Lee (eds.), *Reward for High Public Office*. London: Routledge.

—— —— —— (eds.) (2003). *Reward for High Public Office*. London: Routledge.

—— James, O., Peters, B. G., and Scott, C. (eds.) (2004). *Controlling Modern Government*. Cheltenham, UK: Edward Elgar.

Hood, T. (1911, orig. 1836). 'Poetry, Prose, and Worse', in W. Jerrold (ed.), *The Complete Poetical Works of Thomas Hood*. London: Oxford University Press, pp. 477–9.

Hooghe, L. (2001). *The European Commission and the Integration of Europe*. Cambridge: Cambridge University Press.

Hori, H. (2003). 'Changes in the Japanese Political System after 1993: Incapacitated Cooperation between the Liberal Democratic Party and the Ministry of Finance', D.Phil. thesis, University of Oxford.

Horn, M. (1995). *The Political Economy of Public Administration*. Cambridge: Cambridge University Press.

Hornung, K. (1975). *Staat und Armee*. Mainz: v. Hase & Koehler Verlag.

Horowitz, D. (1985). *Ethnic Groups in Conflict*. Berkeley, CA: University of California Press.

Hsieh, P. C. (1925). *The Government of China, 1644–1911*. Baltimore, MD: Johns Hopkins University Press.

Huber, J. D. and Shipan, C. R. (2002). *Deliberate Discretion? The Institutional Foundations of Bureaucratic Autonomy*. Cambridge: Cambridge University Press.

Huntington, S. (1991). *The Third Wave*. Norman, OK: University of Oklahoma Press.

Hutton, Lord (2004). *Report of the Inquiry into the Circumstances Surrounding the Death of Dr David Kelly C.M.G.*, HC247. London: HMSO.

Ingraham, P. (1993). 'Of Pigs in Pokes and Policy Diffusion: Another Look at Pay for Performance', *Public Administration Review*, 53: 348–56.

—— (2001). 'Linking Leadership to Performance in Public Organisations', PUMA/HRM(2001)8/Final, June 2001.

—— and Ban, C. (eds.) (1984). *Legislating Bureaucratic Change*. Albany, NY: State University of New York Press.

James, O. (2003). *The Executive Agency Revolution in Whitehall*. Basingstoke: Palgrave.

Johnson, C. (1982). *MITI and the Japanese Miracle*. Stanford, CA: Stanford University Press.

Johnson, H. C. (1975). *Frederick the Great and His Officials*. New Haven, CT: Yale University Press.

Jones, B. D. (2003). 'Bounded Rationality and Political Science: Lessons from Public Administration and Public Policy', *Journal of Public Administration Research and Theory*, 13(4): 395–417.

Kalecki, M. (1943). 'Political Aspects of Full Employment', *Political Quarterly*, 14: 322–31.

Kasza, G. J. (1988). *The State and the Mass Media in Japan 1918–1945*. Berkeley, CA: University of California Press.

Keeling, D. (1972). *Management in Government*. London: Allen & Unwin.

Keynes, J. M. (1952). *Essays in Persuasion*. London: Macmillan.

King, D. (1995). *Separate and Unequal: Black Americans and the US Federal Government*. Oxford: Oxford University Press.

Klöti, U. (2001). 'Consensual Government in a Heterogeneous Polity', *West European Politics*, 24(2): 19–34.

Knill, C. (1999). 'Explaining Cross-National Variance in Administrative Reform: Autonomous versus Instrumental Bureaucracies', *Journal of Public Policy*, 19(2): 113–97.

—— (2001). *The Europeanisation of National Administrations*. Cambridge: Cambridge University Press.

Kreps, D. M. (1990a). *Game Theory and Economic Modelling*. Oxford: Clarendon Press.

Kreps, D. M. (1990b). 'Corporate Culture and Economic Theory' in J. E. Alt and K. A. Shepsle (eds.) *Perspectives on Positive Political Economy*, Cambridge: Cambridge University Press.

Krislov, S. (1974). *Representative Bureaucracy*. Englewood Cliffs, NJ: Prentice-Hall.

Kugele, D. (1976). *Der politische Beamte*. München: tuduv Studie.

Lee, L. K. (1998). *The Singapore Story*. Singapore: Times Editions.

Lee, G. O. M. (2003). 'Hong Kong—Institutional Inheritance from Colony to Special Administrative Region', in C. Hood and B. G Peters with G. Lee (eds.), *Reward for High Public Office: Asian and Pacific Rim States*. London: Routledge, pp. 130–44.

Lehmbruch, G. (1998). *Parteienwettbewerb im Bundesstaat*, 2nd edn. Opladen: Westdeutscher Verlag.

Levy, B. and Spiller, P. T. (1996). 'A Framework for Resolving the Regulatory Problem', in B. Levy and P. T. Spiller (eds.), *Regulations, Institutions, and Commitment*. Cambridge: Cambridge University Press, pp. 1–35.

Lijphart, A. (1968). *The Politics of Accommodation*. Berkeley, CA: University of California Press.

Lijphart, A. (1984). *Democracies*. New Haven, CT: Yale University Press.

Lipsky, M. (1980). *Street Level Bureaucracy*. New York: Russell Sage Foundation.

Locke, J. (1960/orig. 1680–90). *Two Treatises of Government* (ed. Peter Laslett). Cambridge: Cambridge University Press.

Lodge, M. and Hood, C. (2005) 'Competency and Higher Civil Servants', *Public Administration*, 83(4): 779–784.

Lodge, M. and Hood, C. (2003). 'Competency and Bureaucracy: Diffusion, Application and Appropriate Response?' *West European Politics*, 26(3): 131–52.

Lynn, J. and Jay, A. (1981). *Yes, Minister*. London: BBC.

McBarnet, D. and Whelan, C. (1991). 'The Elusive Spirit of the Law: Formalism and the Struggle for Legal Control', *Modern Law Review*, 54(6): 848–73.

McFarland, A. S. (1991). 'Interest Groups and Political Time', *British Journal of Political Science*, 21: 257–84.

McFaul, M. (2002). 'The Fourth Wave of Democracy and Dictatorship: Noncooperative Transitions in the Postcommunist World', *World Politics*, 54: 212–44.

McGarry, J. and O'Leary, B. (eds.) (1993). *The Politics of Ethnic Conflict Regulation*. London: Routledge.

—— —— (1999). *Policing Northern Ireland*. Belfast: Blackstaff Press.

McLean, I. (2001). *Rational Choice and British Politics*. Oxford: Oxford University Press.

McNamara, K. (2002). 'Rational Fictions: Central Bank Independence and the Social Logic of Delegation', *West European Politics*, 25(1): 47–76.

Machiavelli, N. (1961, orig. 1532). *The Prince*. London: Penguin.

Mackenzie, W. J. M. (1975). *Explorations in Government: Collected Papers (1951–1968)*. London: Macmillan.

Maier, H. (1966). *Ältere deutsche Staatslehre und westliche politische Tradition*. Tübingen: Mohr.

Majone, G. (1997). 'From the Positive to the Regulatory State: Causes and Consequences of Changes in the Mode of Governance', *Journal of Public Policy*, 17(2):
139–68.

Maor, M. (1999). 'The Paradox of Managerialism', *Public Administration Review*, 59:
5–18.

March, J. and Olsen, J. P. (1989). *Rediscovering Institutions*. New York: Free Press.

March, J. G. and Simon, H. A. (1958). *Organizations*. New York: Wiley.

Marquand, D. (1988). *The Unprincipled Society*. London: Jonathan Cape.

Mars, G. (1982). *Cheats at Work*. London: Allen & Unwin.

Marshall, G. (1965). *Police and Government*. London: Methuen.

Mayntz, R. (1985). 'German Federal Bureaucrats—A Functional Elite between Politics
and Administration', in E. Suleiman (ed.), *Bureaucrats and Policy-Making*. New
York: Holmes & Meyer.

—— and Scharpf, F.W. (1975). *Policy-Making in the German Federal Bureaucracy*.
Amsterdam: Elsevier.

Merton, R. K. (1940). 'Bureaucratic Structure and Personality', *Social Forces*, 18(4): 560–8.

Meyer-Sahling, J.-H. (2004). 'Civil Service Reform in Post-Communist Europe: The
Bumpy Road to Depoliticisation', *West European Politics*, 27(1): 71–103.

Mill, J. S. (1910/orig. 1861). *Representative Government*. London: J. M. Dent & Sons.

Miller, G. (1992). *Managerial Dilemmas*. Cambridge: Cambridge University Press.

—— (2000). 'Above Politics: Credible Commitment and Efficiency in the Design of
Public Agencies', *Journal of Public Administration Research and Theory*, 10(2): 289–327.

Mintzberg, H. (1993). *Structure in Fives*. Englewood Cliffs, NJ: Prentice-Hall.

Moore, B. (1959). *Soviet Politics—The Dilemma of Power*. Cambridge, MA: Harvard
University Press.

Moore, M. H. (1995). *Creating Public Value*. Cambridge, MA: Harvard University
Press.

Moran, M. (2003). *The British Regulatory State: High Modernism and Hyper-Innovation*.
Oxford: Oxford University Press.

Moynihan, D. P. (1969). *Maximum Feasible Misunderstanding*. New York: Free Press.

Mueller, H.-E. (1984). *Bureaucracy, Education and Monopoly: Civil Service Reform in
Prussia and England*. Berkeley, CA: California University Press.

Nakamura, A. and Dairokuno, K. (2003). 'Japan's Pattern of Rewards for High Public
Office: A Cultural Perspective', in C. Hood and B. G. Peters (eds.), *Reward for High
Public Office: Asian and Pacific-Rim States*. London: Taylor & Francis, pp. 105–18.

National Commission on Terrorist Attacks upon the United States (2004). *The 9/11
Commission Report: Final Report of the National Commission on Terrorist Attacks
upon the United States*. New York: W.W. Norton.

Naylor, J. F. (1984). *A Man and an Institution: Sir Maurice Hankey, The Cabinet Secretariat
and the Custody of Cabinet Secrecy*. Cambridge: Cambridge University Press.

Neustadt, R. (1960). *Presidential Power: The Politics of Leadership*. New York: Wiley.

Neumann, J. von and Morgenstern, O. (1947). *Theories of Games and Economic
Behaviour*. Princeton, NJ: Princeton University Press.

Nicolson, H. (1934). *Curzon: The Last Phase 1919–1925*. London: Constable.

Nishio, T. (2004). 'Japan: Where Mutuality Reigns Supreme?' in C. Hood, O. James, B. G. Peters, and C. Scott (eds.), *Controlling Modern Government: Variety, Commonality and Change*. Cheltenham: Edward Elgar, pp. 145–51.

Niskanen, W. (1971). *Bureaucracy and Representative Government*. Chicago: Aldine Atherton.

Nordhaus, W. D. (1975). 'The Political Business Cycle', *Review of Economic Studies* 42: 169–90.

Northcote, S. H. and Trevelyan, C. E. (1854). *Report on the Organisation of the Permanent Civil Service*, London: HMSO.

Nove, A. (1958). 'The Problem of "Success Indicators" in the Soviet Economy', *Economica*, 25(97): 1–13.

—— (1980). *The Soviet Economic System*, 2nd edn. London: Allen & Unwin.

Nowak, K. F. and Thimme, F. (eds.) (1932). *Erinnerungen und Gedanken des Botschafters Anton Graf Monts*. Berlin: Verlag für Kulturpolitik.

Nunberg, B. (1995). *Managing the Civil Service*. World Bank Discussion Paper 204. Washington, DC: World Bank.

Oakley, A. J. (1998). *Parker and Mallows: The Modern Law of Trusts*, 7th edn. London: Sweet and Maxwell.

O'Donnell, G. (2005). 'The Relationship between Economy and State', in Civil Service Commissioners (eds.), *Changing Times*. London: Office of the Civil Service Commissioners, pp. 61–72.

—— Schmitter, P.C., and Whitehead, L. (1986). *Transitions from Authoritarian Rule: Comparative Perspectives*. Baltimore, MD: Johns Hopkins University Press.

OECD (1995). *Governance in Transition*. Paris: OECD.

O'Neill, O. (2002). *A Question of Trust*, Cambridge: Cambridge University Press.

Oppenheim, L. H. (1999). *Politics in Chile*. Boulder, CO: Westview.

Orwell, G. (1994/orig. 1946). *Animal Farm*. London: Penguin.

Osborne, D. and Gaebler, T. (1992). *Reinventing Government*. Reading, MA: Addison-Wesley.

Otto, B. (2001). *Fools are Everywhere*. Chicago: Chicago University Press.

Page, E. C. (1997). *People Who Run Europe*. Oxford: Oxford University Press.

Painter, M. (1990). 'Values in the History of Public Administration', in J. Power (ed.), *Public Administration in Australia: A Watershed*. Sydney: RAIPA/Hale and Iremonger, pp. 75–93.

Parrado, S. (2004). 'Politicization of the Spanish Civil Service: Continuity in 1982 and 1996', in B. G. Peters and J. Pierre (eds.), *Politicization of the Civil Service in Comparative Perspective*. London: Routledge, pp. 227–56.

Parris, H. (1969). *Constitutional Bureaucracy*. London: Allen & Unwin.

Parry, R., Hood, C., and James, O. (1997). 'Reinventing the Treasury: Economic Rationalism or an Econocrat's Fallacy of Control?' *Public Administration*, 75: 395–415.

Pempel, T. J. (1974). 'The Bureaucratization of Policymaking in Postwar Japan', *American Journal of Political Science*, 18(4): 647–64.

—— (1978). *Patterns of Japanese Policymaking*. Boulder, CO: Westview.

—— (1982). *Policy and Politics in Japan: Creative Conservatism*. Philadelphia, PA: Temple University Press.

Pempel, T. J. (1992). 'Bureaucracy in Japan', *PS: Political Science and Politics*, 25(3): 19–24.

Peters, B. G. (2004). 'The USA: High on Oversight, Low on Mutuality?' in C. Hood, O. James, B. G. Peters and C. Scott (eds.), *Controlling Modern Government*. Cheltenham: Edward Elgar, pp. 138–45.

Peters, T. J. and Waterman, R. H. (1982). *In Search of Excellence*, New York: Harper and Row.

Pettit, P. H. (2001). *Equity and the Law of Trusts*, 9th edn. London: Butterworths.

Phelps, E. S. (1968). 'Money-Wage Dynamics and Labour-Market Equilibrium', *Journal of Political Economy*, 76: 678–711.

Philips, H. (2004). *Review of the Honours System*. London: Cabinet Office.

Pierson, P. (2000). 'Increasing Returns, Path Dependence, and the Study of Politics', *American Political Science Review*, 94(2): 251–67.

Polidano, C. (1999). 'The Bureaucrat that Fell under a Bus: Ministerial Responsibility, Executive Agencies and the Derek Lewis Affair in Britain', *Governance*, 12(2): 201–29.

Pollitt, C. and Bouckaert, G. (2004). *Public Management Reform*, 2nd edn. Oxford: Oxford University Press.

—— and Talbot, C. (eds.) (2004). *Unbundled Government*. London: Routledge.

Polsby, N. (1984). *Political Innovation in America*. New Haven, CT: Yale University Press.

Posner, R. A. (1986). *Economic Analysis of Law*. Boston, MA: Little, Brown.

Protherough, R. and Pick, J. (2002). *Managing Britannia*. Harleston: Edgeways.

Public Administration Select Committee (2002). *These Unfortunate Events: Lessons of Recent Events at the Former DTLR*, 8th Report of Session 2001–2, HC 303, London: HMSO.

Pusey, M. (2001). *Economic Rationalism in Canberra*. Cambridge: Cambridge University Press.

Putnam, R. (1973). 'The Political Attitudes of Senior Civil Servants in Western Europe: A Preliminary Report', *British Journal of Political Science*, 3(3): 257–90.

Quah, J. (2003a). 'Paying for the Best and Brightest: Rewards for High Public Office in Singapore', in C. Hood and B. G. Peters with G. Lee (eds.), *Reward for High Public Office*. London: Routledge.

—— (2003b). *Curbing Corruption in Asia: A Comparative Study of Six Countries*. Singapore: Times Media.

Ramseyer, J. M. and Rosenbluth, F. M. (1993). *Japan's Political Marketplace*. Cambridge, MA: Harvard University Press.

Rauderaad, N. and Wolffram, D. J. (2001). 'Dutch Administrative Culture in a Historical Perspective', in F. Henricks and T. A. J. Toonen (eds.), *Polder Politics: The Reinvention of Consensus Democracy in the Netherlands*. Aldershot: Ashgate.

Review Body on Top Salaries (2005). *Twenty-Seventh Report on Senior Salaries*. Cm 6451. Norwich: HMSO.

Rhodes, R. and Weller, P. (2001). *The Changing World of Top Officials: Mandarins or Valets?* Buckingham: Open University Press.

Riker, W. H. (1986). *The Art of Political Manipulation.* New Haven, CT: Yale University Press.

Roach, J. (1985). 'The French Police', in J. Roach and J. Thomaneck (eds.), *Police and Public Order in Europe.* London: Croom Helm, pp. 107–14.

Roberts, A. (2005). 'Spin Control and Freedom of Information: Lessons for the United Kingdom from Canada', *Public Administration*, 83(1): 1–23.

Röhl, J. C. G. (1994). *The Kaiser and His Court.* Cambridge: Cambridge University Press.

Rose, R. (1980). *Politics in England.* London: Faber and Faber.

Rousseau, J.-J. (1993). *J. J. Rousseau-the Social Contract and Discourses*, ed. G. D. H. Cole, London: Dent.

Rouban, L. (1999). 'The Senior Civil Service in France', in E. C. Page and V. Wright (eds). *Bureaucratic Elites in Western European States*, Oxford, Oxford University Press.

Ryan, S. (2002). 'Administrative Improvement in the Commonwealth Caribbean', in S. Ryan and A. M. Bissessar (eds.), *Governance in the Caribbean.* St Augustine, Trinidad: University of the West Indies, Salises.

Savoie, D. (1995). *Thatcher, Reagan, Mulroney.* Pittsburgh: University of Pittsburgh Press.

—— (2003). *Breaking the Bargain.* Toronto: University of Toronto Press.

Schaffer, B. B. (1973). *The Administrative Factor.* London: Frank Cass.

Scharpf, F. W. (1997). *Games Real Actors Play.* Boulder, CO: Westview.

Schelling, T. (1960). *Strategy of Conflict.* Cambridge, MA: Harvard University Press.

Scherzer, L. (1997, orig. 1988). *Der Erste.* Berlin: Aufbau Verlag.

Schick, A. (1996). *The Spirit of Reform: Managing the New Zealand State Sector in a Time of Change.* Wellington: State Services Commission.

Schmidt, M. G. (1989). 'Learning from Catastrophes: West German Public Policy', in F. G. Castles (ed.), *The Comparative History of Public Policy.* Cambridge: Polity.

Scholtz, J. T. (1991).'Cooperative Regulatory Enforcement and the Politics of Administrative Effectiveness', *American Political Science Review*, 85(1): 115–36.

Schroeter, E. (2004). 'The Politicization of the German Civil Service: A Three-Dimensional Portrait of the Ministerial Bureaucracy', in B. G. Peters and J. Pierre (eds.), *Politicization of the Civil Service in Comparative Perspective.* London: Routledge, pp. 55–80.

Scott, J. C. (1998). *Seeing Like a State.* New Haven, CT: Yale University Press.

Shaw, C. (1992). 'Hegel's Theory of Modern Bureaucracy', *American Political Science Review*, 86(2): 381–89.

Siavelis, P. (2000). *The President and Congress in Post-Authoritarian Chile.* Pennsylvania, PA: Pennsylvania State University Press.

Sieber, S. (1981). *Fatal Remedies.* New York: Plenum Press.

Silberman, B. S. (1993). *Cages of Reason.* Chicago: Chicago University Press.

Simmel, G. (1950). *The Sociology of Georg Simmel*, ed. Kurt H.Wolff. Glencoe: Free Press.

Sisson, C. H. (1976). 'The Civil Service after Fulton', in W. J. Stankiewicz (ed.), *British Government in an Era of Reform*. London: Collier Macmillan.

Sjölund, M. (1989). *Statens Lönepolitik 1986–1988*. Stockholm: Publica.

Skowronek, S. (1982). *Building a New American State*. Cambridge: Cambridge University Press.

Smith, A. (1937/orig. 1776). *The Wealth of Nations*. New York: Random House.

Southworth, J. (1998). *Fools and Jesters at the English Court*. Stroud: Sutton.

Sowell, T. (1990). *Preferential Policies*. New York: William Morrow.

Stepan, A. C. (1971). *The Military in Politics*. Princeton, NJ: Princeton University Press.

Stiglitz, J. E. (1974). 'Wage Determination and Unemployment in LDCs', *Quarterly Journal of Economics*, 101: 513–42.

Subramaniam, V. (1967). 'Representative Bureaucracy: A Reassessment', *American Political Science Review*, 61(4): 1010–19.

Suleiman, E. (2003). *Dismantling Democratic States*. Princeton, NJ: Princeton University Press.

Taylor, H. (1993/orig. 1836). *The Statesman*. Westport, CT: Greenwood.

Theakston, K. (2003). *Winston Churchill and the British Constitution*. London: Politico's.

Thelen, K. (2003). 'How Institutions Evolve: Insights from Comparative Historical Analysis', in J. Mahoney and D. Rueschemeyer (eds.), *Comparative Historical Analysis in the Social Sciences*. Cambridge: Cambridge University Press, pp. 208–40.

Theoharis, A. G. and Cox, J. S. (1988). *The Boss: J. Edgar Hoover and the Great American Inquisition*. Philadelphia, PA: Temple University Press.

Thomas, R. (1978). *The British Philosophy of Administration*. New York: Longman.

Thompson, F. (1993). 'Matching Responsibilities with Tactics: Administrative Controls and Modern Government', *Public Administration Review*, 53: 303–18.

Thompson, M., Ellis, R., and Wildavsky, A. (1990). *Cultural Theory*. Boulder, CO: Westview.

Tocqueville, A. de (1946, orig. 1835). *Democracy in America*. London: Oxford University Press.

Tsebelis, G. (2002). *Veto Players: How Political Institutions Work*. Princeton, NJ: Princeton University Press.

Turnbull, Sir A. (2005). *Valedictory Lecture*. Available at www.civilservice.gov.uk/publications/speeches/pdf/sat_valedictory_lecture.pdf.

Turner, J. (1988). ' "Experts" and Interests: David Lloyd George and the Dilemmas of the Expanding State, 1906–19', in R. MacLeod (ed.), *Government and Expertise*. Cambridge: Cambridge University Press.

Tversky, A. and Kahneman, D. (1991). 'Loss Aversion in Riskless Choice: A Reference-Dependent Model', *Quarterly Journal of Economics*, 106 (November): 1039–61.

—— —— (1992). 'Advances in Prospect Theory: Cumulative Representations of Uncertainty', *Journal of Risk and Uncertainty*, 5: 297–323.

United States Office of Personnel Management (2001). *Guide to the Senior Executive Service*. Washington, DC: Office of Personnel Management.

Voslensky, M. (1984). *Nomenklatura.* Garden City, NJ: Doubleday.

Wagner, M. (1998). *Ab morgen bist du Direktor.* Berlin: Edition Ost.

Walker, D. (2005). 'Fings Ain't Wot They Used To Be', *The Guardian Public Magazine,* 3 March.

Weaver, R. K. (1986). 'The Politics of Blame Avoidance', *Journal of Public Policy,* 6(4): 371–98.

—— (1988). *Automatic Government.* Washington, DC: Brookings Institution Press.

Weber, M. (1968). *Economy and Society,* Vol. 2, eds. G. Roth and C. Wittich. Berkeley, CA: University of California Press.

—— (1980/orig. 1921). *Wirtschaft und Gesellschaft,* 5th edn. Tübingen: JCB Mohr.

Weiner, M. (1984). 'The Pursuit of Ethnic Equality Through Preferential Policies: A Comparative Public Policy Perspective', in R. B. Goldmann and A. J. Wilson (eds.), *From Independence to Statehood.* New York: St Martin's Press.

Wildavsky, A. (1966). *The Politics of the Budgetary Process.* Boston, MA: Little, Brown.

—— (1971). *The Revolt Against the Masses.* New York: Basic Books.

—— (1979). *Speaking Truth to Power.* Boston, MA: Little, Brown.

Wilde, A. (1999). 'Irruptions of Memory: Expressive Politics in Chile's Transition to Democracy', *Journal of Latin American Studies,* 31: 473–500.

Willeford, W. (1969). *The Fool and his Scepter.* Evanston, IL: Northwestern University Press.

Williamson, O. E. (1986). *Economic Organization.* Brighton: Wheatsheaf.

Whitehead, L. (2002). *Democratization.* Oxford: Oxford University Press.

Wilson, J. Q. (1989). *Bureaucracy.* New York: Basic Books.

Wlezien, C. (1995). 'The Public as Thermostat: Dynamics of Preferences for Spending', *American Journal of Political Science,* 39: 981–1000.

Wolseley, G. J. (1869). *The Soldier's Handbook for Field Service,* London, Macmillan and Co.

World Bank (1993). *The East Asian Miracle.* Oxford: Oxford University Press.

Zach, M. (1997). *Monrepos oder Die Kälte der Macht.* Hamburg: Rowohlt.

Zifcak, S. M. (1994). *New Managerialism.* Buckingham: Open University Press.

Index